THE

HEA

THE
YOUNG
ATHLETE'S
HEALTH
HANDBOOK

A Guide to Sports Medicine and
Sports Psychology for Parents,
Teachers, Coaches, and Players

Douglas W. Jackson, M.D. and
Susan C. Pescar
ILLUSTRATED BY MICHELE PREDISIK

New York   EVEREST HOUSE   Publishers

#7171372

Library of Congress Cataloging in Publication Data:

Jackson, Douglas W
　　The young athlete's health handbook.
　　Bibliography, p. 299
　　Includes index.
　　　1. Physical education and training. 2. Sports—
Physiological aspects. 3. Sports—Accidents and
injuries. I. Pescar, Susan C., joint author.
II. Title. [DNLM: 1. Sports Medicine—Handbooks.
QT 260 J12y]
GV711.5.J32　　613.7　　80-27448
ISBN: 0-89696-124-9

Contents

Acknowledgments

No book can be completed without the help and support of many others who give freely of their time and expertise. The authors gratefully acknowledge the following individuals who were interviewed or whose assistance was sincerely appreciated.

(In alphabetical order): Dan Bailey, head trainer, California State University, Long Beach, California; Mike Bisk, head coach, Monarchs Gymnastic Team; Luci Collins (U.S. Olympic Gymnastics Team) and her parents, Ulysses and Claire Collins; C. Carson Conrad, executive director, President's Council on Physical Fitness and Sports; Cliff Crase, editor, *Sports 'N' Spokes*; Patrick Griffin, director, Recreation Therapy, Rancho Los Amigos Hospital; Gene (Topper) Hagerman, Ph.D., exercise physiologist, U.S. Olympic Training Center, Colorado; Norman Kaplan, founder and executive director, Foundation for the Junior Blind; Beth Kline (U.S. Olympic Gymnastics Team) and her parents, Bob and Bitsy Kline; Herb Kramer, the Special Olympics; Joe Fritsch, Men's Athletic Director, and Jerry Jordon, Gallaudet College, Washington, D.C.; Elizabeth Menze, research assistant; Christine A. Nelson, M.D., Associate Adjunct Professor of Pediatrics, University of California (Irvine) College of Medicine, and Pediatric Education Coordinator at the Earl and Loraine Miller Children's Hospital Medical Center, Long Beach, California; James Nicholas, M.D., member of the President's Council on Physical Fitness and Sports, founder and director of the Institute of Sports Medicine and Athletic Trauma, Lenox Hill Hospital, New York City; Mark D. Pescar, whose help was invaluable in completing this book; Don Peters, head coach of the Southern California Acro Team; Clifton Rose, M.D., team physician, California State University, Long Beach, California; John Soto (11-year-old record holder for the mile) and his parents, Ron and Janis Soto; and Dale Toohey, Ph.D., sports sociologist, California State University, Long Beach, California.

A very special added thanks to Jerry Gross, our editor at Everest House, for his diligent and energetic work on this book; and Glenn Cowley, our literary agent, for his continued support, assistance and faith.

Introduction

THE YOUNG ATHLETE'S HEALTH HANDBOOK is a tool for parents, players, teachers, coaches and school nurses. The first section provides information vital to "The Making of An Athlete"—information about growth and development, conditioning and training, nutrition, competitiveness and aggression, alcohol and drugs, matching physical and psychological traits to sports areas, and much, much more.

Part Two, "Sports Medicine and the Care of the Injured Athlete," contains vital information not only about injuries, but the total care of the young athlete, including important medical and orthopedic considerations in sports participation, injury prediction and prevention, where and how to find a sports medicine specialist, sports-related injuries, the uses and abuses of medications, diagnostic and treatment procedures for sports injuries, and safety and first aid tips.

Reading the book from cover to cover will give you an excellent overview of healthful sports participation for the young athlete. But its purpose is twofold—to lay a solid foundation for the overall care and nurturing of the young athlete, and to be a resource guide to specific sports injury information. Considering the enormous numbers of young people participating in organized and unorganized athletics today, there is great need for young athletes, parents, and people working with athletes to understand how to make sports participation and working toward physical fitness safe, enjoyable and as rewarding as possible.

From marbles to kick-the-can, baseball to soccer, football to tennis, swimming to gymnastics, running to jumping—our children will always be involved in some form of activity. And we have a responsibility to do all we can to ensure safety as well as enjoyment.

Certainly, the influence of sports on our children is dramatic. Most of them participate in sports in one way or another and watch competition on television or in person. Indeed, children are encouraged to participate and to excel in some form of athletic competition regardless of their social or economic backgrounds. Sports participation has become a way of life for millions of youngsters across the country. Twenty-nine to thirty million youngsters aged 6 to 21 took part in organized sports in this country in 1979. Of those, 6.4 million were involved in high school interscholastic sports and 540,-000 in intercollegiate sports. And, too, there is a wave of enthusiasm for young girls' participation in athletics to a much greater degree than ever before.

The above statistics are offered by the President's Council for Physical Fitness and Sports, and show how widespread athletic participation is today. Yet, they do not even include the vast numbers of youngsters who play at recess, before or after school, or on weekends in leisure-time activities.

Because of this increased interest and participation in both organized and free-play sports, more research is underway to add to what has been completed in the past. New information has given us some very useful knowledge about the unique needs of the young athlete. Information about nutrition, physical and psychological growth and development, conditioning, prevention and treatment of injuries, adequate and complete recovery from injuries, administration of medication, and selection of and participation in specific sports all allow parents to make a somewhat informed decision.

To help our children develop life-long physical fitness habits, we must first understand the major elements involved, from proper conditioning to the care of injuries.

Lenox Hill Hospital's Institute of Sports Medicine and Athletic Trauma reported that "there were more sub-lethal casualties in this country last year from leisure-time activities (adults and children combined) than there were from all this country's wars put together." According to this report, more than 17 million people required services of a physician due to leisure-time activities. This number included all recreational, amateur and professional athletics and activities. The Institute also notes that one in every three youngsters up to age 15 will experience some type of injury each year in recreational activities and organized athletics. And many of these will be "repeaters."

Today, those who work with children are beginning to look into the individual child's physical and psychological traits because it appears that matching certain individuals with certain sports activities with expertness and precision may result in fewer injuries. It also appears that some specific traits may protect the child from certain injuries and help maximize enjoyable participation and minimize injury and frustration.

Proper equipment and good facilities, safety precautions, conditioning and supervision also reduce the number of injuries and make sports more enjoyable. An awareness of children's unique physical makeup will help further in reducing the incidence of certain injuries.

Ideally, we should strive to have an athletic trainer or trained personnel assigned in every school. This experienced person would be aware of the injury risk factors, assure rehabilitation and recovery from previous injuries, supervise sports activities in hopes of reducing injuries, and identify injuries that need further evaluation and treatment. But, since injuries can occur any time and any place our children are active, it is vital also that others who work with children be able to recognize an injury that needs to be seen by a doctor. The best possible situation would be to educate teachers, coaches, school nurses, parents and others who work with children about sports and the needs of the young athlete.

Why? Because whenever and wherever an accident happens, a decision must be made to go to the doctor's office or the emergency room, or treat the injured athlete at home.

Although we do have some idea of how many young people play organized sports and the general number of injuries, further work needs to be done to determine whether injuries are the result of activities during recess, after school, or during weekends. With most minor injuries treated by coaches, parents, friends of the athlete, and less frequently by a doctor, many of these go undocumented. Experts believe these numbers to be extremely high.

Certainly, we don't want our children, as a result of injuries, to be precluded from enjoying physical pursuits at age 40, 50, 60 and beyond, because of arthritis or musculoskeletal deformities and restrictions. Some athletic or free-play activities during childhood can result in damage that lasts for a lifetime. Athletic injuries can cause some degree of pain or discomfort, or even lack of useful function of a joint, arm, leg, back or other area forever. Certain injuries may even prevent a child from reaching his or her potential during formative years and beyond.

And, if a child wants to become a champion, besides careul conditioning and injury prevention, other factors come into play such as growth and performance potential. No child becomes a champion without support from a parent or another supportive adult, sacrifice by the youngster and the entire family, and a dedication to working out as much as two to four hours every day. It also helps if that child is exposed to the best available coaches and facilities. This means a serious commitment, often one to spend a great deal of money in the development of a champion in such sports as ice skating, gymnastics, swimming, tennis, golf and skiing, just to mention a few.

Even if a child does not want to compete at championship levels, but wants to be skilled enough to enjoy and participate in sports, it's important to understand how to care for the youngster. Direction into specific sports based on physical and psychological traits will allow the child to enjoy sports by reaching his or her potential rather than experiencing early frustration.

Remember, children have only so much time during these formative years. And their enjoyment of active sports should not only be a childhood experience, but a life-long experience—so they do not become merely spectators as they grow older.

If you are a parent, this book will prove to be a helpful and useful guide—a tool—to use in your all-important role of directing your children into enjoyable, rewarding and safe sports participation. If your children are very young, it will give you a welcome head-start in encouraging healthful physical activity and in having reasonable expectations of the children's performances as they grow up. It will also help you direct your children into sports areas best suited for them physically and psychologically—those which can be most rewarding and enjoyable for a lifetime of physical fitness.

If you are a player, you are responsible to a great degree for your own good health and physical fitness. You will decide what role sports will play in your life and how much energy you want to put into them. You also need to get the record straight when it comes to many of the old wives' tales you've probably heard over the years. You should understand what's healthful for you and what isn't when it comes to sports participation, and how best to prevent injury. You have a major role to play in your own participation; the more you know the more aware you will be.

If you are a teacher, particularly in an elementary or junior high school, you work with young people day-in and day-out. Often you're the one responsible for activities at recess, during physical education class or after school. For you, understanding the scope and nature of physical activities, conditioning, stretching, nutrition, competitiveness and aggression, the plight of the late bloomer, and the frustrations of the adolescent, will help you perform your job better. Often, too, you will be the one to evaluate the extent or severity of an injury or problem—and you must make a decision. Should the paramedics be called? Should the youngster's parents be called and the youngster sent home with a recommendation to take him or her to the nearest emergency room or the family doctor? Should the young person simply rest and stay off the injury for the remainder of that day, or can he or she resume activity?

If you are a school nurse, you'll often be asked to evaluate a young person injured during physical education class or on the playing field. A better understanding of sports and athletic injuries, safety, first aid, and rehabilitation will enlarge your scope of knowledge and your ability to handle the problems. And, like the teacher, you may have to decide how extensive the damage is and what steps to take to ensure the safety and well-being of active youngsters who are injured during sports participation.

If you are a coach, whether professional or amateur, you have a big responsibility for the fun, well-being and safety of other people's children. In injury evaluation, emergency care and preparedness, safety precautions, handling aggression and competitiveness and instilling healthy attitudes, you can have a major impact. Understanding what young people can do and cannot do at certain ages and stages of growth and development, matching physical and psychological traits, and understanding and encouraging the participation of the late bloomer will help you better perform and enjoy your work and your team, too.

When it comes to our children, it is our responsibility to emphasize the importance of life-long physical fitness and the enjoyment of a sound body, before competition in organized athletics begins. It is there that most attention should be directed—there we can have the greatest impact in helping to develop a healthful and beneficial experience in sports for all children, a part of their lifestyle they can enjoy all their days.

THE YOUNG ATHLETE'S
HEALTH HANDBOOK

The Making of An Athlete

1.

Ages and Stages of Growth and Development

GROWTH AND DEVELOPMENT, two of the most phenomenal features of childhood, extend into the teenage years and sometimes the early twenties. If you observe closely, you can see an orderly progression of changes in what children look like (physique) and what they can do (performance) even over a period of several weeks. The physical development and emotional maturation of the body influence their ability to perform certain athletic tasks and physical feats, and determine their psychological reactions to sports and competition.

Growth

Growth, simply stated, involves not only weight gain, but an increase in height and in the size of all body parts. Each body system has its own pattern of growth. For example, the head and the brain inside it grow very rapidly during the first year of life, reaching two-thirds normal adult size by the end of that first year. Muscle growth, on the other hand, proceeds much more gradually, and a significant increase in muscle mass does not normally occur until several years later, peaking during adolescence.

It is important to remember that each child is an individual and his or her growth is determined by many factors. You've often heard, "He's so tiny, he can't be six," or "She's so tall, she looks much older than she is"—or the other way around. The final size a child reaches is influenced to a great extent by his or her genetic background; that is, the potential for growth is a result of many generations of both parents' families. Not only is the ultimate size determined by family characteristics and potential, but the rate of growth is also dependent upon family traits. Consider the fact that youngsters at age 12 are of various shapes and sizes—and continue to change at different rates over the next few years.

Muscle types and body builds are also fairly well determined by genetic inheritance. Some children are born with more slow-firing (slow-twitch) muscle cells and will do better in endurance activities, while others are born with fast-firing (fast-twitch) muscle cells and will probably do well in activities requiring speed and quickness. Children are also born with either "loose joints" or "tight joints."

Nutrition is another factor which influences how tall or heavy or muscular a child is, not only in infancy but all through the growing years. Early in infancy, diet influences whether a child is well proportioned or fat or thin. This early growth pattern might continue into early childhood and even adulthood.

Although it is impossible to predict exactly how tall or heavy a child will be at any given age, and exactly what his or her ultimate size will be, it is possible to make some generalizations about the physical characteristics at a given age, and about growth patterns. It is probably best to group children based on size and physical characteristics rather than on age, at least to determine physical capabilities.

Development

Development, the complement to growth, also proceeds in an orderly fashion. It refers to the increased complexity of function of parts of the body, a maturation rather than an increase in size. Maturation is both physical (skills, abilities) and psychological (thought processes, reasoning, reaction).

"Just as with physical growth, development is an ongoing process. It seems that youngsters are never quite the same from day to day or week to week in their capacity to perform certain tasks," Christine A. Nelson, M.D., explains. Dr. Nelson is Associate Adjunct Professor of Pediatrics at the University of California (Irvine) College of Medicine, and Pediatric Education Coordinator at the Earl and Loraine Miller Children's Hospital Medical Center in Long Beach, California. "One of the very real goals of parents and others concerned with the well-being of children," she notes, "should be to maximize the process of growth and development in order to allow and encourage children to reach their full potential with the most satisfaction—and the least frustration and injury. Understanding growth and development better and knowing the basics of what youngsters can do at certain ages and stages may be helpful and result in reasonable expectations of the young person."

Stages of Growth and Development

The Infant and Toddler

The infant first learns how to control the head without bobbing, then gradually gains control over the back muscles. The muscles of the shoulders and hips then begin to mature, so that the nine-month-old is able to stand. Cautious steps will occur when the child is between ten and thirteen months of age. These achievements require a complex combination of strength, balance and coordination translated into graceful, efficient movement.

"Next time you see an infant or toddler, carefully watch how he or she struggles to do things most older people perform with ease. Notice the amount of determination—and the frustration if the child fails—but he or she will try again and again. These developmental tasks are very difficult and often strenuous work for the learner. In fact, this process is analogous to the athlete's conditioning and training to develop and learn new skills or routines, or enhance endurance or strength. If you really look at the two processes, then you realize they really only represent a difference in level of sophistication. The human body was meant to be physically active and the infant's determination to be active and to perform is innate," Dr. Nelson emphasizes.

After many of these basic gross motor skills are learned, those which allow the infant to control the larger movements of the body, he or she begins to also learn fine motor skills. These skills require the use of the smaller muscles of the body, especially those in the hands, and depend upon the refinement of hand-eye coordination. This neuromuscular (brain-nerve-muscle) maturation takes time and involves the development of physical reactions, reflexes, perception and coordination.

By the end of the first year, toddlers can begin the real business of exploring their environment—and proceed with the fine-tuning of their skills. At this stage the activity level of most young children is at a very high point. They stop only when completely exhausted. They run, climb, and stoop incessantly and children at this age have little regard for their own safety. Curiosity is at a peak, and they "practice" tasks until they get them right. This is the stage, Dr. Nelson explains, of the "great imitator."

The Preschooler

Between ages two and five, children begin to try almost everything shown to them, and slowly start to master tasks. Ball-throwing, kicking and running are improved and they enjoy somersaults, tumbling and jumping. At this point, all movements become progressively more "fluid" and graceful. Many four- and five-year-olds, although not all, can begin to hit a large ball with a bat or racket, and may become interested in some of the activities and sports their parents enjoy. This new-found progress results in increasing confidence in their ability and they take pride in doing things right.

However, these children are easily frustrated if pushed too hard, or if adult expectations are too high. The same applies if they are playing with children much older than they or who are capable of better performance. Ironically, Dr. Christine Nelson notes, for some, this is just the needed incentive to perform and remain active, while for others it is the source of the worst type of frustration. Therefore, it is vital that, at this age, children be praised for participating and encouraged to try a wide range of activities, not pitted against older children or forced to achieve standards set by adults.

The School-Age Child

School-age children, from five to twelve or so, are increasingly capable of physical tasks which require both strength and coordination. During grade school, the physical activity interests and skills of the coming years are easily cultivated or discouraged; peer pressure influences what children will or will not do. At this time, speed and agility improve, while the energy and determination to continue activities until the point of exhaustion remains.

Stamina and attention span are vital areas to consider when directing a youngster into athletics. The younger the child, the shorter the attention span is likely to be. This makes it difficult for a young child to be dedicated to any one sport, and it is unreasonable to expect or impose such discipline on a child not ready for that kind of intensity. Also, children will usually only participate and compete in any one thing for a very short period of time before losing interest or stamina. It simply becomes just not fun any more.

This is one of the reasons, particularly with younger children, why organized or competitive sports events are shortened: the number of innings in baseball or softball, or the length and number of periods in basketball, hockey, volleyball, etc., are reduced. The lengths of races and other such events are also shortened to meet the needs of this age group. It should be noted that those adjustments are also made for safety's sake, and to reduce the threat of injury due to fatigue and loss of concentration.

The Teenager

As many young people approach adolescence, the importance of succeeding in whatever they do becomes vital. Competition is essential. To continue any sport or athletic endeavor, an activity must be very interesting and pose a continual challenge. Unfortunately, working out simply for the sake of good health or for the benefits of training is rare, unless this attitude has been emphasized over the years or parents have taken an active role in the young person's conditioning during the formative years. The teenager usually works out because of a "goal" to compete for or because he or she enjoys sports and being involved.

The pre-adolescent and adolescent will begin to do a great deal of picking and choosing. Those successful in a certain sport will pursue it if they see themselves continuing to improve and wish to compete on higher and higher levels. Others who either feel themselves to be or are truly less successful will change to a different athletic activity or quit altogether. Some who are very talented, but do not wish to maintain a rigorous training schedule, will also either change sports or stop activity.

During adolescence, the athlete's ability to complete certain feats varies, depending upon the individual's stage of growth, as well as training. Youngsters must continually adapt to changes in body size and agility, and can become quite frustrated if they perceive (in their own estimation) that growth is proceeding either too fast or too slowly.

Body image is important to adolescents. Parents often hear that John is bigger, stronger or better skilled; that Tom even has hair on his chest, looks like he may soon need to shave, and always talks about sex. They also hear that Susan is stronger, more athletically inclined and skilled, has larger breasts, and started her menstrual periods earlier than others; that Karen makes all the school teams and seems able to do just about anything; or that all Tracy talks about is boys.

Because children grow and develop differently (and this has nothing to do with being more or less a man or woman), adolescence is a very difficult and frustrating time for the young person. Many at this age feel (indeed are convinced) that something is wrong with them. Some have even suggested to their parents that they might need hormone shots in order to be normal or to "catch up." This is certainly nothing for parents to laugh at! The young person needs, it would seem, all the reassurance in the world that he or she is maturing on schedule and that nothing at all is wrong. Empathy and understanding are vital at this time of tremendous changes. So much happens to youngsters physically and psychologically that it's important to remember that their confusion and fears are *real* to them. If need be, the young person should be seen by a physician to relieve the anxiety and to reinforce the fact that all is well.

Because the ability to compete in certain sports depends upon the rate and pattern of growth and development, new and overwhelming frustrations can occur. The boy who always played organized youth football and excelled, but is a so-called "late bloomer" in high school, will not very likely do well on the school's football team in his sophomore year, and will have difficulty understanding why. The formerly tiny and adept female gymnast whose breasts suddenly develop accompanied by considerable weight gain in her hips and thighs, may find she is not as agile as her lighter friends who are maturing more slowly; she is at a loss over this. The young girl who was always used to being the best softball, volleyball and basketball player finds in her high school years that everyone has caught up with her, adding more frustration and insecurity to her adolescent years.

Youngsters of both sexes have similar strength potential until puberty, but then the young male begins to develop greater muscle mass and strength than the young female, due to increased production of male hormones. His bones become heavier and larger, partly as a result of his production of testosterone. The teenage girl also develops strength during adolescence but not to as great a degree as her male counterpart. Yet, it should be noted that, physiology aside, the difference in strength is also related to the male's many years of activity in sports which develop upper body as well as lower limb strength. The strength differences between the male and female are more a result of environmental factors than physiological ones.

In one study, young boys and girls (under age ten) were asked to throw a ball overhand with their dominant arm. The boys could throw much, much farther. But, when both groups were asked to throw the ball with their non-dominant arms, both groups threw, in general, an equal distance.

The differences in ability and performance after puberty will be based on body type and shape (percentage of body fat), growth and development, the size of the lungs and ability to process oxygen, and whether or not the young person has been involved to any significant degree in those activities which promote strength, such as throwing, running, swimming and so forth.

Skeletal Growth

Because youngsters' skeletons are growing and constantly changing, the possibility of injury to bones and their related structures—tendons, ligaments, cartilege—exists when forces are too great. Specifically, injuries to the growth plate are of concern, not because these injuries are always disabling (in general, with appropriate care, growth-plate injuries will heal normally), but because there is a risk of growth deformity if the injury is not recognized and treated. Some growth-plate injuries and tendon injuries are particularly serious and may plague the youngster for the rest of his or her life. (For details, see Chapter 15.)

Psychological Traits for Each Age and Stage

A youngster's psychological traits at any given age will have a major bearing on his or her attitude toward athletics, sports and activity. Both the physical and psychological characteristics of each child must be considered when determining at what stage he or she may be.

Very young children—ones under three—are essentially preoccupied with learning things and exploring the environment. They are unlikely to be very interested in what others, especially other children, are doing.

Although very young children will play games with adults, their ability to really play "with" other children is limited. Not until they are three or four years old do they have the ability to play cooperatively with children of the same age. It is at this stage that children begin to understand the "give and take" of interactive games and sports, and for several more years, each one is more interested in his or her own performance and participation than in the progress of the game.

At this stage, any attempt to involve children in team games is frustrating at best. Their attention spans are very short and they are more interested in impressing adults and performing by themselves than participating with others. For example, a child may work very hard at hitting a baseball, but not be at all willing to give up his or her turn at bat to another. Adults have witnessed screaming episodes because of this, but everyone must understand that the child's reaction is a natural one for this stage. Creative thinking on the part of adults may help deal with this phenomenon, but the child's selfishness and aggressiveness in insisting on doing all the "fun" things in games and activities is normal. They are also inclined to change the rules of the game to suit their needs and wants, which they can't understand as cheating. It's just changing them for the better.

Although in various sports children begin training at age two or three, it is important to understand that "training" has quite a different meaning in this case than "training" as we know it. In gymnastics, for example, Don Peters, head coach of Southern California Acro Team (SCATS) in Orange County, which has produced Olympic gymnasts since 1968, says that the little tots learn flexibility, balance and strength along with some basic gymnastics skills— they tumble, roll, do somersaults, jump and run to music. Emphasis is placed on building coordination, developing a joy in active participation—and fun.

"From two to six years of age, children are not ready for any serious training schedule or the stresses of competition," Peters says. "The point is to prepare these youngsters for the feeling of, let's say, being upside down and to experience what their bodies can do. We want them to enjoy the physical activity itself and be proud of their participation. We emphasize agility, physical fitness for each age group and fun. Physically, developmentally and psychologically, that's where the emphasis should be."

Other programs in various sports also include the very young, but care is taken to make their experience enjoyable and rewarding, not demanding and strenuous physically and emotionally.

As children approach school age, they become more capable of interactive and cooperative games but their drive to compete remains very high. Those children who are clumsy—later in developing coordination than their classmates—are likely to be very frustrated with team play. If the strengths of such children are not recognized and fostered, they are likely to become more and more inactive, and less and less likely to participate in any activity as the years go by.

The result is a sedentary child, prematurely either frustrated or rejected because he or she has been given up on by adults as "unathletic" or "impossible."

One of the basic dynamics of childhood is the need to gain the approval of adults—especially parents, teachers, coaches and other significant authority figures in their lives. All children will try their best to impress their parents and will continue an activity relentlessly to the point of utter exhaustion if they receive the reward of encouragement and support. This is where parents and others need to be prudent and cautious. Youngsters can be pushed and prodded beyond the point of safety and reasonability, both physically and psychologically. Those who have such influence over a child must learn where encouragement and support stop and pushing and expectations begin.

Parents in particular, and others (as the child grows older) play a tremendous role in encouraging the youngster to attempt new tasks and activities, as well as discouraging a budding athlete or active young person if no support or approval is offered. If physical activity and participation as a healthy and enjoyable part of life is encouraged, the young person will usually maintain this same attitude as he or she grows. If, on the other hand, winning in sports is deemed the only reason to participate, the young person will also accept this criterion. In the long run, he or she may become so frustrated or pressured that participating in sports doesn't seem worth the pain, and a sedentary life becomes an attractive alternative.

Peer Pressure

Not until later childhood and adolescence do youngsters begin to feel intense pressure from their peers to perform at a certain acceptable level. At that time, youngsters might try sports for which they are not suited, simply because being a football star or a varsity forward on the school's basketball team, or a girls' varsity volleyball, basketball or tennis star seems to carry a little more glory, recognition and prestige to them than other sports. The real drive to please their peers and to be part of a special group is commanding. One brilliant American swimmer decided to be a cheerleader because she thought it would be more acceptable than being a championship swimmer! But eventually, if the youngster is not physically and psychologically equipped to excel in a certain area of athletics, he or she will become frustrated, either returning to the activities that were most rewarding or quitting athletics altogether.

The Importance of Growth, Maturation and Sports

Among the saddest of states for any youngster is progressive inactivity. Physical activity is a powerful and vital form of expression for both the body and the mind. Inactivity deprives children and people of any age of physical expression, and cheats them of fitness and fun.

Yet, inactivity has become a feature of American society and modern society throughout the world. As children grow older, there is an increasing and alarming tendency to sit for longer and longer hours in school, at friends' houses and in front of television sets. Parents provide transportation almost anywhere the young person wants to go. This is partly for safety's sake, but more frequently it is due to the young person's laziness or desire for convenience. The "soft life" has come a threat to the well-being of modern society, not only because it discourages physical activity and fitness but because it encourages the idea that a sedentary existence is "the good life."

With automation and gadgets available to do many tasks for us, and a great emphasis on playing sports only to win, the idea of conditioning and fun through athletics as an important and enjoyable part of life isn't easy to sell. One of the prime goals of parents and others who work with children and young people should be to encourage continued activity, emphasizing not just winning, but the challenge of physical tasks, and participation itself as the accomplishment. They should do all they can to encourage more walking and running instead of sitting and riding. And, as the youngster matures, they should emphasize the fact that sports are a special part of life and vital for good health. Most importantly, they should do all possible to direct children into sports and activities in which they are physically and psychologically adept, so rewarding and exciting experiences result for them.

Obviously, the child who remains fit from infancy on by remaining physically active will, in most cases, be much healthier than one who is rewarded for staying still and not bothering the adults.

It should be equally obvious that it is just as damaging to push a child or young person too far, and expect too much, based on his or her developmental level and physical features, as it is to discourage activity. Some children who are pushed too hard and too soon will continue to participate to the point of serious physical or emotional injury in order to please parents, teachers, coaches, or friends. Others will give up all activity early because of discouragement over their inability to perform at the level expected of them or "burn-out" because the pressures are very great and the rewards simply not worth it. Certainly, neither of these is desirable.

The best possible attitude would be for everyone involved in supervising children and young adults to actively encourage continued participation in the sports enjoyed most—and to emphasize fitness, participation and the challenge of physical activity as the reward. Understanding the young athlete psychologically, knowing his or her physical traits, and correctly identifying stages of growth will help adults maximize and enhance the youngster's efforts. With care, this will be translated into a lifetime of sports activity, physical fitness and fun.

If young people wish to further pursue an area of athletics and have the talent and drive to do so, they must feel that they have accomplished something simply by participating and enjoy the challenge of scaling new heights. With this attitude they are true winners.

If, by chance, they achieve national or international acclaim, they will also receive the greatest rewards—those of high self-esteem and involvement in the never-ending effort to train, condition and to extend the limits of the human body's physical performance, agility and endurance.

AGE	GROWTH AND DEVELOPMENT	PSYCHOLOGICAL TRAITS	ACTIVITIES TO ENCOURAGE
0–6 mo.	Head and trunk control; interest in surroundings	Complete dependence on parents for all physical and emotional support	Sit-ups w/ help; prone activities; rolling games
6 mo–1 yr.	Standing; crawling; rolling; walking; sitting up	Continued dependence; beginning interest and curiosity about environment; interaction with others starts; fear of strangers and separation	Rolling games; crawling; chasing; standing; walking; being near familiar surroundings and faces
1–1½ yr.	Walking; running; throwing; "games"; climbing	Essentially self-centered; will play with adults; very curious, exploring environment; into everything	Running; squatting; throwing safe things; climbing in harmless places
1½–2 yrs.	Running well; climbing; jumping; throwing	Characterized by "I'd rather do it myself"; play is self-centered, can amuse self—"loner" but will imitate others; learns best by demonstration; show-off stage	Climbing; jumping; running; hide-and-seek; enjoys playing with balls; stunts like "wheelbarrow" with supervision
2–4 yrs.	Graceful running; tricycle riding; throwing and catching; jumping; hopping	Starts cooperative play with other children; still more interested in own performance and participation than game itself; wants to do all the "fun" things; relatively short attention span; will change rules to suit needs; starts becoming competitive	All of above, including hitting as well as catching balls; throwing; begins to refine all stated above
4–6 yrs.	Hopping; running; jumping; throwing; hitting; improved eye-hand coordination; balance improves; bicycle riding	Restless; relatively short attention span; more cooperative in interactive games; tends to be showoff; persistent and tireless; needs much approval	All of above; skating; skiing; balance beam; bicycling; racket sports; baseball; swimming; running

6-10 yrs.	Improvement in all of above; late developers must not be frustrated by too much push to participate, or will drop out; recognize differences in rate of growth and ability; little or no differences in strength, agility or stamina of males and females other than those based on participation and training in various sports areas.	Attitudes, personality and likes become apparent; enjoys imaginative activities and interactive games; easy to prod; thrives on approval; important to encourage participation and challenge, not winning; peer approval starts to become important; team spirit high; loyalty to friends	Nearly all sports and activities within reason; ready to start training (apropos of age) in athletic area of interest if wishes to achieve higher level of performance, but should not be pushed beyond level. Serious competition is not recommended or healthy, either physically or psychologically
10-18 yrs.	Improvement in stamina and fine-tuned performance; final growth spurt; males become stronger due to hormones (greater muscle mass and heavier bones) of puberty; females experience puberty with menstrual cycle, breast development, higher percentage of fat on body, possibly greater lower body strength; differences in strength between male and female much less than thought, and can be overcome to a great extent by conditioning and activity	*From 10-13*: peer approval and participation hand-in-hand for some; better prepared for serious training and some degree of serious competition if desired; need encouragement of parents, teachers, coaches and others for involvement; easily frustrated by poor performance—encourage participation for right reasons; parents start to be replaced by other adults as "idols" *From 13-18*: Peer pressure significant; faced with difficult decisions about commitment to sports vs. social aspects of high school, parties and experimentation; majority involved in sports for fun and prestige and challenge rather than for fitness or serious competition; if encouraged to do so, may learn to incorporate activity into lifestyle; those wanting to pursue high levels of competition need much support; trying time with many psychological changes and adaptation to more independent existence. Team spirit, drive to compete high for some.	All sports and athletic activities; conditioning and training complementary to sports areas important; teenager will do more choosing of activities of interest; encourage participation in areas of sports which can carry over into adulthood for health and physical fitness, as well as fun and relaxation.

AGE:	GROWTH AND DEVELOPMENT	PSYCHOLOGICAL TRAITS	ACTIVITIES TO ENCOURAGE
18-21 yrs.	Some may continue to grow and physically mature (especially males)	For those continuing in school: Continued dependence in certain aspects of life, and "carefree" existence while attempting to find life niche; competition and team needs may peak for some, but conflict with individual needs may remain. For those beginning to work or raise family: shift to more sedentary, routine life, with decrease in participation and activity; individual sports prevail. May be uncertain about ability to perform vs. peak of performance	All sports and activities possible; beginning emphasis on fitness and conditioning rather than competition for most; individual sports that can be done for many years to be encouraged for most.
Over 21 yrs.	Beginning of "de-growth," or ageing. Physiological maturity; peak of performance met at varying ages, with subsequent decline; fitness needs harder to meet for many.	Adapt to demands of lifestyle; some better than others at self-discipline needed for continued activity and participation; does things for personal reward and pleasure, rather than approval of others	Encourage maintenance of fitness and activity to promote lifelong health.

Table 1   Characteristics of growth and development as they relate to athletic participation and activity. (Courtesy of Christine A. Nelson, M.D. Printed with permission.)

2.
Matching Physical Traits and Characteristics to Sports

EACH PERSON IS BORN with certain physical attributes which will influence his or her ability to excel in a specific sport or sports. As youngsters engaged in a sport advance to higher, more demanding levels of competition, they will probably be excluded somewhere along the line if they do not have the physical traits necessary for that sport. Even youngsters not involved in competition may become frustrated with free play because they never seem to perform adequately.

But, if a youngster with the physical attributes necessary for a given sport is matched with the right coaches and facilities, and there is parental or equivalent support, then there is a good chance the young athlete will be able to reach a high level of performance.

Certainly, some youngsters can compensate for not having the physical characteristics required for a specific sport by starting their conditioning and training at an early age. However, no matter how early an age a youngster may begin, he or she may be eliminated from the ascent to the top when a level of competition is reached at which ability makes the difference between the good athlete, the outstanding athlete, and the "champion."

"Ability," therefore, becomes not merely the manifestation of one physical attribute, but the interplay of multiple physical factors, psychological traits, coaches, parents and facilities, hormones and chemistry.

For example, a young female gymnast who can place her hands on the floor without warming up does so because of the length of her legs and arms, as well as the flexibility of her back and other joints of her body. The level of skills she has acquired through training depend on her psychological makeup, that is, her willingness to discipline herself to train; safe and supervised facilities; the advantage of good health that sustained her through a prolonged period of training; and coaches skilled in teaching and providing for her well-being and safety.

All these are important parts of the "ability" puzzle. For many sports such as ice skating, gymnastics, tennis, golf, and skiing, you must add another factor—the cost of coaching and facility fees.

In some countries, physical evaluation and testing are being experimentally completed on youngsters at a very early age to determine traits and potential athletic ability. This testing is an attempt to direct children toward those areas of athletics in which they will be most likely to succeed. This approach, however, is still in its infancy.

In the United States, we have been trying to develop physical assessments and psychological tests which would accurately match a young person's potential with athletic areas to which he or she is best suited both physically and psychologically. This could be important not only in terms of competition, but for directing children into sports where they will experience the least frustration and the fewest injuries.

In this research it would be important to determine those characteristics which might make certain youngsters "injury-prone" if they participated in certain sports. By doing this, we could direct young children to athletic experiences in which they would be less likely to be injured and which they would more likely enjoy and be successful at throughout their lifetimes.

James Nicholas, M.D., a member of the President's Council on Physical Fitness and Sports, and Founder and Director of the Institute of Sports Medicine and Athletic Trauma at Lenox Hill Hospital in New York City, has done extensive study on the physical demands of 61 sports. He is well known for his work in profiling the physical demands of sports.

"The point is, there are some traits that are trainable, like strength and endurance, and others which are not, like speed. But we have to be careful with this kind of information. Profiling for sports performance is not really our concern, and there are certainly ethical considerations involved too. Youngsters, in particular, should not be eliminated from a sport because they do not meet a specific profile. We all too often place too much emphasis on performance and not enough on the health benefits of sports. Profiling does have merits in injury prediction," Dr. Nicholas emphasizes, "and directing young people into sports areas where there is less likelihood for them to sustain injuries because of their physical characteristics is the direction we need to take."

Certainly, injury potential should greatly influence the sports chosen. Studies show that individuals with marked generalized laxity and flexibility tend not to be as good at some sports as at others and should be directed into those not associated with a high degree of joint injury. On the other hand, less flexible individuals, with tight muscles and ligaments, are more susceptible to strains of the muscle groups. They can help prevent injury by stretching and conditioning early on. Carefully done, such exercises and conditioning may keep them from being restricted in their participation.

Other characteristics that play a role in the choice of sports are eye-hand coordination, fine motor responses in precise sports, mental quickness, endurance vs. quickness, and vision and agility.

Does all this mean a child cannot and should not participate in whatever sport he or she chooses? No! Children should be encouraged to participate and enjoy physical fitness and fun from childhood on. But the child participating to reach a high competitive level will most likely benefit from having the physical attributes associated with success in that sport. The child who doesn't have all of the ingredients will probably eventually be eliminated from competition or from winning as he or she approaches the highest attainable level in that sport.

Desire, psychological makeup, determination and the young person's ability to adapt his or her body to the requirements of the sport may allow some to overcome all the obstacles. But this situation is the exception, not the rule.

Assessment of the young athlete, however, would allow youngsters to develop skills in a sport (or sports) which would be less frustrating for them and would alleviate the tremendous waste of time and effort in trying to do something they can't because of their physical traits.

One example: A superbly conditioned and disciplined athlete had spent most of his life training to become a world-class high jumper. His ability and skill were recognized early and expectations were high. Thin and flexible, he had excellent spring-bounding ability, both from a standstill and on the run, and possessed excellent muscle and body control.

In fact, he had all the makings of a champion high jumper except one—his height—a factor over which he obviously had no control. He had reached his full stature and maturation early. Although he was a young champion, he saw many pass him by who had physical traits that no amount of training and discipline on his part could match. Only 5'9" tall, he could jump 7'4" high—a spectacular feat. Considering the fact that he was able to jump 19 inches above his head, he was essentially out-jumping his 6'5" opponents who were jumping only 12 inches above their heads.

But when it came to competition and winning, he was eliminated; in high jumping there is no height classification or judging based on inches jumped above one's height.

Look, too, at the odds against someone playing in the NBA if he is less than six feet tall. He will meet frustration prior to the professional level—simply because he is too short for that sport.

For sports such as boxing and wrestling a player's height or weight is a consideration. In these sports, certain physical attributes allow one person to be more effective than another equally good athlete. But other sports are concerned with different traits in different team members: football, for example, is one of them. The small, quick defensive back certainly looks and functions differently from the large offensive tackle.

Almost no sports, save the decathlon, require a *single* athlete to excel in many ways. Yet, years ago, the great athlete was one who had reached the highest achievement in several sports. Today, however, athletic competiton is so keen and so specialized that, more often than not, the young athlete must confine his or her time and commitment to one sport. It seems almost a matter of natural selection. But, if this sport is not best suited to the young athlete's physical traits, or if there are not enough facilities or coaches available, the athletic endeavor will be a potential source of frustration.

You've heard people say: "He looks like a basketball player" or "That guy has to be football material" or "She'd be a good gymnast" or "Look at the shoulders on that brother and sister—they'd make fantastic swimmers." But appearance alone does not make champions, or even athletes.

What *are* the traits that make a basketball player, or a gymnast, or a football player, or a swimmer or those in other sports? The answer is a combination of a person's physical and psychological traits.

Experts at the U.S. Olympic Training Center in Colorado

Springs, Colorado, perform assessments and evaluations on athletes to determine their strengths and weaknesses, and to aid them in achieving their goals through the development of specially designed and individualized conditioning/training programs. As part of their assessment, physical tests are performed. These tests are as specific to the athlete's sport as possible. Testing includes flexibility and power determinations; an evaluation of body composition; strength, power and endurance assessments of specific muscle groups; and metabolic tests to evaluate maximal oxygen consumption. Experts do not compare an athlete in one sport to an athlete in another, nor do they compare those in the same sport to each other.

"In order for an athlete to be evaluated at the training center, usually a request from his or her coach must be approved by a national governing body of the U.S. Olympic Committee," explains Gene (Topper) Hagerman, Ph.D., an exercise physiologist at the center. "Our job is to evaluate strengths and weaknesses, and from these tests identify areas an athlete needs to work on, and design a program that will do just that. But I'm always asked, 'Can you predict whether or not someone can be a world champion—Can your tests determine that potential?' Certainly we have some indicators based on what others in the same sport are capable of doing. For example, if you look at oxygen consumption, let's say, during a treadmill test, those on the high side of the scale for that sport will usually do better than others in the same sport who have a lower oxygen consumption capacity. However, it's a fine line. You can get someone with a lower capacity who utilizes oxygen better than the one with the higher capacity. So, there are variants. There will always be someone unique who will not fit a pattern."

Dr. Hagerman also points out that muscle strength, power and endurance testing can tell the experts whether an athlete is in the same performance range as others in the same sport, but won't necessarily predict success in that sport. Body composition (percentage of body fat, lean muscle mass and body build) is another important aspect. Experts see a range of 8 to 12 percent body fat, on the average, in males (5 to 6 percent in marathon runners), and 16 to 18 percent, on the average, in females (12 to 14 percent in distance runners). If a person's anatomical size is large with a great deal of muscle bulk and a greater percentage of body fat, then more than likely that person will not be a distance runner.

"In Russia, they are now looking to mothers and fathers to establish profiles on youngsters at an early age. Physical traits and characteristics are determined, and based on those determinations—body size, build, flexibility, agility, eye-hand coordination, speed, muscle strength, balance, coordination, power and other components— sports profiling is done. If the child's profile is consistent with those of top-level athletes, the child is nurtured in that direction.

"In the United States," Dr. Hagerman emphasizes, "our athletes are given many avenues to follow. Predicting the best sport or sports for them is difficult because there are so many variables in this country, unlike in the Soviet Union. Here, training, coaching, geographic area, parental support and encouragement, the social aspects of sports and our culture, all make it difficult to arrive at any specific and easily identifiable pattern of traits for profiling. Certainly, there are overall physical traits which are helpful in directing a young person to a given sports area, but it's important to remember that everyone is unique and not all will fit the ideal picture. We have to leave room for exceptions, allow our children to try many sports, and learn basic skills of balance, coordination, and agility up to their potential level of ability. Then," Dr. Hagerman says, "they can proceed to learn the specific skills for the sport or sports of their choice when they are ready. We should use physical-trait profiling as helpful a guideline in directing youngsters to sports which they will enjoy most, because they have the physical make-up for these sports areas. That type of use would be very beneficial."

Physical Traits

Height

With today's specialization in sports, not all young men and women who want to be basketball stars, for example, will be. Although most of these young athletes can learn to dribble and shoot a basketball at an early age, the ones who are going to be on the high school team or earn a college scholarship will practice one to two hours every day of their teen years. Many who competed against each other in grammar school will be unable to make the team after the junior high school level. From there the statistics for participation in scholastic basketball plunge drastically. But for those who love the sport, there are organized intramural, YMCA, club and church leagues in which their ability and commitment can be met. Even of the 200,000 young men who play high school basketball each year, fewer than 1,500 of them will be able to make college teams. Of those who graduate from college, fewer than 200 will be given a chance to play with the pros. Of the 200 given the opportunity, a mere 55 will actually obtain a professional basketball contract, and for several years only a handful of the 55 who make it each year will get off the bench.

Today's high school, college and pro basketball players are more often than not over 6'5" tall, muscular but slender-looking with a low percentage of body fat, and have good endurance and speed. Their ability to perform a standing vertical jump as well as a standing broad jump correlates well with their overall skills. On the court they move, start and stop quickly and are agile, flexible, and in superb condition.

Women's basketball teams do not have the same height as their men's counterparts, but also prefer the taller athlete when recruiting. The women playing on the top teams tend to be much taller than the average woman and must have the physical capabilities of quickness and agility much as the men players do.

Without these physical traits, the chances of succeeding in serious competitive basketball are quite low. Young athletes discovered late may take too long to develop to make a specific team; e.g., the young athlete who has a six- or eight-inch growth spurt and then decides to take up basketball. The younger one begins playing a sport, the easier it is to develop the necessary coordination patterns and the instinct to play the sport well.

Flexibility

Other sports have noticeable groups of specific traits, too. Gymnasts are usually shorter, lighter in weight, more flexible and quite strong compared to the general population of the same age level. These athletes spend anywhere from two to four hours a day working out, beginning at a very early age, and have that added ingredient of parental support and encouragement.

Interestingly, 93 percent of junior high school female gymnasts examined in a study were able to bend over and touch their palms to the floor without first warming up. It seems that if a young female cannot perform this, her chances of being a top-level competitor are slight. Our top international gymnasts all have this capability. The ability to do this is dependent on spinal and hamstring muscle flexibility, and the length of the arms and legs. In essence, it is a summation of necessary traits. But the ability to put one's palms on the floor can be acquired by most individuals, particularly if conditioning starts early in life. "Tight" individuals may never be able to do so, however, and would be frustrated in gymnastics; it is an area of athletics toward which they should not be directed.

The National Junior Volleyball Team is a good example of a similar "mold" for volleyball players. If you lined up all the team members, you would find some at each end a little taller or a little shorter. But, as a rule, the entire team would look very similar in structure, shape, percentage of body fat, and conditioning. They would also be similar in how much and how often they practice, their motivation, and so on.

What about young people who do not wish to compete at a high level, but want to be involved in athletics? A physical assessment is still worthwhile in these cases. These youngsters want to do something that they are good at and enjoy. They don't want to continually sustain injuries, or be frustrated because they don't do well. Here again, a look at the child's physical and psychological makeup will give you a fair idea of the kind of athletic participation best suited to him or her.

Sometimes the choice of sports should be based also on the youngster's ability to continue the sport into adulthood. Many people choose tennis, swimming, volleyball, ice skating, golf, skiing and other sports which do not always require organized activity or team participation.

Muscle Type

Although physical traits are determined genetically, and some may be altered by early training and conditioning, many can never be changed. It is important, then, that young people not suffer because of something they cannot alter. For example, explosive power and speed are pretty much inherited. The capacity for great endurance is also innate but can be enhanced by training. There are also different types of muscle fibers. The child with slow-firing muscles is better off in endurance sports. The child with fast-firing muscles will probably excel in explosive sports.

Matching Athletes with Sports

Parental Influence

Certainly someday it will be possible to perform an early assessment of all children to help guide them toward areas of athletics best suited to them physically and mentally. Until that time, parents, teachers and coaches alike should provide the opportunity for children to experiment with different sports, whether they want to compete at a high level of performance, or just enjoy the activity.

In any case, children in free play learn quickly who is the best at a given activity. When the parent or coach chooses "the best," another set of judgments is placed on those who will excel and those who will be frustrated. Or, when expectations rise and the young athlete *wants* to excel—to be the best—physical traits superimpose their effects, the stakes become high, and the sports event changes in character and goals.

Natural Selection: the Athlete's Choice

Interestingly, most children will choose an area of athletics in which they do best, even if they thought they wanted to participate in another sport. In most cases, the one in which they do best is usually the one best suited for them. They do well because they are physically and mentally equipped for the sport. So we should learn to listen to what our children say.

For example, Danny was light and thin, but strong for his size. He loved to play sports at an early age, but never seemed to do well in Little League Baseball or Pop Warner Football. His father had played both sports in college and had married one of the cheerleaders. Both parents very much wanted Danny to excel. Danny still did very poorly, looking almost uncoordinated when he batted or tried to catch a pass. Danny's father was very upset and disappointed that his only son would not be the sort of top athlete he had been. His father and mother pushed him, hoping he would catch on soon. But at the age of 13, after failure and frustration, Danny quit all team sports. He simply didn't want anything to do with them.

Ironically, after being left alone for a few years, Danny decided to go out for the cross country and track teams. Although he had no experience in either sport, he made both teams in his sophomore year. And even though he was plagued by a knee injury sustained in pre-high school football, Danny lettered in both areas and was conference champion in his senior year. He also did well in his weight class in wrestling.

In college, he continued to grow and develop. Danny was simply one of those young people who had matured later than his classmates.

Because of his endurance and strength, in college he switched to crew. Again, he was successful, representing America in several rowing competitions. By this time Danny was considered an outstanding and accomplished athlete. Although his father was now proud of his son, he still did not completely understand Danny's forms of physical expression and some of the reasons behind them.

In most cases a child does not want to disappoint a parent. Danny kept trying and kept quiet because he wanted his father to be proud of him. He might have subtly mentioned that he was the fastest runner in class. But if he did, it went right past his father, who just didn't hear him, perhaps because he still wanted his son to be a baseball or football star.

A parent may hear, "I got to be the quarterback today, and I threw a touchdown"; or "I was captain of the basketball team at recess and I made more baskets than anyone"; "I came in second in swimming at the pool"; "You should see how fast I run and can kick the ball"; or "Look at the somersault I can do. I figured it out all by myself."

The list goes on and on. But if we listen, our children will tell us what they do best and enjoy most. We should encourage them in these areas, relinquishing our own biases and criteria for athletic enjoyment.

If nothing else, parents should do all they can to help their children move in directions in which their physical attributes are not detrimental to them. This also applies to teachers and coaches. Children are easily hurt by unnecessary failure, peer embarassment or a parent's, teacher's or coach's disappointment. We must be careful not to set them up for these.

The most important part of athletic participation for the majority of all people, young and old alike, is fitness, its associated health benefits, and fun. We must emphasize these. The importance of winning—being a champion—is secondary and a very individual matter. Without the fitness and fun, the young person will be involved in sports for less healthful reasons.

Pushing children into sports they either dislike or don't do well can only be detrimental to them in the long run, either physically from unnecessary injuries, or psychologically from the constant failure to experience satisfaction.

A sense of well-being and life-long fitness is a far more important benefit than a college athletic scholarship, or being the local champion in a given sport. If we can teach our children that, then we will have done them a great service.

3.
Matching Psychological and Personality Traits to Sports

FOR YEARS, SPORTS psychologists have been interested in the "making of the athlete." Obviously athletes are both born (in that genetics determines the physical build and body type) and made (many non-genetic factors having positive or negative influences). Success in athletics (excelling to one's ability level) is probably based not only on genetics but on many other variables: growth and development; environment; intelligence and learning; the development of innate physical traits and attributes; amount of practice; training method and coaching direction; personality traits and characteristics; and support and encouragement.

Sports psychologists have posed many questions and have been striving through various studies to find concrete answers. Are there differences between the personalities of athletes and non-athletes? Do certain personality traits or characteristics direct people to a certain sport or sports (team sports vs. individual athletics) or even a certain position in a sport? Or, conversely, does involvement in sports competition influence personality or psychological makeup? Are there specific personality differences between the champion athlete and the average competitor? Do female athletes have different personalities from non-athletic females? Do certain personality traits or a specific psychological makeup predispose an athlete to injury? If so, can the identification of these traits help direct young people into sports in which they will experience fewer injuries? Can psychological tests help direct a young person into sports that best suit his or her psychological makeup and personality traits?

Personality Testing

"Most experts involved in the psychosocial aspects of sports agree that a variety of traits and characteristics probably determines a person's likes and dislikes, how he or she behaves in certain situations and the response to any given situation," Dale Toohey, Ph.D. has noted. "What a young person experiences, his/her environment, and what he/she has inherited physically and psychologically, to a great degree will determine attitudes, abilities and even values. Psychological testing is not new, but there is tremendous disagreement in the field about the methods of testing and interpretation of results."

Dr. Toohey, an internationally known sports sociologist at California State University in Long Beach, has long been interested in athletes as a distinct group of people. Psychological testing, he says, is performed through personality profiles and inventories. These can be performed subjectively through personal interview or observation, or through the use of more objective paper-and-pencil tests.

"Personality unto itself is complex, and understanding it has challenged mankind for all time. For years we've heard people say, 'He or she is the athletic type.' Most people have heard something like this, and have even said it about someone. Then psychologists and sociologists started to investigate. Is there really an athletic type? If there is, what is it, and what traits and characteristics 'type' or direct one person and not another into sports? These are not simple questions and they do not as yet have simple answers. What we're really talking about here is dismantling and reassembling personalities to determine specific variables and constants. If constant common denominators can be distinguished and identified through valid, accurate testing, then predicting, let's say, if a young person has an 'athletic personality' or which sports areas would better suit him/her psychologically, would be possible."

Other Variables in Matching Athletes to Sports

Some experts believe that a certain body type predisposes a young person to a certain set of personality traits and success in athletics. In this case, genetics would determine personality, but environment would merely determine the extent of development of that personality makeup. Others feel that environment plays a much more significant role than genetics (that is, heredity would determine potential physical skill, but environment would dictate personality and whether physical skill would be used, enhanced or suppressed). Still others in the field of sports psychology believe that certain traits and personality characteristics themselves will determine success in athletics, as well as each person's preference for individual or team sports. The trend seems to be toward the development of testing measures which evaluate *all* the variables: genetics, environment and personality traits and characteristics.

Are There Differences Between Athletes and Non-Athletes?

When Lowell Cooper, a well-known expert, compared athletes' with non-athletes' personalities, reported in the *Research Quarterly*, 1969, he found athletes to be more outgoing and socially confident, more aggressive and dominant; they were leaders instead of followers. He said that they were rated by teachers and peers as having higher social adjustment, prestige and social status, as well as self-confidence. Athletes also seemed to be less compulsive and more impulsive, and possessed a greater tolerance for physical pain and discomfort.

In Albert V. Cannon's book, *Social Psychology of Sport*, he cites the work done by sports psychologists Shurr, Ashley and Joy which identified differences among three types of athletes versus non-athletes. Their study showed that team sports athletes, when compared to non-athletes, were more extroverted, dependent, and possessed less abstract reasoning ability and weaker egos. When individual sports athletes were compared to non-athletes, they too seemed to have less abstract reasoning ability, were more dependent and objective but were less anxious. And those athletes involved in direct competition with others (tennis, football, baseball, hockey, etc.), when compared to non-athletes, were more independent, extroverted and objective.

But there are other studies which show little difference between athletes and non-athletes, so care must be taken not to generalize these findings. However, common sense alone dictates that becoming a top athlete takes determination, a strong drive to excel, discipline, and self-confidence, considering the long and gruelling workouts each sport demands year after year. Most people without drive, commitment and the ability to discipline themselves will more than likely be unable to compete at higher levels of performance.

Even the recreational jogger or other non-competitive athlete who wants either to stay physically fit or surpass his or her present ability level must be disciplined enough to continue a routine, have a strong drive to excel, and display the self-confidence to perform tasks well. The youngsters who don't do well disciplining themselves, don't have the confidence to compete, nor the determination to practice and condition, will probably not engage in highly involved and competitive sports in which these traits are essential.

The question does arise, however, as to whether these traits were developed because of early sports participation or were part of these individuals' personalities before participation in athletics occurred. That question remains unanswered because most testing has been performed on adolescents or older populations. Few studies have dealt with the young child and followed through on a long-term basis to identify results. Until this is done, it won't be known whether the "athletic personality" is born, or develops as a result of sports participation.

Does the Team Athlete Differ from the Individual-Sport Athlete?

Introverts and Extroverts

You've heard people say, "He must be a runner, he's so shy," or "I'll bet she plays volleyball, she has such a nice outgoing personality!" This stereotype of the individual-sports athlete and the team-sport athlete has been around for years. The football player who is outgoing and congenial. The tennis player who is quiet, reserved and shy. The hockey player who is outspoken and involved in school activities. The swimmer or gymnast who hardly ever speaks. The basketball player who always seems to have something to say and "cuts up" in class. For most people, these personality types are well accepted as the norm for participation in specific sports—team or individual. But are they myths? Or is there a basis in fact? Scientists are trying to find out.

Some research has already shown that world-class marathon runners are introverted and that world-class wrestlers are extroverted. Other studies have shown that athletes involved in collision/contact sports score high on extroversion, while those athletes in non-contact sports tend to score lower in that area. Further studies have noted that extroverts seem to be more tolerant of pain than are introverts. In one study of high school football players, defensive players appeared to be more extroverted and less rule-bound; offensive players tended to be more introverted and more rule-bound. Overall, athletes seem to have a greater degree of pain tolerance than non-athletes. All of this research seemed to concur with the general beliefs about team players and individual-sports athletes.

Another study showed that individual-sports athletes, when compared to team athletes, appeared to be less emotional, less dependent, less anxious, more introverted and more objective. Those involved in direct competition with others appeared to be more aggressive, while those involved in indirect competition (against records, points or themselves) were less aggressive.

Exceptions to the Rule

However, there are other studies which point in the opposite direction. There are marathon runners who are extroverts and have a very high tolerance for pain. There are tennis players who are outspoken. There are football and hockey players who are shy, aloof, easily injured and with little tolerance for pain. There are top-level gymnasts who are crowd-pleasers because of their extroverted personalities, and figure skaters who fit that description, too. There are also youngsters who enjoy and excel in many sports, both in team participation and individual athletics; some have more extroverted and others more introverted personalities.

The point is that there are exceptions which cannot and should not be overlooked. To determine a child's area of athletic participation based on personality type alone would be unfair to many young people. It would be an injustice to direct a shy youngster into individual sports and an outgoing youngster into team sports solely on the information now available. Again, the question arises whether personality traits are enhanced and influenced by participation at an early age, or whether they are a unique and specific part of each person's character. Since sports participation can be a socializing experience for youngsters, it's best to provide them with many and varied opportunities, allowing them to grow and to evaluate their likes and dislikes, and then choose the sport or sports they enjoy and in which they excel.

World-Class Athletes vs. Other Competitors

At the Institute for the Study of Athletic Motivation (ISAM), at San Jose State University in California, Thomas T. Tutko and Bruce C. Ogilvie studied personality traits of the high-level competitor. The Athletic Motivation and Inventory Test, developed at ISAM, reportedly identifies traits associated with athletic achievement. Profile sheets of athletes also indicated the degree to which a certain athlete possessed an identified trait. These traits were further broken down into desire factors and emotional factors.

The traits Tutko and Ogilvie identified are: drive, determination, coachability, emotionality, self-confidence, mental toughness, responsibility, trust and conscience development, intelligence, aggression, leadership, and organization. Although they believe that outside influences, such as parents, other family members, boyfriends and girlfriends, teammates, and teachers can have either a positive or negative influence on success, their research showed that the champion athlete (when compared to others) has a great need to succeed, is resistant to the stresses of competition, has psychological endurance, and is self-assertive and confident.

Dr. Tutko, in a book written with Jack W. Richards, noted that: "Although each athlete is uniquely motivated to compete, the athletes who are successful compose a very select group of people. The basic thing these individuals share is talent or the ability to perform a particular skill well. A large number," the authors said, "tend to share certain traits, combined with physical talent, make [sic] possible the selection of those athletes most likely to succeed in high-level competition."

In another study, champions as a group were easily distinguished from other athletes. This study noted that the superior athlete will be one who is extremely aggressive, self-assured, with a high degree of aspiration and the need to achieve. Champions will have, they said, a higher anxiety level and greater emotionalism.

However, another study's results said that there were **no** distinguishing factors between athletes as a group and the champion. All athletes seemed to be determined, disciplined, self-assured and self-assertive.

Obviously, more research must be completed before any definitive answers about possible differences can be ascertained.

The Successful Female Athlete

Is She Different from the Non-Athlete?

Studies of the personality traits of the female athlete are sketchy at best. With studies of her male counterpart called contradictory, inconclusive and often unproductive, more information and testing will need to be done on the female athlete's profile before many criticisms or insights can be applied. However, a few of the studies already completed may give some hints about her psychological make-up.

William P. Morgan, a noted sports psychologist, in his article, "Personality Dynamics and Sport," noted a study in which female team-sport athletes were compared to individual-sports athletes. All women in the study were either members of the Olympic Team or played AAU basketball in the same year. Dr. Morgan said the study pointed out that individual-sport female athletes were "significantly more dominant and aggressive, adventurous, sensitive, imaginative, radical, self-sufficient, resourceful, and less sophisticated than the team-sports group." Individual-sports athletes also appeared to be more introverted than the team-sports athletes, but both were emotionally stable. "These female athletes were found to be more intelligent, conscientious, persevering, and aggressive than female non-athletes of similar age and educational background."

One cross-cultural study of American and Hungarian female Olympic athletes proved very interesting. All those involved in the study were either swimmers, track and field stars, gymnasts, skiers or fencers, and the study showed more similarities in personality than differences. Jean M. Williams, Ph.D. in her article, "Personality Characteristics of the Successful Female Athlete," writes that "Athletes from both countries scored highest on achievement, autonomy, and aggression and lowest on affiliation. In addition to the similarities in personality profile, there were several identical patterns in the developmental dynamics of the two groups. All of the girls talked about themselves as energetic and very active children and as having a strong drive to excel, to be the best. Another recurring theme was the desire to move and the love of movement." Dr. Williams also mentioned the fact that families played a supportive and crucial role in all the athletes' values and ideals.

A study by Eva K. Balazs of 24 female Olympians who represented the United States in the 1972 games found that "All subjects had a strong and early drive to achieve, to 'be the best in something,' 'to be somebody.' They internalized this need early in childhood and set a goal for themselves in sports." She went on to say that, "Fathers were described by almost all as 'available.' . . . The support of both father and mother was positive and consistent . . . [and] in these families everyone believe[s] that sports are worthwhile endeavors and being outstanding in a sport is all right for girls. Sports do not make a girl unfeminine seemed to be the message . . . heterosexual relations were described as satisfying and important to the subjects . . . and 25 percent of the athletes were already married." Dr. Balazs' conclusions from the case studies were that these female athletes had a "strong drive to excel"; conducted "early goal-setting" and followed through to the original goals; held "positive self-images"; displayed "well-developed heterosexuality"; enjoyed "family atmospheres in which support was coupled with high expectations"; and identified as a "main motivating force—parents and the coach."

If these studies are conclusive in any way, it appears that female athletes, on the average, do differ in a number of personality traits from non-athlete females who were less aggressive, less imaginative, less resourceful and self-sufficient, less intelligent, and less goal-oriented.

This research, however, is still in its infancy and much more work will have to be completed with more objective measurements to validate these conclusions.

The Accuracy and Validity of Psychological Testing in Sports

In an attempt to determine the accuracy of psychological testing in identifying successful athletes, William P. Morgan and others studied the 1972 Olympic freestyle wrestling team. Forty athletes competing to make the Olympic team were psychologically tested prior to final selection. The ten athletes who did make the team had lower scores in depression, mental fatigue, tension and confusion than the others. That same team went on to win six Olympic medals.

Dr. Morgan again tested sixty athletes vying for a spot on the 1974 National Rowing Team. He found that testing to determine success was accurate in 70 percent of cases. He noted, however, that the 30 percent margin of error was too high to validate the selection or elimination of athletes on the merits of psychological testing alone. He pointed out that testing methods will need to be made more precise and further investigations must be performed before predictions will be reliable in all cases.

Finding the link between personality and competitive success will be an arduous task. Considering only all the possible variables and subtle differences in people will make it difficult to say who will be better in one sport than in another, or who will be the champion or just an average athlete. This kind of testing will have to be done in conjunction with physical-traits testing and performance testing to better achieve and determine consistent results.

Personality Assessment of Athletes and Non-Athletes in the United States

In the United States, research into personality testing, as well as physical-traits profiling, have not been aimed at eliminating individuals from sports. There are some very real ethical concerns about potential misuse of such profiles, and experts acknowledge that no one should be eliminated from sports activities because of his or her profile.

On the other hand, there are some very real benefits from profiling youngsters at earlier ages if the results are used effectively and practically. Psychological and physical-traits profiling can help direct youngsters into sports areas they would enjoy most and in which they could excel. More probably, they would then continue the sports activity throughout their lives (with the benefit of physical fitness), would be less likely to be injured, and would be less frustrated.

Another benefit of profiling would be to identify the basic personality traits of champions, not as a means of eliminating players from sports, but in order to identify those who have the basic factors to move on to the highest levels of competition without frustration and injury.

In addition, knowing more about the different personalities of athletes could help coaches in their work. With more information about the relationship between personality and sports, the management of tension and anxiety could be improved; methods of sports coaching would be enhanced; techniques of teaching composure and self-confidence in competition could be developed; and many other areas would evolve, based on individual needs and desires, to help the average or the champion athlete improve his or her participation.

In the United States, the direction of personality and physical-traits profiling seems to be aimed at finding ways to better help the aspiring athlete to meet his or her goals. Generalizing or using these methods for the elimination of athletes would not be productive for a free society in which each person can choose his or her own endeavors.

U.S. champion athletes will continue to achieve their preeminence through competition, experience and training. The use of psychological and/or physical-traits testing will probably be of benefit in helping these high-level competitors in training methods, coaching methods, game psychology and sports preparation, But, as Robert N. Singer writes in his book, *Coaching, Athletics, and Psychology*: "There is a remarkable difference in personality traits from athlete to athlete. The lack of consistency in patterns has made it difficult to generalize about the behaviorial expectancies of all athletes. The same is true of superior athletes. Certain traits are frequently encountered in superior athletes, but unique differences make it necessary to deal with all athletes on an individual basis." Dr. Singer has been the sports psychology coordinator on the Sports Medicine Committee of the U.S. Olympic Committee.

Personality Assessment in the Soviet Union

In Russia, a great deal of work is being done in personality assessment, psychological traits and qualities of top-notch performers.

N. Norman Schneidman in his article, "Soviet Sports Psychology in the 1970s and the Superior Athlete," says that, "It is claimed that one of the tasks of contemporary Soviet sport psychology is to compile lists of the most important psychological traits and characteristics that have been scientifically substantiated and tested in practice for different sports, and on the basis of them to establish models of 'ideal' athletes for each sport discipline."

It is believed that in the Soviet Union more than 300 sports psychologists and others are doing studies on sports psychology in 23 institutions for physical culture, 91 facilities of physical education and a number of scientific-research institutions. Experts are attached to National Teams to conduct research, to implement findings to better help the teams develop, and to find aspiring candidates for the teams.

Schneidman goes on to say that research findings are rarely published as they relate directly to the preparation and performance of the Soviet National Teams, "because they are viewed as important weapons in the combat of Soviet athletes and teams against representatives of other countries." Therefore their findings and their implementation will be known only as small bits and pieces leak out to the West or are made available in scientific exchanges.

4.

Conditioning and Training—
Keys to Success

JOHN SOTO IS AN eleven-year-old record holder for his age group in the mile run.

"One day John, then seven years old, came home from school all excited, with a flyer in his hand," his father, Ron, said. "His teacher had given him the flyer and said he could run in the city's cross country race that Saturday if he wanted to. John had never really run to any degree, except the usual things children do. He asked me to coach him, but I wasn't a coach. He seemed so excited about it that I decided that if he really wanted to do this, we'd better go out the Friday before the race and let him try it once."

John practiced the race Friday and set a new city record at the meet on Saturday—much to everyone's amazement, except John's. He took it all in stride. Soon after, John was set to race in the Southern California finals, but had to go to the bathroom as the race was about to begin. The race was delayed for him, and he finished fourth. "Dad," he said, "I want you to be my coach and I want to beat the record next year."

Although Ron Soto had enjoyed running and been interested in athletics, he was not a track coach and even suggested they find a professional if John wanted to achieve on the competitive level. But John would not be convinced, so his father began to read everything he could get his hands on, talked to coaches and trainers, and attended seminars and talks given by doctors and trainers. Then, he carefully devised what he felt to be an appropriate conditioning and training program for John, considering his age and developmental level.

"Basically, John was very small for his age, but was self-motivated. We really felt we had a choice—try to do what was best for him by being supportive, involved and helpful, or let him tackle this alone, without supervision and help. Janis [John's mother] and I decided we would be as supportive as possible if this was what John wanted, and let him decide how far he wanted to go with this. Some coaches and trainers," Ron Soto said, "expect too much of the young ones and pressure them if they don't meet their expectations. We didn't want this for John. Win or lose, we wanted him to be active in a sport of his choice and to be as physically fit as possible."

The Sotos understand that some traits are inherited, but that champions are made through conditioning and training as well. But they felt that this decision and commitment must come from John and not from them. His father says John has "stick-to-it-iveness" and seems to thrive on running. The family makes it a point to be with John at his races, and Ron Soto is always there when John is working out. John's older brother Tim, now 17 years old, is also a superb athlete, and he and John seem affectionately admiring of each other. Both parents support all the endeavors of their sons—school work, social experiences and athletics. They don't believe anyone should ever force a young person into participation or competition, but believe in opening up the avenues which would allow them to do so if they wish. This healthy attitude has allowed John to compete because he wants to, and Tim *not* to compete because he isn't interested in doing so.

John Soto has won many awards. When he was nine, he ran the fastest mile ever run in his age group at the Nationals in Omaha. Then, he set a record in the 10,000-meter race on an AAU course. It was the fastest 10,000 meters ever recorded for anyone through the age-thirteen group—and John was only ten.

If you ask John about all of this success, he puts it very simply. "Well, it just came on slowly. I won a race and thought it was fun, so I kept on going. I work out six days a week and rest one. After track-and-field season, my parents make me take six weeks off, and I take a few weeks off after cross-country. You know, it feels good to run. And my life's been pretty exciting. I've been to meets in Oregon, Nebraska, Canada and other places with my family. I like that, too. And, my brother's a surfer—he's great!"

When asked if others his age or younger should be encouraged to participate in a sport so intensely, John says they should "do what they feel like doing, but should talk it over with their parents first, to make sure it's okay."

Who knows what John Soto will do at eleven, or after? But one thing seems certain—he appears loved by his family, fun to talk with and energetic. "As long as he loves to run and wants to compete and is happy," his father said, "then he'll run. And, if he changes his mind, all of us feel that there are other exciting and important things in life that John can do and enjoy. We think that's the way it should be and encourage that attitude."

Basics about Conditioning and Training

It was evident some years ago that those athletes who trained and conditioned in addition to fine-tuning their sport's skills were performing better and winning more than those who did not follow a specific conditioning and training program. The conclusion was that athletes were more effective in their sport if they attained fitness first.

Conditioning refers to those tasks and skills that make the cardiovascular system more efficient: the ability of the heart and lungs to support and adapt well to increased physical demands and muscle activity. It also involves specific activities, usually repetitive, which also build strength and endurance in muscles.

Training, on the other hand, involves developing skills that are necessary for a specific sport or physical activity. This sport-specific conditioning is the traditional "practice" for a given sport: the repeated throwing in baseball or volleying in tennis or ball-handling in basketball.

Sophisticated training begins at earlier ages than ever before. So experts in the field of sports medicine are stepping in and evaluating the safety of early training both physically and psychologically. Although research is continuing and some questions still need specific answers, from these ongoing studies come recommendations for safe and sane participation.

Conditioning and Training for Every Stage

Early Years

Before the age of six or seven, children should be encouraged to experiment with a variety of sports and activities. In the pre-school years, children learn specific skills best if they think they are fun, or if they see others doing the same things. They are great imitators. They will, therefore, be very interested in learning to swing a bat if an older sibling can, and likewise with other skills. If children of this age are exposed to stretching and conditioning, it should be in the spirit of fun and "doing things with daddy or mommy." Agility, coordination, flexibility, balance and physical activity are the benefits, but fun should be the focus of the activity. Strength and endurance training beyond what the young child does without encouragement are not necessary.

School-Age Children

At age seven or eight, an informal conditioning program may be incorporated into the sports program. It should not be intense or competitive. Exercises such as sit-ups, push-ups, chin-ups, leg-lifts and running are sufficient for strength-building and endurance. Weight training seems inappropriate at this age and is usually not done. Physical activity should be emphasized for fitness and fun alone.

The Pre-Adolescent Years

As the youngster grows older, the training and conditioning program may increase in intensity and duration. But, before the adolescent years, these programs should be carefully and reasonably planned, with the physical and psychological health of the youngster in mind. Most experts agree that somewhere between ten and thirteen years of age (depending on the child's growth and development), more intensive training and conditioning programs may begin, along with more intense competition.

The Teenage Years

As youngsters begin puberty, both the male and female will develop greater strength and muscle mass, but the male will develop more because of his male hormones; it is at this point of puberty that weight training may have marked benefits for the young male athlete, in particular, and for all young athletes, in general. This is also the time that, for both sexes, more strenuous programs involving exercises, interval training, and endurance conditioning can be appropriately added to fine-tuning the skills necessary to succeed in a specific sport. Young males at this age become more conscious of body image and actually seek out weight training on their own.

Achieving Fitness—Can It Be Done through Sports Alone?

Physical fitness is difficult to achieve through sports alone. Consider the baseball player who requires bursts of energy, or the football player who comes in and out of the game, the tennis player who spends a great deal of time picking up balls, or the golfer who has waiting time before playing. Fitness, by definition, should provide health-related benefits: cardiovascular function should be improved; percentage of body fat should be reduced; and ability of the body to function and carry out activities for longer periods of time without fatigue should increase. Achieving physical fitness means that all systems of the body benefit as one approaches tip-top shape. This requires an active, ongoing process, not a passive one, and one not dependent entirely on participation in sports.

Children, though, are more likely to achieve physical fitness through sports than adults. This is because of the amount of time spent on sports and the intensity of the activity. For example, the youngster who shoots baskets, running around the court for an entire afternoon three or four times a week, can become physically fit through this activity, as may the tennis player who rallies and runs for two or three hours. But those who hit a few tennis balls, or shoot a few baskets, or pass a football around, or ice-skate now and then, will probably not gain physical fitness from such casual and intermittent activity.

Sports that do have physical fitness built into them are running, jogging, swimming, rowing, cycling, and cross-country skiing. In athletics today, more emphasis is placed on conditioning and training, in addition to the time spent playing the sport itself. Attaining fitness has reduced injury rates for the well-conditioned athlete.

The Difference between Conditioning for Fitness and Training for a Specific Sport

A football lineman may not be able to run a mile in under eight minutes, but he can easily "run" for an entire sixty-minute game in which play lasts three to five seconds at a time, with brief periods of rest in between. The sprinter may become extremely fatigued when asked to run a distance, only to lose despite being so physically fit for his own race. There's a very distinct difference between physical conditioning for physical fitness, and training for a specific sport. Today most experts believe that a combination of conditioning and specific sports training will provide the best results for health and attainment of goals.

Although a youngster who plays youth baseball, soccer, football, softball, volleyball, and swims may not be conditioned, he or she can participate nonetheless. However, those who *excel* in several sports, particularly as they grow older, are usually the ones who are more physically fit. Those in junior high or high school who are well conditioned seem to be the better athletes, and will probably be the stars of the volleyball team, first string players on the basketball team, or play varsity tennis or other competitive sports.

Although many sports require explosive, short bursts of power, these activities alone will not, in general, result in physical fitness unless the intensity and duration of activity is great enough to stress all the systems of the body. Only total body conditioning results in total fitness.

A young person who appropriately conditions for his or her growth and developmental stage will build stamina and endurance (through cardiovascular fitness and enhanced pulmonary function); achieve strength and muscle tone (which is dependent upon the efficiency of the heart and lungs, as well as muscle condition); and develop greater agility, flexibility, coordination and balance (as the athlete gains control of his or her body while in motion). Success in sports almost always depends upon appropriate conditioning to achieve physical fitness—to extend the limits of the human body—as the child matures into adolescence and adulthood.

Making Physical Fitness Conditioning Yield Dividends

Highly intensive endurance conditioning and sports training programs can be harmful both psychologically and physiologically for young children who are not as yet prepared for an undertaking which sacrifices much of the play time and socializing healthful to childhood. But, because of both great exposure to athletics and great emphasis on winning, conditioning and training programs sometimes get out of hand.

Pressure to excel places the greatest amount of stress on young people who want to be Olympians or professional athletes. The young swimmer, for example, hears that another competitive swimmer is now working out five hours a day, seven days a week, and changes his training and conditioning schedule to meet that same timetable, with hopes of keeping up with or besting the other youngster. Even the local newspaper or television news show announces that athletes in East Germany are identified and nurtured early. They may be sent to special schools where they work out each day, beginning at very young ages. The pressures on the young athlete build and build, because of competitiveness inside the system. The risk is that this trend may not end until the system is overloaded. This stress will continue to increase with the continued emphasis on international competition and winning.

But, in the United States and in some other countries, dedicated coaches and trainers have proven that reasonable methods of training and conditioning, as well as realistic performance expectations at early ages, can pay off too and successful world champions can be nurtured and trained.

Benefits of Beginning Early and Gently

Don Peters is head coach of the SCATS program in Orange County, California, which has successfully placed Olympians on the United States gymnastics team since 1968. He says their training is no secret—they institute reasonable performance expectations and appropriate training and conditioning for youngsters at each level. SCATS pre-school participants, besides doing somersaults and cartwheels, running, tumbling and jumping to music, learn some basic gymnastic skills—but only when they are ready and able to perform the tasks. All coaches emphasize the fun of physical activity, and aim for agility, flexibility, coordination, balance and fluidity of movement. When the children are about six, Don Peters and his staff will begin at a higher level of skills training and informal conditioning.

Starting Competition

No serious competition is allowed until age ten, and it remains relatively low-key until age twelve or thirteen, when training and conditioning programs intensify to meet the young gymnasts' needs. At this time they are ready, both physically and psychologically, to deal with the rigors of training, and to decide whether they wish to make a serious commitment to the sport or not. SCATS has an outstanding record of achievement, yet has not in any way pressured or pushed their young athletes to perform or even to participate. Their approach to conditioning and skills acquisition and their emphasis on slow, careful and appropriate training have not hampered their ability to produce outstanding world-class athletes. Indeed, it appears that this attitude has made them so successful—and the youngsters so involved and enthusiastic.

Making Competition Safe

Coach Peters' SCATS program is an example of many fine programs in Southern California and throughout the United States. Only a small percentage of the girls who use these facilities in this female-only organization move on to the top level of competition. Most participate at a non-competitive level for their own enjoyment and body development

And many concerned coaches are making gymnastics safer by making the demands of competition more reasonable. One of them is Mike Bisk, a competitive gymnast in high school and college, and presently coach of the Monarchs Gymnastic Team in Thousand Oaks, California. This non-profit organization's program serves 400 to 500 young people, and provides a well-respected team development program for top gymnasts.

"We now have a rule change in competitive gymnastics which states that a girl is eligible to compete internationally as long as she is 15 years old by the time of the competition. This is official all over the world," Mr. Bisk notes, "as of the 1980–81 year. There is also a strong movement to raise the age to 16 in the next year or two. This would affect all international, World and Olympic championships. The point is, the girls were burning out and retiring from the sport long before they were women. It was widely felt that the sport was also losing its artistic value and turning into little kids performing difficult acrobatic tricks. We all felt that a mature team would not only be better as artists, but also be better prepared mentally for the pressures of competition. It's simply a positive step. Young girls will be able to mature, we may see fewer injuries and less burn-out, and preparation for the sport can be slowed down."

Like Don Peters, Bisk believes in the careful, gradual building of skills with emphasis on the basics. His program serves not only tiny tots, but provides beginning, intermediate, and advanced training and conditioning; youngsters move up as they are ready both physically and psychologically.

"Of course we'd all like to train and nurture top-level gymnasts, and, in the team programs, we do. But, the point of all these programs is to also allow active and involved participation by as many young people as wish to be part of an exciting sport like gymnastics. We'll probably see a Junior Elite Program which will be developed to allow the under-age to compete on an experience and fun basis. The fact is that," Mike Bisk says, "this rule change concerning age will result in fewer coaches pushing kids to get them into the World Games or Olympics, because the youngsters simply won't be old enough. With less pressure, the young people can enjoy participation and their level of competition without undue stress."

Exercising, Competition or Not

Dan Bailey, head trainer at California State University, Long Beach, agrees that careful and appropriate conditioning and training in any sport, based on a child's age, size, ability and development, is the proper way to go. "Pushing or prodding young people into an intense program too early," he says, "when they are not prepared for it, can only be detrimental for them. The important thing is for parents and others to encourage and allow children to do something which requires endurance and fitness every day. This is the best way to instill the importance of physical activity without pressure or stress. Physical activity then becomes another special part of their lives."

He also points out that when most children are left alone, they will find a happy medium for themselves, if the opportunity to be involved in physical activities exists. "Most of the time," Bailey notes, "the young person will not harm himself or herself, and will not play if something is wrong. It's when an aggressive parent, trainer or coach gets involved that a child can be pushed beyond the limits of reason and good health, both mentally and physically."

Physical Factors in Sports Training

How can a parent and others know what the ideal conditioning and training effects at a certain age in a given sport are? What nutritional requirements are vital for which kinds of program? What psychological risks exist at various ages and stages if a child specializes in one sport?

Part of the problem in answering these questions is that when we talk about young people, we're dealing with different maturational and developmental levels, so it's difficult, if not impossible, to generalize. And generalization might be an injustice to some youngsters; they will simply not fit into a clear, easily identifiable category. The result? Parents and others who work with children sometimes have to "play it by ear," particularly in the early years.

But one thing is certain. Damaging a child physically at a very young age has no place in athletics. The important goals should be: to allow children to participate; to foster their own good opinion of themselves and their accomplishments; to help them learn to deal with failure as well as success; and to understand their abilities and limits. With these goals and an emphasis on fitness and fun, most children will do well with fitness and training programs.

Ideal Weight

Young people who participate in athletes should achieve an ideal weight based on their body type and activity level. Ideal weight involves the percentage of fat on the body more than the actual weight in pounds or kilograms. It is achieved through a balance of caloric intake (how much and what kinds of food the child eats) and the exercise level (how many calories are used). As the young athlete pursues a conditioning program, he requires more and more calories to satify his body's need for fuel. As participation and training intensify, this balance changes.

Interestingly, but not surprisingly, a youngster weighing 130 pounds with 10 percent body fat would be more fit than the youngster of the same height who weighed only 120 pounds but had 20 percent body fat.

The percentage of body fat is determined by using calipers to measure the amount of fat at the waist, thigh, behind the upper arm and elsewhere. It can also be determined more accurately and scientifically by a test which involves submerging the athlete in water while on a special scale. But parents can easily get a rough idea of the percentage of a child's body fat. Simply pinch the subcutaneous tissue (fatty area) on the thigh, waist and the back of the upper arm. If the fold that results is more than an inch thick, the youngster has a greater percentage of body fat than desirable.

Height and weight charts are also helpful guidelines in assessing body fat, but are not absolute indicators. A child with an increased lean muscle mass and large bone structure may appear to be overweight when, in fact, the body fat is relatively low. However, the child with a small bone structure and muscle mass may have increased body fat and still not appear to be overweight when using height and weight charts.

Metabolism—the Body's Energy-Producing Functions

The conversion of fuel (food) into energy is the basis for the body's activities. Fuel-producing substances—sugar (glucose), glycogen (a storage form of sugar), fat, and sometimes proteins—are "burned" to produce energy. Food intake supplies the basic raw materials, which are converted through digestion into immediate or stored fuels. These energy sources are kept ready for use by the body through one of its two types of metabolism.

Aerobic metabolism is a complex chemical reaction which depends upon oxygen to convert the fuel into energy. In anaerobic metabolism, on the other hand, the fuel is converted into energy without the help of oxygen (the fuel is found in the muscle tissue itself).

Each of these forms of metabolism happens normally in everyone, but each individual can be stimulated to greater efficiency through specific conditioning for each.

Let's look at each of these systems, and the appropriate training and conditioning for each, in more detail.

Conditioning Methods for Sports Training

Endurance Training (Aerobic Metabolism)

The goal of endurance training is to achieve an excellent aerobic metabolism capacity. Sustained muscle activity is dependent upon heart/lung fitness, and chemically requires the "burning" of sugar or fat with oxygen to produce energy. Exercises which require endurance and stamina place great demands on aerobic metabolism. Likewise, aerobic metabolism is greatly dependent on the ability of the heart and lungs to provide efficient, oxygen-rich blood flow to the muscles and other systems of the body. Without this efficiency, the chemical exchange will be less than optimal, and the body will feel fatigued and uncomfortable.

Activities which stimulate the heart and lungs to function efficiently result in conditioning of the aerobic system of metabolism. When the lungs exchange oxygen efficiently and the heart's pump is working at its peak, oxygen is supplied to the tissues, and glucose is utilized to produce energy.

Aerobic exercises, when performed as part of a regular, planned program, contribute to physical fitness. Examples of such exercises include running, jogging, bicycling, swimming, cross-country skiing and brisk walking. With these exercises, activity should be increased in both intensity and duration over a period of weeks or months. Ideally the youngster will continue the endurance training exercises for a lifetime, not just for a particular sports season.

Quickness Conditioning (Anaerobic Metabolism)

The complement to aerobic metabolism is anaerobic metabolism, which results in bursts of energy production from explosive activity. Anaerobic metabolism does not depend on oxygen for energy release. Fuel for this type of metabolism is stored in the muscle fiber itself. The carbohydrate glycogen is instantly released with the start of activity. Lactic acid is a by-product of this chemical reaction in the muscle, and the build-up of this chemical results in fatigue and muscle discomfort. One of the goals of anaerobic conditioning is to train the muscles to withstand the presence of lactic acid. Many experts believe that anaerobic training also increases the enzymes which process the glycogen in the muscle, and may be beneficial in conditioning the fast-twitch muscles (those responsible for explosive power or strength).

All activities require anaerobic metabolism to some extent, but those in which it is the rule are: baseball; football; sprints in such sports as swimming, running and speed skating; figure skating; and downhill skiing. All of these are characterized by short bursts of intense activity. Anaerobic conditioning involves training through repeated short bursts of activity separated by rest periods.

Putting It All Together

Even in those sports which require short bursts of energy with accompanying rest periods, most top-level competitors condition both their anaerobic and aerobic metabolism for the best possible results. If we look at world-class competitors, most perform aerobic and anaerobic conditioning in their programs, as well as train to perfect the skills necessary for performance in their specific athletic area (sport-specific conditioning). It is helpful to maintain generalized fitness between seasons.

Two Types of Training Regimens

Research has proven that there are different types of muscle fibers, but that two are particularly significant to the athlete: the slow-twitch and fast-twitch muscles briefly discussed in Chapter 1. The abundance of one type of muscle fiber over another is determined by heredity (inheritance), but conditioning and training can have a major impact on improved performance of both muscle types.

Slow-twitch muscle fibers are generally used in sports or activities requiring stamina and endurance. This type of muscle fiber is most efficient and effective in aerobic metabolism. *Fast-twitch* muscle fibers are associated with performance in events requiring speed, quickness and explosive power with short bursts of energy, and their functioning is primarily dependent on anaerobic metabolism.

If a youngster has an abundance of fast-twitch muscles, he or she may find endurance activities more difficult. In the same sense, those young people with an abundance of slow-twitch muscle fibers will meet frustration in speed events. Youngsters with fairly equal numbers of both muscle types will improve with appropriate conditioning and training, but may not excel as they might if a specific muscle type were favored.

In most athletic events, endurance and speed are both important. Therefore, most young athletes will need a conditioning program which includes both aerobic exercise and anaerobic training. This training might include running short sprints as fast as possible, then resting briefly, then doing it again and again, coupled with longer slower runs.

Strength Training for All Athletes

Basically, there are three techniques for development of muscle size and strength: isometric exercise, isotonic exercise, and isokinetic exercise. All use muscle contractions to increase the power of the muscle.

Isometric Exercises

Although muscle contractions occur in isometric exercises, they happen without significant shortening of the muscles and without joint motion. Simply, such exercise involves tightening the muscles in a specific area as tight as possible for a maximum of ten seconds, then releasing the tension on the muscle, then tightening and releasing again. As resistance builds up, more repetitions are performed.

Isometric exercise is very useful when an extremity is injured, because it doesn't require shortening the muscle or joint movement. These exercises can be done even while an extremity is in a cast, or when joint motion must be restricted. Isometrics can be performed while standing, sitting, or lying down, don't require any equipment, and can tone and build muscles in any part of the body simply by increasing the number of times the repetitive tightening and relaxing is done.

Isotonic Exercises

Isotonic exercises are among the most popular methods used for strength-building in athletes. Here, weights and various exercise machines aid in muscle development. Included in the group of isotonic exercises are sit-ups, pull-ups and push-ups, because the body itself acts as the weight being lifted, pulled or pushed. During this kind of exercise, the muscle which is shortening is said to be undergoing *concentric* contraction; when it lengthens, the contraction is *eccentric*. As an example, let's look at what happens when a weight is lifted by bending the elbow. When the weight is lifted toward the body, the biceps muscle in the front of the arm tightens (undergoes concentric contraction). When the arm is straightened, the biceps lengthens (eccentric contraction). During this kind of exercise, although the weight itself remains the same, the force the muscle exerts may vary because of the changing relationship of the muscle to the bone, and the "lever" action at the joint is different in different positions. So, with weight-lifting, there may be a throwing effect; that is, as one starts to lift the weight quickly, there is an initial burst of muscle activity. Once the inertia of the weight is overcome, a throwing effect occurs as a result of the explosive power of the muscle.

Isokinetic Excercises

Recently, sophisticated machines were developed which eliminate the ballistic (throwing) effect of weight-lifting. Essentially, these machines accommodate changes in the lever arm as the muscles shorten. No matter how hard someone pushes, the weight will move only so fast. This controls the speed at which the muscle contracts, adjusting to explosive power and coordinating and training it.

The primary purpose of isokinetic exercise is to enhance this explosive power, necessary in the performance of many sports. In most coordinated movements in athletics, there is a balance between explosive contractions and more graduated contractions. This varies by sport.

The principle that for every action, there must be an equal and opposite reaction is true in muscle function. When one muscle on one "side" of a joint contracts, another muscle must relax. And, in order to reverse the movement, the relaxed muscle must contract, and the contracted muscle must relax again. This kind of reciprocal action happens in a fluid movement, as it does in running—one set of muscles draws the leg forward, and another set contracts to stop the forward movement, and pull the leg backward. The process is repeated with the other leg.

Although most experts feel that sports-specific strengthening can be achieved without the use of expensive equipment, most also agree that the use of equipment is perhaps a more efficient method in closely supervised programs. All young athletes who wish to excel in sports will probably include such muscle building and strengthening as an integral part of training.

Stretching and Flexibility

As the young person grows older, stretching and maintaining the range of motion of joints and muscles become more important as a part of conditioning and exercise. Aging results in a tendency to become less flexible and there is a loss of the extreme range of motion of the joints. The extent of this phenomenon varies from person to person and is also dependent upon whether or not he or she has "tight" or "loose" joints to begin with.

Stretching exercises are vital in all sports, and proper and adequate warm-up helps prevent injuries. Stretching and flexibility exercises vary according to the demands of each sport.

If a parent doesn't know the best means of stretching and warming up for a particular sport, he or she can find the most up-to-date information by: (1) talking to the coach or trainer of the local high school or college; (2) viewing a practice session of the local college team in that sports area; (3) arriving at a professional sports event early enough to watch the warm-up drills; (4) seeking out seminars or lectures by professionals on physical fitness and training; (5) asking a sports medicine specialist to suggest appropriate warm-up drills aimed specifically at the desired sport or activity.

Training with Pain

Some discomfort is associated with intense conditioning and training. Changes result when new or repetitive demands, or both, are placed on muscles, tendons, joints, ligaments, bones and other structures. This can be largely avoided with off-season conditioning and a program to build endurance, strength, agility and quickness started slowly, lengthened and intensified over a period of time—weeks to months. If a young person experiences minor discomfort due to a new program, this should disappear during the warm-up stretching and flexibility exercises.

But overdoing it—too long or too strenuous exercising—bears the potential of causing an injury to the growth plate, joint or bone. Or the young person may experience muscle strain, sprain or contusion (see Chapter 14 for details) due to inappropriate training or accidental injury. So young people *should not* "work through" pain when conditioning or playing in an event. If pain is repeatedly present in a shoulder, elbow, knee, hip, ankle, neck, or the back, the youngster should cease the aggravating activity and be seen by a physician. And, if there is sudden, severe pain—at any time—the young athlete should stop that activity and be evaluated.

Pain is the body's natural warning sign. This warning should not go unheeded. If it is ignored, further injury or a life-long handicap could result.

Heavy Days and Light Days

Attaining a high level of conditioning is hard work and is best accomplished through a planned progressive program of exercise and activity. Most experts agree, however, that maximal efficiency is accomplished if the program involves heavy days of workout interspersed with days of lighter activity.

Heavy days of conditioning and training are aimed at pushing the body to its maximum performance and endurance. These hard days usually are followed by a recovery day or lighter day. Lighter days involve enough activity to keep the body at the previously attained level, a plan designed to prevent the athlete from getting too fatigued and "burned out"—both physically and emotionally. Programs are individualized to the athlete and sport, but most serious athletes exercise strenuously three days a week, and lightly for three days, and rest one day. For the less serious athlete, shorter or lighter programs than this may be desirable, but should still involve a combination of harder and easier conditioning.

Training and Conditioning Can Only Do So Much

Even the best and most appropriate training and conditioning can carry an athlete only so far. Many other things influence whether or not the young person will excel at a high level of performance. The length and proportion of the bones—lever arms—affect the efficiency of the muscles.

The amount of oxygen available for metabolic exchange in the body is also important in determining the athlete's vital capacity; and this is dependent on chest size and the condition of the lung tissue itself. The relative proportions of fast-twitch or slow-twitch muscles will further determine the performance of the young athlete. All of these are dependent on heredity, things which cannot be changed, but can be trained and conditioned—to a point.

Another intangible is the young athlete's ability to tolerate "pushing" the body as he or she reaches higher and higher levels of competition. Setting a world record is usually painful—it's pushing the human body to extremes. If you look at world record holders, you will notice that some could perform at a maximal level only once, while others can continue to perform at greater and greater levels on successive occasions. Whether success results from a combination of physical attributes, mental readiness and psychological drive, or one of these more than another, is presently difficult to measure or predict. But being a champion requires all aspects of performance to be at their peak at performance time. Although a few are able to accomplish awe-inspiring feats, it will be some time before *all* the mechanisms which control this ability to soar beyond normal human limits are totally understood.

Points to Remember

➤ Physical fitness requires a sustained program of conditioning. It is difficult to become physically fit through playing games alone.

➤ Conditioning and training for children and young people should be designed with the youngsters' level of growth and development in mind. What is desirable for a teenage athlete is not necessarily ideal for the younger child.

➤ Conditioning and training for young children should involve more play than sustained hard work. As a youngster approaches puberty, he or she responds more dramatically to programs to maximize strength, endurance and speed.

➤ Conditioning and training should be directed at development of both aerobic and anaerobic fitness.

➤ A training program should include both heavy and light days of conditioning and activity.

➤ Proper conditioning and training not only have long-lasting health benefits for the youngster, but can also be instrumental in preventing or minimizing injuries related to participation in athletics and strenuous activity.

5.

Nutrition and the Young Athlete

THERE HAVE BEEN MANY and varied dietary plans touted as being "the best" for athletic performance and physical fitness. But the nutritional requirements of the young athlete are easy to follow and do not necessarily include specialized foods, nutrients or supplements.

Years of research into the effects of various diets on performance show that there is no "miracle diet" and that a well-balanced nutritional plan developed around the four food groups (defined later) will supply the athlete with necessary energy and fuel. In most cases, the only special requirements for those involved in strenuous activities and conditioning regimes will be greater food intake to meet the body's increased energy needs.

Vitamin Supplements, Megavitamins and Minerals

A well-balanced, healthful diet is capable of supplying all the energy an aspiring young athlete needs. The use of vitamin supplements, megavitamins, minerals, additional protein or amino acids is unnecessary—unless the youngster has a specific deficiency which his or her doctor has identified and for which a supplement has been prescribed. Widespread publicity of various supplements encouraged budding young athletes to swallow them. But this has resulted in great controversy over the years. Folklore developed as one heard that a great star used this or that food supplement or dietary plan. Young people felt that imitating a star would improve their performance. And sometimes performance improved—not because of the supplement or regime, but as the result of a psychological impact. This is the well-known placebo effect. Because the young person believes something will improve performance, speed or endurance, it does. The fact is, there is presently no scientific data which unequivocally proves that the use of any vitamin, mineral or supplement will improve an athlete's performance—if he or she is receiving adequate and proper food on a daily basis. It's foolish to spend great sums of money on them.

In fact, some vitamins or minerals or combinations in large quantities can be dangerous and even life-threatening. An excess of Vitamin B complex will simply be excreted by the body, but nicotinic acid (niacin) in excessive doses may cause damage to the heart muscle with or during strenuous activity. Vitamins A and D are toxic in large amounts and are not quickly excreted. Both can jeopardize the young athlete's health, as will excessive iron, which is also toxic.

A daily multivitamin tablet will do no harm as a supplement to a young athlete's diet. However, even these are usually unnecessary if the young person is following a well-balanced nutritional plan. A large number of young athletes, for various reasons, do not eat a balanced diet and the daily multivitamin may be a consideration.

The Well-Balanced Diet and the Young Athlete

Today's emphasis on fast foods—the convenience of grabbing something at school or at home or at the hamburger stand up the street— has resulted in poor dietary habits for many young people. Parents and other influential adults should encourage good health habits with eating nutritious food being an important part of those habits. Foods are often overcooked, eliminating most of their vitamin and nutritional components. So much more is now known about the effects of foods on the body that a healthful, easy to follow diet on a recommended schedule can help avoid crash dieting, improper nutrition and fad food programs.

Nutritional requirements are based first of all on the calorie as the unit for energy and body fuel. Proteins, carbohydrates and fats are burned by the body and converted into energy (calories) for all organ systems and tissues of the body—including the heart and other muscles—through metabolism. For optimal health, a young person needs certain kinds of foods, as well as a specific number of calories. The number of calories required is based on body size, desired weight, and activity level. Although the basic food groups remain constant for all ages and body types, the portions (caloric intake) do differ greatly.

For example, the child of four will have an average weight of perhaps 36 pounds, and, if moderately active, will require roughly 1,450 calories a day, preferably derived from a well-balanced assortment of foods from the four food groups listed below. The average youngster of fifteen, by contrast, will weigh about 122 pounds and will need 3,000 calories a day. Of course, these figures vary according to each individual's growth and development, physical build and activity level.

The Four Food Groups

Meats and Other Proteins

Includes beef, pork, veal, fish, lamb, poultry, and eggs. Two servings daily of these high protein foods (about four or five ounces per serving) will meet the young athlete's minimum daily requirement for protein.

Dairy Products

Consists of all dairy products: whole or skim milk, half-and-half, evaporated milk, buttermilk, cheddar, American or other cheeses, cottage cheese and ice cream. Daily minimum requirements can be met by two or more servings.

Fruits and Vegetables

Includes citrus juice (and other fresh juices), deep yellow and dark green vegetables, fruits and potatoes. Four servings meet the minimum daily requirement.

Grain and Cereals

Consists of cereals and breads made of whole, enriched or restored grain. Four servings each day meet the minimum daily requirement.

Tailoring Eating Habits

Eating according to these food groups will give the young athlete all the nutrients, proteins, carbohydrates and fats minimally required, but will probably not provide the needed number of calories for an active young person. The types and servings above are the baseline nutritional requirements for daily food intake. As the youngster grows, his or her caloric intake will increase and as the activity level increases even more food will be needed. Preferred foods or extra helpings of choices from the four food groups should be added to meet the youngster's caloric needs. In general, a nutritious diet is comprised of 50 percent carbohydrates, 35 percent fats, and 15 percent proteins. The young person should be encouraged to eat either three regular meals or more frequent smaller meals distributed at regular intervals throughout the day. This provides a constant source of energy and allows for proper digestion. One large meal a day or irregular snacking won't do this.

Most young children, given the proper food and not prodded to overeat, will eat servings appropriate for their energy needs, and will request more food if their need increases. In most cases, a young person will follow a dietary plan learned early on: the overeater may continue to overeat, and the youngster who learned well-balanced nutritional habits will, in general, continue to follow a similar plan as he or she grows older, particularly if he or she is involved in a fitness program or sports conditioning.

The Dangers of Sugars

Essentially sugar has no specific nutritional value except adding calories to a diet. The designation "empty calories" is a good one. Unfortunately, there are still some people who feel that sugar or sweets are important energy-producing foods before or during physical activity, and recommend dextrose pills, candy, sugar cubes or honey as energy builders. Drinks containing sugar should be limited during activity, with water and small amounts of fruit juices substituted for them. Water should not be restricted during activity as many people have believed.

The Pre-Game Meal

Everyone has questions about the athlete's pre-game meal. There has been much confusion because in the past the heavy training meal was a ritual. Recently, the pre-game meal has been revolutionized because of better understanding of nutrition and its effects on the body's energy supply. That means the huge steak is out! Protein is not an efficient energy fuel, because it takes time and energy to digest.

Carbohydrates and fats, the main sources for the body's energy,

are efficient energy fuels, and are more easily digestible. Protein requirements should be met within forty-eight hours of athletic participation; the young athlete will want energy fuel such as spaghetti or
pancakes before competition or participation. Because it takes at
least two hours for these foods to get through the stomach, a heavy
meal of carbohydrates and fats should be eaten at least three to six
hours before the events, if not the night before.

For those who have the problem of a touchy or jittery stomach
before competition or participation, a liquid meal is sometimes the
answer. Liquid meals were first developed for use in hospitals for patients who could not tolerate solid food, and will supply the young
athlete with fluid and some energy. They cause less stress on the gastrointestinal system before competition than a solid meal might.
Most coaches can recommend an appropriate type of liquid meal
from those now on the market. Small quantities of liquid meals can
be sipped up until time for the event. Sipping decreases the possibility of nausea or vomiting associated with stomach jitters, and jitters
usually disappear once the competition starts.

Carbohydrate Loading

Carbohydrate loading has been given a great deal of attention in recent years, but is not as applicable to the young athlete as to the
adult. Young athletes involved in high school competitive long-dis-
tance running, intensely long tennis matches, or other endurance
events, for example, may wish to try carbohydrate loading only for
special competitions.

At the beginning of the week before the competition, the athlete
limits his or her carbohydrate intake and trains heavily. Three to four
days before the competition, the athlete changes to a basic diet (four
food groups) but supplements it with a large carbohydrate intake,
and trains lightly. Essentially, the glycogen in the muscle is depleted
when the athlete is on the low carbohydrate diet and training heavily. When the athlete changes to a high carbohydrate diet with light
training, glycogen is restored and "overloaded"—stored—in the
muscle. Glycogen is the substance in the muscle which produces energy. The theory is that if glycogen is doubled by carbohydrate overloading, then energy levels will be increased.

Athletes who do not perform for two continuous hours or more probably will not benefit from carbohydrate overloading. And most young athletes will not be involved in competitions of this sort unless they are at the world-class level—and are marathon runners or those with the same demands of such an endurance event.

A word of caution—depleting glycogen during vigorous training may interfere with a demanding training schedule and actually be a hindrance instead of a benefit in the long run if it clearly affects the athlete's ability to train. There have also been reports of stiffness and "heaviness" in the muscles due to carbohydrate loading, as well as some incidences of chest pain and altered electrocardiograms. Very excessive amounts of glycogen can also destroy muscle tissue, so the practice should be restricted to very special competitions and only used by the well-developed adolescent—if his or her level of competition demands it and he or she can tolerate it. It is not recommended for children or pre-adolescents, and has no reasonable place in their sports activities.

Iron Deficiency

Various surveys have shown that many and varying populations appear to be in a state of iron deficiency risk. Mild degrees of iron deficiency have been associated with limitations in learning ability as well as reduction in the ability to perform physical tasks.

Ten to fifteen percent of women are found to have some form of iron deficiency, but fewer are actually anemic. (Anemia is a potentially serious problem in which there is less than the normal amount of hemoglobin, the red pigment in the red blood cells which carries oxygen to all parts of the body.) Although iron deficiency is not the only cause of anemia, it is one of the most common causes of this problem.

Nathan Smith, M.D., a professor in the Departments of Pediatrics and Orthopedics at the University of Washington in Seattle, and a well-recognized expert in the nutritional aspects of sports, points out in an article published in the October, 1978, issue of *Pediatric Annals*, that a mild level of iron deficiency is probably present throughout the years during which a woman has menstrual cycles. By contrast, iron deficiency in males is usually limited to adolescence, when boys are experiencing a rapid growth spurt and may have inadequate and unpredictable diets.

A blood test is necessary to determine whether or not they are anemic and to assess their iron status and may be a part of the complete pre-participation physical examination. This will allow prescription of appropriate supplements, when indicated. This is particularly important for the increasing numbers of young women who are participating in a variety of sports.

In general, following a proper diet is preferred. For those not taking the four food groups as recommended, a daily multiple vitamin with iron as insurance will provide all the necessary vitamins and nutrients including iron for all age groups. No one should self-prescribe more iron than this for their youngsters, because excessive amounts of iron can be toxic and even fatal. If supplements are prescribed to iron-deficient or anemic young people after an appropriate blood test, the recommended dose should be carefully followed. All vitamins and iron supplements should be kept well out of the reach of small children, in whom overdose is potentially deadly.

Poor Nutrition and Its Effects

In the same article in *Pediatric Annals,* Dr. Smith addresses another important and often forgotten point about nutrition and young athletes: that doctors, parents, coaches, school nurses and others who work with youngsters should be aware of young athletes who, while trying to be competitive in sports, are unable to have their nutritional needs met. Most often this happens because the athlete comes from a home which is unable to supply sufficient food to meet the high requirements of an active, growing youngster.

Insufficient food intake, for whatever reason, can at worst limit a young person's growth and development, and at the very least can result in a low energy level. Athletics places additional demands on the body and its energy needs (food intake). If the energy sources are inadequate, the athlete cannot perform on the level that would be possible if his or her nutritional needs were adequately met. Poor nutrition can affect a young person's school work as well. Although lack of adequate food intake can affect young people of all ages, it seems most pronounced in the adolescent. The adolescent experiences a growth spurt which results in additional nutritional requirements. If the demands of sports participation are added to this already increasing need, the problem is obvious. Coaches in particular should be keenly aware of this potential problem and, if possible, steps should be taken to supplement the youngster's diet. In some areas, the school or athletic department may have an existing program to assist in such matters. If not, it may be possible to develop one.

Weight Control in Athletics

Weight Loss

Weight is lost or gained according to the balance between the number of calories ingested daily and the level of physical activity performed on a routine basis. In weight-specific sports such as wrestling, crew, and boxing, great concern has developed over the years about methods of weight control.

The controversy surrounding weight-control programs has centered on the use of crash diets, inappropriate liquid-restricted diets and medications to hasten weight reduction. A few days away from competition, many youngsters find themselves practically starving or inappropriately restricting fluids and inducing sweating in order to meet the required weight for their class. This is not only unhealthy, but avoidable. A well-planned, long-range program for weight reduction based on good health principles is best when it comes to meeting a certain weight.

In an ideal weight-reduction program, the percentage of body fat present is determined, and the amount of safe weight loss to meet optimal fitness is projected. The reduction plan is based on a diet that provides foods from all four food groups so that all nutritional needs are met. But caloric intake (the amount of the various foods eaten) is slightly restricted. The young athlete is also encouraged to increase his or her activity level to "burn off" more fat. Weight loss is accomplished easily and without abusive measures, over a period of several weeks. By eliminating 500 calories from the normal daily diet, a weight loss of one to two pounds each week can be accomplished, depending upon the amount of activity. This can be continued until the optimal weight for that young person is reached. A maintenance program is then initiated to ensure the stabilization of the weight loss.

This type of weight-reduction or weight-control program must be started long before the sport is begun, so that the youngster is at the desired and healthy weight when the sport season starts. Then the young athlete has only to continue his or her maintenance program and activity level in order to keep the unnecessary fat off. Parents should be wary of any quick reducing plans, because they can have an adverse effect on the youngster's growth, development and energy level.

There is no place in sports for weight-reduction medications of any kind—"uppers," thyroid pills, over-the-counter weight reducing pills, and such. ("Uppers" or stimulants increase the body's rate of metabolism, and may have harmful effects on the cardiovascular system. Thyroid pills given to a youngster have a potential for destroying the natural hormonal balance in the body. Over-the-counter weight/appetite control drugs combine stimulants and sometimes antihistamines to suppress appetite. These may have adverse effects on the cardiovascular system.)

A common-sense nutritional plan, which slightly reduces the number of calories eaten, complemented by an increase in activity level, will not cause problems with growth and development, and will judiciously remove unwanted fat from the body while still maintaining lean muscle mass.

Weight Gain

"Bulking up" is the term used for quick weight gain, and is most frequently heard with reference to football, weight lifting and other strength-dependent sports. The problem with "bulking up" is that young men (in particular) and women do not follow a reasonable nutritional plan, and end up adding 20 to 50 pounds of fat instead of lean muscle mass. This is done by eating foods rich in saturated fats, cholesterol and sugar—all associated with an increased risk for cardiovascular disease.

Obesity is not the answer when it comes to healthy weight gain for better performance or strength. Neither is the use of drugs to stimulate muscle growth. In most cases, the use of these drugs for weight gain, bulk and strength, are not particularly effective, and can be dangerous. Anabolic steroids (male sex hormones), for instance, are potentially dangerous drugs which mimic the action of certain hormones in the body. Some of the effects may be irreversible.

Liquid diets and supplements used for weight gain are popular. But they, too, add only calories to the body—meaning fat. Obesity puts greater stress on the heart muscle and its vessels, and packs fat around other organs and tissues. The body has to work harder to carry the useless heavy load.

Adding meaningful weight—lean muscle mass—can be sensibly accomplished through a reasonable nutritional plan coupled with exercise aimed at increasing muscle mass. Addition of muscle mass can be accomplished only through hard work, coupled with the right diet. The usual exercise program to increase muscle mass requires an addition of extra calories (not "empty" ones, about 1,000 a day) to the already balanced diet, which contains the four basic food groups. By working out in some form of weight-training program four to six days a week, an athlete can add one to two pounds of lean muscle mass to the body. If, for instance, the young athlete wishes to gain twenty pounds of muscle mass, then it would take two to three months.

Before the young athlete begins a weight-gaining program, the percentage of body fat may be determined (by measurement with calipers or a special submersion test). To ensure that weight gain is not due to an increase in body fat, this should be checked periodically throughout the weight-gaining program. If the percentage of body fat increases, the athlete's diet will need modification until the ratio of body fat to muscle decreases. The young athlete may cut caloric intake, but should maintain his or her training program (and may even increase it) if this happens. This type of weight-gaining program requires some far-sightedness on the part of the young athlete, coaches and parents alike, because it must begin long before the specific sport's season. But it is one way for a youngster to gain weight healthily.

6.
Alcohol and Drugs—
Handling the Problem

WHETHER FOR PLEASURE, out of curiosity, to lift depression or because of peer pressure, the use of drugs (including alcohol) among young people today has reached epidemic levels. It is foolishly naive to assume that drug use could not be a serious problem for a young athlete, or that the drug culture could not filter into the population of athletic youngsters.

Although it appears that young people who get involved with drugs and alcohol tend to drop out of sports because they cannot keep up with the physical and emotional demands of conditioning, it's important for parents to be aware of the problem, know the warning signs and learn what to do if they suspect a problem.

Unfortunately, some young people also take certain drugs because of a mistaken belief that the drug will help them reach maximum performance. So far, all scientific studies fail to show that the use of any drug improves the athletic performance of normal youngsters. This is particularly true in those sports or activities which require fine motor skills and coordination, but applies also to those involving explosive power and speed.

Athletic performance can only be hindered by drug use. Drugs—any drugs—also have potential and current dangers to the health and well-being of youngsters. And that includes the substances discussed below.

Alcohol

You've probably heard someone say, "He couldn't be an alcoholic—he's only 11 years old," or "That's utterly ridiculous! You're talking about my daughter—don't tell me she drinks all the time. You're wrong!" The fact is that the most commonly abused drug in the young population, athletes included, is alcohol. And this problem includes children from grade school through high school.

Obviously, alcohol is easily abused and overused because of its availability at home or at friends' homes. Most children will experiment with alcohol; that is, simply try it. And athletes tend (although this is admittedly a generalization) to be more outgoing, aggressive and experimental, wanting to try different things. Fortunately, most will simply try it and that will be that. Youngsters who are intensely involved in their sports are on such vigorous training programs and are so keyed up to perform on the highest possible level that they really can't become very involved with the use of alcohol. If they do, it is almost impossible for them to continue their intense conditioning program or compete with the others.

But the majority of young athletes are not seeking international competition or a professional career in sports. Rather, they are involved in sports because they enjoy the challenge, the competition, the exercise, the chance to excel and the sociability. Although their participation in sports activities shows a propensity for good health and exercise, they are susceptible to experimentation. Particularly for the under-21 group, there is still tremendous peer pressure to drink. Even though alcohol consumption can diminish an athlete's performance, wanting to be "in" often means drinking with friends or buddies.

One athlete interviewed in a recent issue of *The Physician and Sports Medicine* noted that he started smoking pot during eighth grade, and began drinking at 13. He had been involved in football, basketball and baseball. After the first summer of his drinking, he went out for football, but had to quit because he could not "take the physical exertion and still drink and smoke heavily." He was getting pressure both from those he was hanging around with—his drug-using friends—and at the same time from his athlete friends who did not use marijuana or alcohol. But he didn't make it back into sports until after treatment for alcoholism and drug abuse.

His parents didn't want to admit or accept that he had an alcohol problem. They felt, he said, that he was going through a "stage." He noted that when he was in junior high school, others were also getting drunk frequently, and that when he was in high school, getting drunk was an every-weekend event.

Alcohol is a drug, although the use of alcohol, unlike other drug use, is more socially acceptable. Youngsters see their parents, their parents' friends, their own friends drink. They watch television commercials in which sports stars praise a certain beer or alcoholic beverage. Chic, tanned and athletic models—very young-looking—also advertise alcohol. It's all very appealing, and no one talks about the devastating effects of alcohol abuse, physically and emotionally, on youngsters and adults both.

Alcohol is said to cause feelings of euphoria, relaxation, lost inhibitions and increased confidence. Yet little is said about the decrease in fine motor coordination and alertness alcohol causes. Even less is said about the serious effects of alcohol abuse: alcohol dependence; liver, brain and kidney damage; serious ulcers and stomach bleeding; delirium; painful and dangerous withdrawal. Excessive use of alcohol can affect every organ system in the body, destroying one after another.

Alcohol is *not* only an adult problem. A 1978 report by the Department of Health, Education and Welfare (HEW) said that 3.3 million of the more than 9 million problem drinkers in the United States were between the ages of 14 and 17. And alcoholism among young children, even 7 or 8 years old, is more common than one would think. The problem is widespread and growing.

There are rules in most schools and organizations providing for the disqualification of athletes caught drinking. In some cases, players can be suspended from participation for a certain length of time even if the drinking took place away from school or the athletic event. Because of a youngster's drive to participate in athletics, he or she may refrain from experimenting with alcohol. But in many cases there is so much peer pressure that the youngster gives in once, and then the question is whether or not he or she will continue to drink with friends.

If the youngster gets caught drinking, and is suspended from participation or otherwise disciplined, it's time for the parent to do more than get angry. He or she must evaluate the extent of the situation. Was this a one-time experience? Or has this been happening for some time? Could the youngster have a serious problem? Professional help—from the family doctor or pediatrician—may be necessary, even invaluable. If the problem appears to be serious, the parent and youngster will be referred to a specialized treatment center.

If a parent notices "watered-down" bottles, or beer or wine missing from the home, or hears that the youngster is drinking, it's very important to find out what's really going on so the young person can be helped, rather than deny a problem may exist. Denial doesn't help anyone. Talking to the youngster, or to his or her coach, trainer or teacher, might also be helpful. The family doctor may be the next step, or perhaps obtaining information about Alcoholics Anonymous.

A self-help program, Alcoholics Anonymous has pamphlets slanted for the young person. Literature can be obtained from a local, central office in any large city in the country. In small cities or in the countryside, a quick look in the telephone directory will tell you whether or not there is a local office and program. If not, a call to the telephone company's information service, asking for the number of Alcoholics Anonymous in the nearest large city will get you the phone number. Requests for literature can be done by either phone or mail. And the public relations chairman and committee of local programs are always happy to send speakers to schools to talk about alcoholism, as well as what Alcoholics Anonymous is and does, and how a teenage alcoholic can be helped. The program does not discriminate because of age, and programs throughout the country have teenage and sometimes even younger members. Their educational programs for schools and youth groups are considered excellent because members of Alcoholics Anonymous themselves talk to the young people about alcoholism, its potential destructiveness, and what can be done to help.

Generally, a frank understanding of what alcohol is and what it does and can do is enough to change the situation for those youngsters who merely wanted to try it, or for whom peer pressure seemed to be the culprit. Education also helps greatly when it comes to the use of drugs, especially when the material presented is factual and honest. If the youngster is at a more advanced stage, more intense steps will need to be taken.

Here are a few things parents should remember:

✓ alcoholism isn't limited to any age group
✓ use among junior high and high school youths is increasing
✓ alcoholism is a disease that can cripple and destroy
✓ youngsters need to be better educated about the physical and emotional hazards of drinking

➤ peer pressure to "join the crowd" will probably always exist and exert quite a strong influence on youngsters
➤ girls are just as prone to alcohol abuse as boys
➤ alcohol-related vehicular accidents are increasing
➤ alcohol is not a good energy source for athletes
➤ the drug cannot benefit an athlete of any age

If a youngster is involved in team sports, it will probably take longer for a problem to be apparent than it would if he or she were involved in individual activities. Simply, the intensity and demands of training and participation will force the young person to make a choice—athletics or alcohol.

Amphetamines (Uppers, Speed, Bennies, etc.)

Better known as "uppers" or "speed," amphetamines are readily available on the street and are quite inexpensive. Essentially, these drugs give a feeling of well-being. The user feels more intensely involved and "revved up." Some describe their effect as providing extra energy.

There is no evidence available today, however, that the use of such drugs in any way helps athletic performance; instead, it may hinder it. But there are many situations noted in the literature on drugs in which a runner or cyclist or other competitor felt he or she had done very well, when indeed the athlete had performed badly. Drugs can affect judgment, and the athlete thinks he or she is doing a fine job, when the fact of the matter is, reaction time and performance are poorer.

An athlete using drugs to try to improve performance is said to be "doping." What's ironic is that athletes have always been viewed as the epitomes of good health—as exhibited through precision performance, speed, endurance or skill. And yet dangerous drugs have found their way into athletic events. Even with such organizations as the United States Olympic Committee, the American College of Sports Medicine and the American Academy of Pediatrics condemning the use of specific types of drugs, and with fairly stringent rules governing competition and enforcing testing, there are still those who believe that uppers will give them that added push needed to excel. So they risk their health, their performance and even their lives.

In the book *Sportsmedicine*, authors Gabe Mirkin, M.D., and Marshall Hoffman quote Bob Bauman, a trainer for the St. Louis Cardinals. His point is noteworthy. "In 1964, I devised a yellow R.B.I. pill, a red shut-out pill and a potent green hitting pill. Virtually every player on the team took them and some wouldn't go out on the field until they took my pills. They worked so well that we won the pennant. We used them again in 1967 and 1968 and also won the pennant. They worked because I never told them that the pills were placebos." (Placebos are false drugs—sugar or other non-active substances made to look like real pills.)

The authors of the book asked more than 100 top runners if they would take a "magic" pill which would make them an Olympic champion, even if they knew that taking the pill would kill them in a year. More than half of the runners said they would take the pill!

You've probably heard people say, "He won that race out of pure determination," or "She said she was going to win the match, no matter what!" Much of what athletes do has some psychological basis—they "psych" themselves up. Sometimes it's a little thing like wearing the same socks during each competition, or having a certain meal the night before. Others give themselves pep talks or hear them from their coach or trainer. Sometimes the "psych up" takes the form of a specific routine right before competition, like seeing an early show or something more elaborate. The point is that pushing oneself to the limit takes courage, conditioning and the belief that it can be done. It doesn't take—or need—uppers.

"Psyching up" isn't exclusive to athletics. It's all around us in everything we do. An executive psychs himself up before an important meeting just as much as an athlete does before an important competition. But neither should "dope up" in hopes of a better performance. Certainly, it's possible that both might feel less anxious and more energetic about getting in there and winning, and each may feel he or she has performed better, but in reality the drug may have cheated each of them of a superb performance. The drugs become their downfall.

Uppers may also mask pain, fatigue, lethargy or the feeling of being down—but don't rid the athlete of these. Drugs that mask pain simply remove nature's warning sign that something is wrong or that the athlete is doing something he or she should not be doing. Once the medication wears off, the athlete comes down hard. This masking of pain, fatigue or discomfort can be deadly in certain situations. The athlete runs a great risk of being injured, often seriously, and some forms of activity are dangerous enough without adding more risk to the situation.

Amphetamines also have an adverse effect on the cardiovascular system (heart and blood vessels) of the body. The drugs, combined with stress and exertion, may induce potentially deadly cardiac arrhythmias (irregular heart beats). Further, there has been some direct association between the use of "uppers" and heatstroke. Heatstroke in itself can result in death. These drugs are habit-forming, too—tolerance builds up quickly, forcing the athlete to use more and more to feel "pepped up." Addiction can lead to overdose and death as things get further out of control.

No athlete then, young or old, should use amphetamines for any reason. And the young athlete should understand that anyone who suggests the use of uppers to enhance performance doesn't know what he or she is talking about, and is endangering the athlete's health and possibly life.

For those youngsters who want to achieve more and more at greater and greater heights of competition, it's important to understand what amphetamines are and what they will—and will not—do. The youngster might have heard that an added boost might come from a little pill. The youngster who begins to use uppers, and continues, will most likely be eliminated from participation at some point. And no one can avoid, with prolonged use and withdrawal, having the drug take its toll both physically and mentally.

If a parent finds that the youngster is taking amphetamines, professional assistance is necessary. The family doctor or pediatrician can best evaluate, along with the parents, the extent of the problem and recommend specialized treatment.

Sedatives and Tranquilizers ("Downers")

Easily found on the street or in many home medicine cabinets, "downers" are habit-forming drugs which must be taken in increasing doses in order to calm, or sedate, a person down. They are known to decrease performance and reaction time, and may lead to injury due to this diminished response.

Several types of sedatives are commonly available. One large group is the barbiturate family—phenobarbital, Seconal®, and others, often called "barbs." Other similar drugs also sedate—for example, Quaalude®, Doriden®, and Placidyl®—and are usually prescribed for sleep. Common tranquilizers such as Valium®, Librium®, Dalmane® and Miltown® also cause problems if used by athletes. All of these drugs are prescription medications, but all are also readily available on the street.

Barbiturates and other sedatives do not in any way enhance performance and do not give a feeling of energy or pep. Under normal circumstances, athletes tend not to use them. However, in the higher levels of competition, the athlete who is constantly on the road, away from family and friends and under great stress because of the pending competition, may use these drugs to get to sleep.

There is no place for use of these barbiturates or other tranquilizers among athletes, regardless of age. If a child is having trouble sleeping due to "nerves," jitters or an anxious stomach because of a competition, medication is not the answer. Some people might make the mistake of giving their child one of their own prescribed pills— such as Valium® or Librium®. Although these are classified as minor tranquilizers, they too have the potential for abuse, are habit-forming and may become an unnecessary crutch to the budding competitor. The parent who does this may be "setting up" the youngster for a life of using uppers to perk up and downers to calm down. After awhile the youngster will feel as if he or she *needs* this medication to perform and to sleep.

Everyone gets nervous, apprehensive and jittery before competitions. Extreme nervousness, however, may be a warning sign, and deserves special attention. Professional help in solving the problem might be of some benefit. Finding another way of calming down before an event, or in order to sleep, is the ideal solution. Some athletes devise special routines which psychologically prepare them for the coming day's events: they may take a hot bath; drink a glass of warm milk; perform relaxation exercises; watch television; practice self-hypnosis; or whatever works best for them—without using medications.

Withdrawal from sedatives and tranquilizers, especially barbiturates, can be devastating, and should *never* be attempted without professional help. As with alcohol, an addicted person may experience seizures, the "shakes," and may suffer brain damage. Educating the young athlete about the serious dangers and the lack of benefits of these drugs is the best deterrent to the problem of abuse. Having no drugs available in the home is an important way to set a good example. But if drugs are available in the home and a parent notices that pills are missing from prescription bottles or has any reason to believe that a youngster is using drugs to calm down or sleep before a competition, professional help should be considered. Again, the family doctor or pediatrician is an excellent source for assistance and referral to an appropriate center or individual counselor.

Marijuana (Grass) and Hashish

The use of marijuana among children, adolescents and adults alike has increased over the past few years, partly because of increased accessibility and partly because of increased social acceptance—much like alcohol. With this increase in use among youth has come a very real concern about marijuana's effect on the growth and development of children and long-term effects on their health.

Marijuana, and its relative hashish, are drugs that calm and relax. They have no known benefits in athletic participation or competition, and chronic use may lead to the youngster dropping out of sports because of poor performance or the inability to endure the rigors of training.

Certainly, it's difficult to discuss a drug which has not been adequately studied specifically in athletes. But studies do show that marijuana and hashish give a feeling of euphoria, and perception may be altered. Time can be confused and the user may be unable to perform even simple mental and physical tasks. The feeling of unreality and dissociation abounds, and anxiety and feelings of panic can result. Hallucinations are also possible. They do not enhance performance, and may increase the potential for injury.

Recent concern has been expressed about the possible effects of heavy marijuana use and early cessation of pubertal development. Reports suggest an association, and further studies are needed and are in progress clarifying this aspect of these drugs.

Parents should understand that with the great accessibility of "pot," young athletes may find themselves in situations of tremendous peer pressure to experiment with these and other drugs. The parent should be sure the child understands what is—and is not—known about the drug, and that use of marijuana may have a harmful effect on performance.

Although apparently not physically addictive, marijuana and hashish are thought to be mentally habit-forming, because they make one "feel good." A youngster who has a serious problem with marijuana use should receive professional help. Those who simply experiment should know the risks in chronic use and the legal problems that can arise from using the drug, not to mention the physical effects. But the peer pressure remains and the parent will be challenged to deal with a youngster early and honestly, so that the athlete understands how marijuana use might affect his or her ability to perform—and what it might do to the growth of the body.

Angel Dust (Phencyclidine hydrochloride, PCP, Sernylan®)

As with the other illicit drugs, there are no definitive studies concerning the use of angel dust and athletes. Known by some 20 names—PCP, hog, dust and others—angel dust is becoming an increasing problem in many localities. It is available on the street in many forms—tablets, capsules, powder, etc.—and almost anyone can make the substance with a little instruction and readily available supplies. Although there is little evidence that athletes have any specific propensity for the use of this drug, parents should be aware that it is commonly used by youngsters of all ages. It is also used to "cut" other street drugs, and is often mixed with marijuana, so an athlete may not know he or she is getting it. The drug can have devastating effects both physically and psychologically, especially if an overdose is taken.

PCP seems to remove all inhibitions in many of the people who use it. They tend to have delusions of super power, feeling almost supernatural and safe from death. There are accounts of people diving out of windows because they felt they could fly, and other such dangerous and life-threatening situations. The drug has been known to cause some who use it to go into an uncontrollable rage. Paranoia may result; the individual suddenly feels threatened by almost anyone—and attacks. The person "flips out." Many young people have had to be institutionalized for treatment after PCP use, some have died because of their actions under its influence, and others have found themselves in situations very dangerous to themselves or others. Most experts agree that the use of PCP is extremely dangerous, and great emphasis should be placed on educating young people about the potential hazards of its use.

A youngster who uses angel dust will probably be eliminated from participation because he or she will not be able to keep up. But, again, if a parent suspects a drug problem—or has heard that the child has been using angel dust—it's best to seek professional help.

Cocaine

Cocaine has regained popularity in recent years because many see it as socially acceptable as alcohol and marijuana, and believe it is not particularly harmful. This drug is generally used primarily by older people because of its expense. An upper which gives one the feeling of extra energy and euphoria, it is administered intravenously, orally or by snorting through the nose. Lately, there has been a trend to smoke it as "free base" (a technique in which a solvent such as ether is used to concentrate the active ingredient in the powder, changing it into a liquid and lacing cigarettes with it).

Although cocaine is the oldest local anesthetic known to man, it is seldom used medically (except for application to eyes, ears or nose) because of its potential adverse effects and the risk for associated drug dependence. In some patients, it has caused excitation, nausea, vomiting, and restlessness, followed by sweating, twitching, pallor, a drop in blood pressure, convulsions and unconsciousness. Large doses taken by mouth have been known to cause trembling, restlessness and hallucinations. The repeated use of cocaine can cause psychological but not physical drug dependence. But those who become psychologically dependent may still develop the drug craving, weight loss, memory loss and potential mental deterioration of addiction.

Classified as a narcotic, cocaine is a stimulant which acts on the central nervous system, and also causes the small blood vessels of the body to constrict. Death may result from massive doses.

Although there is no specific evidence that young athletes are using this drug to a great extent, with the number of illicit drugs available today, it is wise for parents to be aware of its popularity. It would also be wise to explain the dangers of this drug to youngsters who might be inclined to try it. The use of cocaine by an athlete cannot possibly help in athletic performance, and potentially puts his or her health in jeopardy.

Caffeine

To date, there has been no research done concerning the effects of caffeine (as found in coffee, tea, chocolate or cola drinks) on children or athletes. However, one well-known expert in exercise physiology has noted that one or two cups of coffee before a road race would improve *adult performance* to a minor degree. He pointed out that coffee is a safe drink before competition if taken in small quantities. However, the use of caffeine-containing drinks or pills in sports needs further investigation.

Caffeine is known to increase heartbeat and reaction time, and is said to enhance one's ability to work. A stimulant, it can also cause insomnia, restlessness, irritability, some stomach disorders, headaches and heart palpitations in many people.

Because research has been limited to adults and exercise, it would be unwise to recommend the use of drinks containing caffeine as a performance enhancer for young athletes. The potential side effects in themselves are enough to bring into question the reasonability, no less necessity, of caffeine use by growing youngsters.

Tobacco

An estimated 30 million Americans quit smoking cigarettes since the 1964 Surgeon General's report which showed a strong association between cigarette smoking and lung cancer, pulmonary disorders and cardiovascular disease.

But statistics show that 3,200 adolescents between 12 and 18 years of age start smoking every day. These numbers do not include the 10- to 12-year-olds who experiment with cigarettes. Studies have also shown that children of parents who smoke or whose older brother or sister smokes are more likely to smoke at some time during their lives than those in non-smoking households.

Most athletes do not smoke, and most young athletes do not start to smoke because its effects on heart and lung function interfere with their ability to perform well. Nicotine, the drug in cigarettes, is a mild stimulant which increases heart rate and may cause headache, nausea and possibly lack of appetite.

Cigarettes are readily available in schools, from friends and sometimes at home. There may also be peer pressure for the youngster to try cigarette smoking because it's the "in" thing to do. Fortunately, it is usually not the "in" thing for an athlete to do, and this is probably the most helpful deterrent available.

Points to Remember

➤ All parents should understand the enormity of the drug problem among young people today. The temptations and pressures on young people to try all sorts of drugs are great.

➤ Good, solid information should be made available to all young people concerning the effects and dangers of drug use.

➤ Drugs *will not* improve athletic performance—nor help the youngster deal with the stresses and anxieties sometimes associated with competition. Anyone who tells a child that a certain drug will help him or her is endangering that child's health and life.

➤ If a parent suspects a drug problem (including alcohol) may be present, he or she should seek the help of a respected coach, trainer, teacher, family doctor or pediatrician, for starters. If the problem is serious, the doctor can refer to an appropriate treatment center.

➤ Although most drug or alcohol use by athletes results from peer pressure or is experimental, youngsters who try drugs should be considered "at risk" for a problem. Denial by parents or other adults may be the worst possible response, and may result in a much worse problem.

7.
The Female Athlete—
Myths vs. Reality

Two Young Female Gymnasts

In 1968, little Luci Collins saw Cathy Rigby, who was representing the United States, perform in the Olympic Games, on television. She told her parents that she wanted to do that.

"I remember telling her to go outside and play," Claire Collins, Luci's mother, said. "She was simply too young for gymnastics, and frankly, her father and I didn't know anything about the sport. The boys were involved in baseball and other sports, and we knew Luci loved sports, but this was quite beyond our experience. We simply forgot about it."

Four years later, Luci watched Olga Korbut on television. Much to everyone's surprise, Luci said, "I saw that before when I was little and I wanted to do it. Can't I do that? I'd really like it. I'll be in the Olympics in the 1980s."

Because Luci was so energetic and loved athletics even at so early an age, Ulysses and Claire Collins started looking into a sport they knew nothing about. They were able to find a summer program at the University of Southern California in Los Angeles that included gymnastics for children nine years old and up. Luci was only seven, but seemed so skilled when the program directors had her do a few basic moves that they took her into the program.

"You have to understand that we didn't know anything about the right methods, when young people get coaches and anything else about this sport," Mr. Collins said. "All we knew was that Luci enjoyed it and wanted to continue to get better. It seemed like everywhere we went, people would say, 'She has talent; get her a good coach,' but we didn't even know where to look. When she was eleven, she was already a Class III champion with little skills training. At that point, she decided to go into modern rhythmic dancing instead of gymnastics."

Luci's mother enrolled Luci and her sister in a class. She admits that it never occurred to her that Luci was changing her activity because she couldn't go any further without specialized coaching.

"One day while Luci was in her dance class, Zinovy Kinolik, a Master of Sport from Russia, was teaching the bars to his gymnastics class, which works out in the same gym. Luci watched and watched, then went over and asked him if she could try that. He smiled pleasantly and told her to go ahead. After she finished, he and the dance instructor argued back and forth in Russian. I didn't really know what was going on," Mrs. Collins said, "until the dance instructor came over and told me that Luci would be doing gymnastics from now on. When I said, 'No, she wanted to do rhythmic dancing,' Zinovy came over and said, 'You have an Olympic gymnast on your hands.' And that was that!"

Mr. Collins started working two jobs, one for the family and one for Luci's gymnastics. They drove 74 miles round trip from Los Angeles to SCATS gymnastic club in Orange County. The entire Collins family decided that if this was what Luci wanted, they would do all they could to help. And, with five children in the family, sacrifice and help they did. In 1980, Luci Collins made the United States Olympic Gymnastic Team at the age of sixteen, something she had innocently predicted almost twelve years before.

Luci sacrificed too. She said, "Other people were growing up without me. I lost a lot of close friends because I was so involved in training and all, but I made friends in the gym, too. You have to adjust to it all. When I think about if it had been any different, I just can't imagine it any other way." To Luci, just making the Olympic team was exciting, and worth it.

But she and her parents take her involvement in gymnastics day by day. If Luci wants to continue in gymnastics, they will support that, the Collins say, and when she wants to stop and go on to other things, they will support that too. Her parents believe that Luci can do well at whatever she chooses, that she has a marvelous attitude and a great deal of drive. They are proud of her and excited for her, but they say that whether she had made the Olympic team or not, they would still have felt the same way.

Luci Collins is thinking about being a doctor someday. She says that in gymnastics you learn a lot about muscles and other structures, and how the body functions. For her, that's fascinating and exciting. Whether Luci continues on and makes the next Olympic team or not hardly matters, nor does whether she changes her mind about medicine. The point is, she and her family are very happy and loving people. And to them, that's what really counts.

Beth Kline was very small for her age and energetic, yet shy. Both Bob and Bitsy Kline had been involved in gymnastics—he as a gymnast and she as a gymnast and coach. When Beth was very young, she used to watch her mother's team work out. She seemed to pick things up here and there, so Mrs. Kline started instructing her in the basics so she'd learn them correctly and wouldn't hurt herself.

"It's funny how things happen. When Beth was five years old, I knew she had a special talent for gymnastics. She took to it quickly, taught herself, pushed to learn more when we were trying to slow her down, and her upper body strength for her size was amazing," Mrs. Kline said. Because her mother specialized in gymnastics, her parents decided that Beth needed a coach to teach her all the other areas of dance.

"She seemed to love the sport so much that there was no stopping her," Bob Kline said. "We felt if this was something she wanted to do, we would support her 100 percent. We always wanted our children to be involved in athletics—to enjoy the challenge and excitement that sports had to offer—but I really never thought about anyone being a champion or anything like that. We all ride bikes and run and enjoy physical activity. But Beth kept getting better and better and we did all we could to be supportive of her efforts."

Beth made the 1980 United States Olympic Gymnastics Team. She was just 14 years old. When you ask her about it, she says, "I started gymnastics because it was just fun. Then I did things really well and kept on going because it was exciting. It seemed like I couldn't wait to wake up the next day so I could go to the gym. Next thing I knew, I was trying out for the Olympic team, it seemed to happen so fast. Once I got there, it was just like another meet. You become used to it, with five-day-a-week, five-hour-a-day practices. When I realized that I had made the team, it was like a fantasy come true. It sort of hit me all at once. But I love what I do, so I'll keep doing it."

Bob Kline smiles warmly when you ask him if he and his wife are proud of Beth. They feel that it's been an exciting, emotional experience for all of them. "I'll tell you, I always thought it would be thrilling to know someone who had made the Olympic team. But I never thought—not in my wildest dreams—that *that* someone would be my daughter. But whether she had made it or not, Bitsy and I would still have been as proud of her. She's just a lovely person with a fantastic attitude, and that alone makes her special to us."

Beth Kline and Luci Collins represent an elite few female athletes in this country. Both had families who were supportive and sensitive to their needs; both were encouraged by teammates and coaches; both had a drive to excel in a sport; each has her own unique personality, likes and dislikes, and dreams for the future. And Beth and Luci have one more thing in common—they represent the new wave of enthusiasm for sports participation by girls and women in the United States.

Rapid Growth in Female Sports Participation

The number of young girls and women participating in sports today is increasing by leaps and bounds. The statistics are staggering; some call the increase in female athletic participation a revolution. More than 1.6 million girls are active in high school sports and about 100,000 are participating in intercollegiate athletics. The numbers of young girls involved in softball, tennis, swimming, gymnastics, figure- and ice-skating, soccer, hockey, jogging, track and field, basketball, golf, volleyball, handball and a host of others is phenomenal.

Dance (a truly athletic physical activity) was and has always been an acceptable form of activity for females. In Spartan society women were encouraged to be physically active, because it was believed that a physically fit woman was a better childbearer. With the German Revolution of 1848, many teachers came to the United States and organized, to some degree, athletic games for women. By the 1912 Olympics women were participating and competing in basketball (which had remained solely a women's sport until 1910), gymnastics, tennis, ice-skating, bicycling, hiking, golf and boating.

"But with the advent of the 1920s, words like unladylike, physically harmful, and psychologically damaging began to appear, putting an end to women's participation in a wide variety of sports," Letha Yurko Hunter, M.D., Ph.D., said. Assistant Professor in the Department of Orthopedics, Division of Sports Medicine at the University of Washington, Dr. Hunter's article, "Female Athlete" (which appeared in *Resident and Staff Physician*) further explains that it was not until the 1950s "with the increased knowledge of women's physiology and greater emancipation, that the trend of the '20s was reversed. The philosophy that vigorous physical activity is unfeminine was challenged, and people began to realize that women were as physiologically capable of achieving athletic success as males."

Until very recently, the young athletic female was considered a tomboy—and continued participation in athletics carried a stigma for the female who was involved in what was considered a masculine activity—sports. As one study pointed out, being competitive in sports was part of a man's world—where prowess and strength were expressed. The winner was then the dominant figure, and sportsmen were revered as the fittest and most able.

Even though this point of view has changed dramatically in recent years, there are still those who register displeasure or concern. Most people feel it is a function of childhood to play and be active, and rarely are little girls called tomboys simply because they enjoy participating at recess or want to learn to swim, dance or play other acceptable games. Few people and programs emphasize teaching little girls sports skills their male counterparts learn at a very young age and are encouraged to master through continual practice and participation. Simple things like how to throw and catch a ball properly, or efficient and correct running techniques, have generally not been part of a young girl's childhood or even later school years.

Organized programs for young girls where physical fitness, improved coordination, strength, flexibility, endurance, agility and sports-specific training, are emphasized are still relatively new today. Until recently little girls were rarely encouraged to go outside and run or throw a ball back and forth, or perform some other form of strenuous activity for any significant length of time. In some situations, this is still not acceptable to some adults, and organized sports for girls raises a few cynical eyebrows now and then.

When the little girl becomes a young woman (at the time of puberty) there are those who still believe that she should no longer participate in organized sports or strenuous physical activity because it is unladylike, or because she could injure herself and destroy her chances of having children later. Only time can change the attitude of some people that physical activity is unladylike. But parents and others should understand that a young female can participate in almost any sport without a higher risk of injury than a male, and that her participation will not bring about any complications during a later pregnancy.

From ages five to thirteen, boys and girls compete fairly equally. In fact, some girls perform better than their counterpart males in particular sports, because girls tend to mature physically earlier than boys. At puberty, sex hormones in the male contribute to greater muscle bulk and greater resultant strength. Boys also have, on the average, larger bone structures, and a larger rib cage (lung capacity), influencing their ability to perform.

Differences between Young Female and Male Athletes

From puberty onward, females tend to have a greater percentage of body fat and, in our culture, have less upper extremity strength than males. This is largely due to a previous lack of early participation and conditioning on any significant level. But the fact remains, the male, on the average, will be stronger. However, significant early participation and conditioning (or the lack of it) do play a role in the woman's ability or lack of ability to participate in sports.

"It used to be that women didn't get involved in sports until high school, but now we're seeing them start when they are much younger," says Dan Bailey, Head Trainer at CSU. "People always ask me about the differences in the male and female competitor: are injuries different; are training techniques different; are they overly emotional; are they accepted by the men? The female athletes I see work very hard to achieve goals and train the same as men depending on the needs of the sports they're involved in. They have similar injuries to the men's. And today, particularly at the college level, they are not seen as being masculine because they enjoy sports. The fact is, there are very lovely young ladies in sports who are simply fantastic athletes. I think," Bailey says, "it's great that women are finally getting more involved, because sports have many benefits. Everyone has the right and maybe even the responsibility to be physically fit. Besides, athletic participation is exciting."

The list of accomplishments of female athletes is impressive, and too long to enumerate in detail, but it starts with women such as

Gertrude Ederle, who, in 1926, when she was 18, swam from the shores of France to the cliffs of Dover faster than anyone had ever done; Katherine Switzer, who, in 1967, was the first woman to enter and complete the Boston Marathon; Shirley Babashoff, who won Olympic medals in swimming; and the skillful and successful Dorothy Hamill, Billie Jean King, Nancy Lopez Melton, Wilma Rudolf, Debbie Meyer, Robyn Smith, Cathy Rigby, Donna DeVerona, Chris Evert Lloyd, Peggy Fleming, Evonne Goolagong, Tai Babilonia, Suzy Chaffee, Sheila Young, Beth Heiden, Tracy Austin, and on and on.

In her book *Women and Sports,* Janice Kaplan writes that "the image of the ideal American woman is changing, and activities that were once suspect are now admired. Nobody laughs any more if a woman jogs around a park or dashes into a supermarket wearing a sweatsuit. Being in shape is fashionable, and through sports women are affirming their existence as flesh-and-blood entities." The same author later quotes Dyveke Spino, a coach to several Olympic athletes, who says, "Remember the Greek ideal which talked about the integration of mind, body and spirit? Well, you get strong mentally while improving your body, and the whole psyche opens."

Most experts believe that sports activity and physical fitness are just as important for young women as for men. And, as more young girls and women begin to participate, many of the myths about the physical limitations of females in sports activities are being exposed and are slowly beginning to disappear.

Strength

Until very recently it was generally accepted that young girls and young women were virtually weaklings, and those that weren't were somehow more masculine. Masculinity has nothing to do with it, but exercise, early participation in sports, and the development of physical attributes, or lack of the same, will determine a young female's strength. Studies have shown that before puberty young boys and girls have the same relative strength potential. But, if the young male is out playing sports that increase upper extremity strength (such as football, baseball or swimming), and the young female is doing none of these things, then you'll see a marked difference in strength between the two. Before more research was done in sports medicine, it was simply assumed that this difference was physically based, but the truth is, it's culturally determined by the patterns of activity of young girls. Before puberty, young girls who perform the same types of physical tasks, with the same intensity and frequency as men, will have a similar potential for strength, coordination and skills ability. The differences will result from each individual youngster's body type, genetic makeup and psychological traits (see Chapters 2 and 3 for more information); some youngsters are inherently faster, stronger, bigger, more flexible and more aggressive than others. These phenomena will be similar in girls and boys.

At puberty (between the ages of 10 and 15, on the average), a difference in strength is far more noticeable between the sexes. The difference in strength at this time is due to the production of sex hormones in the male. Testosterone stimulates muscle growth and strength.

Although both men and women have some male *and* female hormones, the male will produce much greater amounts of testosterone (male hormone), and the female will produce much greater quantities of estrogen (female hormone).

Even after the onset of puberty, the differences in strength potential between male and female are not as great as previously assumed. Some experts believe males have no more than a 10 percent performance difference from their female counterparts. They base this on a comparison of age-group records and performance standards.

In an article in *The Physician and Sports Medicine,* Jack Wilmore, M.D., said that "there appears to be little difference between the female athlete and her male counterpart in terms of strength, endurance, and body composition. Strength of the lower extremities, when related to body weight and lean body weight, is similar between the sexes, although the male maintains a distinct superiority in upper body strength."

Essentially then, male or female, each individual is equally capable of striving to reach his or her potential. Women do, however, have a greater percentage of body fat, particularly in the hips and thighs, than their male counterparts at the same level of training. And, because the male is simply larger, his vital capacity (ability to take in and process oxygen) will be greater as well. Although these are limitations, the degree of difference is not always striking and the functional effects are not great.

Strength Training

Another long-believed myth surrounds the female and strength-training or weight-lifting. It has been the consensus until recently that young girls and women involved in any physical activity that promoted strength would develop huge muscle mass, similar to that seen in the male.

The truth is, women do not produce enough testosterone to develop this kind of muscle mass or a masculine physique. Weight-lifting programs for female athletes have proven that strength can be markedly increased and the percentage of body fat reduced (when done in cooperation with a conditioning program), but strength-building itself does not produce great muscle mass. Basically, because of physiology and hormones, the woman will retain the female figure or body type, but will increase her strength and endurance.

In some foreign countries, some female athletes have been known to take testosterone to increase bulk and strength of their muscles. This practice is controversial, and may have lasting masculinizing effects. It usually increases body hair, deepens the voice, and may cause sterility. In the United States, the experience has been that if a female athlete lifts weights as part of her conditioning and training, she can still compete on the international level, without taking such drugs. In fact, the use of these steroids (male sex hormones) is discouraged for both males and females alike. Any young woman who is asked to take such a drug to improve strength should be very wary of such advice.

It should be noted that extensive weight-training programs for females and males have not proven to be markedly effective in increasing strength until the youngster reaches puberty, when the hormones work in their favor. Therefore, extensive, vigorous weight training is not recommended until puberty.

The Menstrual Cycle

When a young girl reaches puberty, her menstrual cycles begin. Associated with this physical phenomenon have been many myths, some of them absurd. Fortunately, some have already been laid to rest. Gone are the days of a mother telling her daughter to get into bed and rest because her menstrual period has begun again. Gone are the fears that if a woman or young girl is physically active during her period, this will somehow harm her or limit her ability to have children later. Until much more was known about the menstrual cycle, such myths persisted and young girls were excused from physical education, sports participation and even from school.

There isn't any contraindication to participation during a menstrual period unless the young woman is having an unusually excessive amount of cramping (dysmenorrhea). Refraining from physical activity should be based on the amount of discomfort rather than physiology. In fact, it seems that the more active female will tend to have *less* trouble with cramping than the one who is non-active. And many international championships and Olympic medals have been won, and world records set, by women who were menstruating. There doesn't seem to be any good reason, then, to stop training or sports activities because of menstruation.

But it is well known that women have an increased need for iron intake during the years in which they menstruate. This probably arises from many factors. While not all women who are deficient in iron intake are anemic, chronic iron deficiency can have a long-term effect on everyday energy level, and hence on athletic stamina and performance, because of an impact on the body's ability to carry oxygen. A diet high in iron-rich foods is part of the answer, as is the supplementation of the young woman's diet with an over-the-counter vitamin-with-iron preparation once a day. However, no more than this amount should be taken without the advice of a physician, since excessive iron intake can also be damaging.

One phenomenon noted by experts in sports and physiology has been a cessation of the menstrual periods with strenuous training in some female athletes. Some experts believe that when the woman pushes herself to the limits of training, and experiences a reduction of body fat (below 12 percent), menustration can stop for months or years. However, this does not adversely affect the woman physically, and does not permanently alter her ability to have children. Once vigorous training is stopped, menstruation begins again. So it's something parents and young athletes should not be overly concerned about.

Indeed, many women have maintained their activity level and some have even competed while pregnant. Juno Stover Irwin won her Olympic medal in diving when four months pregnant. Studies have shown that physically active women who continue some degree of activity during pregnancy seem to have fewer problems with labor and delivery, high blood pressure, headaches and fluid retention. However, a woman who is not already very active should not begin a vigorous program of conditioning and activity during pregnancy, and if she attempts to increase her usual level of activity, her progress should be very gradual, with supervision by her physician.

Injuries

Another area of great concern has been that girls and young women will incur more as well as more serious injuries than boys and young men. Not true, say the experts.

Obviously, women have a different physical form than men. Physiologically, the pelvis is wider, so a woman tends to have a little different walking and running gait than a man. In some women, there is a tendency for the kneecap (patella) to be positioned in such a way that there is a greater tendency for it to be dislocated during activity, especially recreational sports. And there has been concern about the greater number of certain injuries seen in females as compared to men. These include: stress fractures (breaks in bone which result from repetitive stresses due to too much activity too quickly); strains (injuries to the muscle-tendon units); sprains (injuries to ligaments); shin splints; and shoulder injuries.

Judy Devine, Assistant Professor of Physical Education and the women's basketball and field hockey coach at Kent State University in Ohio, noted in an article in *The Physician and Sports Medicine*, "Women in Sports—Are the 'Problems' Real?": "Probably one of the greatest factors in the high incidence of injuries among women is related to the fact that women historically have done a very poor job of conditioning before any kind of participation in athletics. One of the biggest advantages of proper conditioning, of course, is injury prevention . . . Again, I think the reason (for the number of injuries) is lack of conditioning, and not so much that the female is more fragile or is more susceptible to those injuries under equal conditions."

Studies performed at U.S. military academies showed that their top female performers were less likely to experience injuries when they were physically fit before the training programs began.

Although many people have felt that young girls have more fractures than boys, this is not true in the younger age groups. The information that says that females statistically have a greater number of fractures is taken from information about women after menopause (change of life—when estrogen production by the ovaries ceases). After menopause, women tend to lose calcium from the bones. This factor, which results in bones that are more prone to breaking, coupled with the woman's longer life expectancy, has led to an increased incidence of fractures in this age group. When you compare *young* males and females of the same age, there is no greater incidence of fractures among the girls, especially when weight and size differences between the sexes are taken into account.

Because young girls and women had rarely participated year-round either in sports or in a conditioning program until recently, they *were* more prone to stress fractures. (When training is started too rapidly or strenuously, the new stresses on the bone are too great for the changing bone to adapt to, and stress fractures occur. These result from repeated episodes of minor trauma to the bone.) Most experts believe that as more young women participate year-round and follow appropriate training programs, the numbers of these injuries will decrease.

Physical Assets of the Female

Some people believe that the female is physically designed for certain endurance events. And women have proven their ability to achieve in endurance sports. The new time for women in the New York Marathon would have beaten all the men's Olympic times prior to 1956. Miki Gorman from Los Angeles ran 100 miles in only 21 hours. Cindy Nicholas performed a round-trip swim from the cliffs of Dover to the French coast in under 20 hours—a speed that was 10 hours faster than that of any other human. Women have successfully competed in endurance sports such as cross-country skiing, speed-skating, marathon running, and swimming. Many experts believe that the female structure is built for endurance, partly because it efficiently utilizes body fat, converting it into energy. Research will have to continue before solid conclusions about the female athlete and endurance events can be drawn.

Coaches and trainers also say female athletes are determined, hard workers. They are committed to physical fitness and enjoy sports participation. Most importantly, the little girl, the young female, and the adult woman all have the capacity and physical makeup to participate in a variety of sports, and should be encouraged to take part in vigorous physical activity on a routine basis for better health and enjoyment.

Should Males and Females Participate Together?

Males will have a size and strength advantage beginning with puberty (for boys, between the ages of 12 and 15, and for girls, between 10 and 14 years of age on average). Until the young male reaches puberty, sexes can participate together and compete without concern about more or worse injuries than if these youngsters were competing against members of the same sex and age or developmental level. And most agree that if older youngsters are matched in size, skills, physical maturation and weight, they can readily participate in a variety of athletic areas to mutual advantage.

One caution, though—most sports medicine experts, along with members of the American Academy of Pediatrics, recommend that girls not participate against boys in collision/contact sports after puberty. The reason is that the risk for significant injury to the female does increase simply because the male has greater muscle mass and therefore greater strength. However, girls and young women can participate against boys and young men in sports such as soccer, tennis, volleyball, swimming, running, skating, skiing and most other non-collision sports as long as they have realistic goals and understand there are some differences in strength.

8.
Competitiveness and Aggression in Sports

IN THE LAST FEW YEARS, a great deal has been written—and discussed—about the issues of competitiveness and aggression in sports. As with all issues, there are at least two points of view—and in some cases, many more—when it comes to what's bad, good or best for young people today.

Although competitiveness and aggression are really two distinct issues, they intertwine. Many experts feel that too much emphasis on competitiveness and winning results in aggressive and destructive behavior. Competitiveness and aggression are serious questions that should be carefully examined. Sports can and should be a healthy and enjoyable experience for all involved, even at higher levels of expertise. A closer look at each of the two issues will bring them into perspective and illumine their relationship to sports participation.

Competitiveness—What Is It?

Any discussion about competitiveness and sports must start with a definition of the term, but being competitive means something different to many people. Is it enjoying a challenge? The expression of excellence? The showing of superiority? Or striving to be the winner?

If you look closely at the various definitions, you find even more confusion. The dictionary defines competition in several ways: contending with another; vying with others for profit, prize or position; and as a contest of skill. To make things more complicated, a look into *Roget's Thesaurus* under "compete" refers you to "contention and opposition." Competitive is listed with words like struggle, fight, battle, enemy, combat, scrimmage and warlike. Many specific sports are also listed. But if you take all of this a step further, back to the Latin root of the word, *competere*, it means "to strive together."

Immediately then, a problem arises. When people talk about being "competitive," depending on their frame of reference, the word will have either a bad or good connotation. Indeed the word in itself may conjure up a response of diametrically opposed value systems. This war of words lends itself to separating competitiveness into two categories: healthy competitiveness and unhealthy competitiveness.

What Is Healthy Competitiveness?

Today, the word "competitive" bears sinister overtones, but that's an easy oversimplication of the problem, and neglects the real issues involved. Man has always been competitive, struggling to achieve certain things, from basics such as food, family and home, to the more abstract parts of life such as dignity, rights and freedom. In a real sense, all these are forms of competition. Some experts feel that, to a certain degree, the competitive spirit is a natural instinct and in itself is not a destructive force. The desire to excel, to be recognized, and to seek one's limits and use one's ultimate abilities is probably natural to most people.

So, good or bad, we live in a competitive society. And much good has come from healthy competition—in science, law, government, technology, medicine, education, availability of consumer goods and athletics, to name a few areas. And it begins early. When children reach school age, they are evaluated by tests, grades, academic standing among their peers, and athletic ability. We see the effects of competition in our children's responses every day.

After the first day of kindergarten, one little girl says to her mother, "The teacher asked a question, but I didn't know the answer. Johnny and Susie knew the answer. I want to know the answers, too. I'm gonna know the answer next time."

A seven-year-old runs home from school one day asking what time his dad will be home. He's anxious. When his mother asks what all the rush and excitement is about, he says he played softball during P.E. and wants to learn to hit the ball better.

Little Jackie asks her parents enthusiastically if she can take swimming lessons during the summer because all her friends are going to.

Before age four or five only 50 percent of children express some form of competitiveness, one study showed. There is an upswing in competitive spirit at school age, when youngsters begin to play games with others, learn to work together for a common result, and begin to notice what others do or can do compared to what they do or can do.

Games and activities can be useful tools in teaching youngsters to share, play fairly, enjoy teamwork, find limits and abilities, and experience social interaction. Children learn a great deal about likes and dislikes through experiencing a variety of activities. Being successful at something certainly encourages a young person to continue participation and to learn new skills. If something is gratifying to them, youngsters will want to learn more, increase their skill levels, and continue to participate. In such cases, healthy participation and competition help them feel more confident, improve their self-image and have an enjoyable, exciting experience. The challenge of healthy competition can then be a fulfilling experience for young people.

How Is Healthy Competition Fostered?

If we accept the premise of mankind's instinctive competitiveness and complement that with a good attitude and values, then healthy competition can be the result. If a young person is encouraged to participate in athletics to achieve excellence, improve existing abilities and enjoy the challenge of rivalry within the bounds of fair play, then competition in sports is healthy.

But this is only possible through good attitudes, learned responses, and the responses of others. If parents, teachers and coaches have reasonable expectations and are supportive of young people's active involvement in sports, youngsters will benefit. If the youngsters know that doing their best and participating enthusiastically are encouraged and supported by those important to them, they will also have a similar attitude about athletic participation and competition. When the joy of competing and the exuberance of doing one's best become more important than the values of winning or losing, then attitudes will be healthy, and the youngster will not be overly goal-oriented.

Nor does a healthy attitude in sports seem to hurt a young or older person's chances of excelling. One study of female Olympians showed that the majority had very mature attitudes about their participation in sports. Winning or losing didn't appear to be as important as doing their best, achieving excellence in their sports area, and enjoying the thrill of competition. And yet these were highly skilled and successful young athletes who had achieved world-class status. Could it be that they weren't competitive or didn't want to win? Certainly they were competitive, but in the best sense of the word, or they would probably not have been where they were. Many world-class competitors have been heard to say things such as, "I figured if I did my best I'd have a good chance to win," or "I gave it all I had," or "I knew if I executed my routine well, I'd have an excellent chance to win a medal."

Although it seems that we become more competitive with age, as some studies show, many of our attitudes in all aspects of life will be based on the values learned early. If children are rewarded for participation, and encouraged to enjoy the thrill of competition, then this attitude will most likely persist.

What Is Unhealthy Competition?

James A. Michener, in his well-researched and widely read book, *Sports in America*, said that "a sense of competition is natural in children, provides healthy emotional outlets and must not be suppressed; but it should not be exaggerated, either. Adults must not dominate the play of children . . ."

When there is too much emphasis on winning at all costs, competition takes on a different meaning and has the potential of being destructive. You've heard the adage "winning isn't everything; it's the only thing." When this attitude encompasses athletic participation, the results can have adverse effects not only for those who lose, but for those who are under the stress of having to continually win in order to receive approval, affection, support and love. When the emphasis is totally on the winner, he or she receives the greatest amount of praise, reinforcement and reward. All others involved then become losers, and being considered a loser at any age (no less in the formative years) can be devastating. If youngsters are evaluated only by their ability to win, with no regard for their attempts to excel to the best of their own ability, the result can be damaging to their self-image, confidence, willingness to try new things, attitudes about others, and their feelings of self-worth. If they must win in order to achieve—when winning means beating or defeating others at all costs—competing takes on an entirely different meaning.

This is seen all around us, not just in athletics. Often, youngsters are pitted against the expectations of parents, teachers, coaches and even their peers. With all these expectations and the jockeying for position, prestige, and acceptance, it becomes easy to push any form of competition, whether academic, social, athletic or professional, beyond the bounds of reason and into the realm of potential destructiveness.

"Competition in sport, in some instances, comes close to being conflict. The 'win-at-any-cost' philosophy carries with it the seeds of its own destruction simply because it implies operating outside of the rule structure if necessary. One must realize that conflict engenders hatred, resentment, and implicit destruction and, in this sense, has no place in sport. If conflict rather than competition is encouraged, then one is risking the very social system one is attempting to establish," says R. B. Alderman, Ed.D., in his book, *Psychological Behaviour in Sports.*

Other experts concur with Dr. Alderman. An article by Edmund J. Burke, Ph.D. and Douglas Kleiber, Ph.D. states, "These highly competitive, adult-controlled sports programs for children may actually discourage the continuation of physical fitness and healthful physical pursuits later in life. It is unreasonable to believe that we can raise our children to be highly competitive in a stressful environment and expect them to reach maturity calm, serene and at peace with themselves." The authors go on to say that "it is probably not the experience of competition alone, but rather the intensity of that experience that may be dangerous."

When youngsters compete in fairly unstructured programs, they set their own rules and determine limitations. But, when adults intervene, set up rules, expectations and value systems, and begin pushing youngsters, eliminating those who are less talented or late-maturing, the results can be disastrous. Winning often becomes paramount, when encouraging participation, physical fitness and the thrill of competition, as well as applauding the young people's efforts no matter what the results, should prevail.

"I was appalled by the politics, trade-offs for better players and the 'blood and guts' seriousness of the meeting to choose teams in one youth baseball league," one coach says. "Kids were eliminated not only because they weren't the most skilled, but also for downright political reasons—they [the organizers] didn't like the parents or a youngster wasn't the killer type. It just seemed that everyone had lost his or her perspective. It seemed to me that we should have been trying to choose teams in order to make them as even as possible—so games would be exciting and challenging for all. It seemed to me that the youngsters had been forgotten in all of this—their needs, their enjoyment. All these adults were doing was fulfilling their own needs. It was their team, their league, their parties, their victories or defeats, and many never let the kids forget that. Those youngsters were simply puppets for the entertainment of adults. Unfortunately, no one could see that. But, see it or not, it wasn't the kids' sport anymore. It was their parents', who were living it through them."

In *Sports in America*, Michener discusses incidents as unreasonable as the one stated above. Mothers wanting their children to play and score highest in games so that the family might receive special treatment—like being invited to a new district where they might receive a house rent-free. Coaches persuading parents of 9-year-olds to move into another district. A youngster leaving his parents and allowing an uncle to legally adopt him so he could play basketball at a better school. Cheating in a soap-box derby in order to win. Ridiculing the youngster who strikes out, misses a pass, or doesn't win. Michener points out that the "evil" begins with the adults who want to win through their children.

Not all organized and structured sports activities involve abuse brought on by overemphasis on competitiveness and winning. There has, however, been a trend for children to begin specialization and stressful competition at earlier and earlier ages because of adult influence. On the other side, there are good, reasonable and sensitive coaches and parents who strive to teach excellence in sports, participation for all, and encourage healthy and meaningful competition.

Reaching a Healthy Balance

Parents should not assume that all organized sports are bad for the young person. Rather, they should do all they can to instill a healthy attitude about athletic participation. Sports can be a superb means by which to challenge the body physically and keep it fit, to meet others and experience teamwork and cooperation and to develop ideals of fair play and the continuing thrill of healthy competition. Some experts recommend keeping a close eye on the emphasis and attitudes fostered in organized sports in which children and young people participate. If a parent feels competition is too keen and overly emphasized, and that the psychological and physical health of a youngster may be jeopardized, the parent should direct the youngster to a different league or sports area.

Other experts recommend that young children before age 12 or 13 be encouraged to enjoy participation and perfecting skills, and not be allowed to compete at any significant level. If this occurs, many feel fewer young people will burn out or drop out of athletics, and more will participate for the benefits of good health, the excitement, the challenge, and the fun.

Aggression

What Is It?

The ultimate extension of unhealthy competition is aggression, described psychologically as the intent to inflict harm to another, or defined in the *American Heritage Dictionary* as "hostile action or behavior or an assault." There is, however, another definition of aggressiveness—that it is the manifestation of "assertive and bold" behavior aimed at meeting goals or objectives without any harm to others.

Some experts say aggression is a learned behavior, while others believe it to be a natural instinct. There are some who feel that sport teaches youngsters to be aggressive, while others believe that society is, on the whole, predisposed to aggressive behavior. Two theories of aggression and sports are presented in an article by Ruth E. Tandy and Joyce Laflin in the *Journal of Health, Physical Education and Recreation*. One says that sports serve as a catharsis, a release of aggression, while the other hypothesis states that sports contribute to a violent society by making people violent. One theory then postulates that athletics has a positive effect on society, while the other proposes that sports feed violence.

Like the word competition, aggression seems to have two distinct meanings. If one defines aggression as hostile behavior, obviously it has the potential to do harm. If, on the other hand, aggression is being assertive—the striving for a goal with no thought of inflicting harm—it can then be positive and channeled into a healthy attitude.

Aggression: Hostile and Harmful

You've heard about the fights during local high school football games—on the field and in the stands; the player who suddenly throws a tennis racket at his opponent; the youngster who has gotten so involved in the game that he or she tries to "bean" the batter with the next pitch; or the runner who trips the opponent intentionally. You've been to games at which adults are yelling, "Kill 'em, nail 'em, flatten that guy," or even "Fight, fight, fight!" To be fair, many don't really mean to be hostile when they say these things. But to others, caught up in winning at all costs, the words take on a literal meaning. Children are easily directed or led. During the formative years, they are learning what is expected of them, and what are acceptable and unacceptable behavior and responses. Most studies show (whether one believes aggression to be instinctive or cultivated) that aggression can be directed or misdirected.

Although still controversial, some studies indicated that overemphasized competition increases the probability of destructive aggression, and that losing heightens aggressiveness. If the young person is rewarded for his or her destructive aggressive behavior, then the response to stress or the desire to win at all costs will heighten or at least continue. If the child is not rewarded and instead admonished for destructive behavior, the response will usually be diminished or stopped.

If aggressive behavior is directed into performing better or doing one's best, instead of "getting" the opponent, it can be an excellent outlet. In fact, some psychiatrists believe that sports participation can relieve natural aggressiveness through healthy physical expression, and that this kind of control over aggressive feelings can be useful in everyday life. J. P. Scott, Ph.D., in his article, "Sports and Aggression" states, "The general principles are that individuals fight in the situations in which they have been trained to fight, and are peaceful in those in which they have been trained to be peaceful." He goes on to say that "one of the first principles of competitive sports is that the person who loses his temper is likely to lose the game, either because he loses his judgment, or through violation of the rules." Dr. Scott feels that sports and games "provide powerful methods, both positive and negative, for training individuals to live together in a peaceful fashion."

It's important to keep in mind that all young people are different. Some will tend to naturally be more determined or assertive, others will tend to be more destructively aggressive, and still others will be a good deal more passive. These differences may be based on genetic differences. But how parents and others direct this behavior is important.

Injuries: Results of Destructive Aggression

Studies show, and experts believe, that the greater the emphasis is on winning and the more a youngster is encouraged to be destructively aggressive, the more likely it is that avoidable injuries will occur—either to the aggressor, or to the opponent against which the action is taken.

The purpose of athletic participation and competition is to perform well, stay physically fit and enjoy the challenge. Injury can, in some cases, eliminate a youngster from further participation. Unnecessary and unwarranted actions which might result in serious injury have no place in sports. Young people should not be pushed or prodded into destructive behavior for the sake of winning.

Healthy Aggression

Assertiveness, determination and boldness are viewed as respected traits in American society. We respect and admire men and women who stand up for what they believe in, or are determined to accomplish a goal, whether social, political, academic or athletic. A free enterprise system encourages healthy competitiveness and aggression. The athlete who dives for a touchdown pass, or tries to steal a base, or runs to retrieve a basketball when it looks as if it will go out of bounds, is viewed as competitive and aggressive. The young person is simply striving to do his or her best, is determined to excel, and enjoys the challenge, without showing hostility or the desire to harm anyone. This kind of drive can be beneficial to those who enjoy aggressive play.

The Parents' and Coaches' Roles

The parent or coach who encourages and rewards destructive, aggressive behavior will see a greater degree of destructiveness and hostility in their young people.

Placing too much emphasis on winning has played a major role in raising the level of destructive aggression in young people. Too much of their self-esteem and social status is risked by whether they win or lose; unhealthy competition and destructive aggression appear. The young person is under the gun to succeed, and succeeding is defined as winning. If the youngster doesn't win, parental or coach support and affection and consequently feelings of self-worth may be lost. Therefore, the athlete is forced to become increasingly aggressive in order to win—because the stakes are too high to lose.

Robert Corran, in his article, "Violence and the Coach," in *Coaching Review*, states that "athletes should be motivated through accentuation of their own positive values and always with a sense of fair play and sportsmanship." He says that violence can be reduced if a positive note is maintained, whether a team or player won or lost; that negative and unkind remarks heighten aggression; that opponents should be seen in a positive way rather than as the enemy; and, that players should be removed from the game if a potentially hostile situation develops.

There is a difference between motivation and determination and hostility and destructiveness. Those who work with young people must teach positive responses to frustration or anger—instilling healthy attitudes about competition and determination—and make a clear delineation between acceptable healthy aggression (motivation, determination, assertiveness) and unacceptable destructive aggression (hostility and anger). By doing so, young people will emulate their example, enjoy the best of what sports has to offer and view themselves with respect, confidence and self-approval.

9.

Levels of Competition—
Local to International

To be involved in sports can mean many things. For some, involvement means simply observing sporting events. For others, involvement means participation in leisure-time activities or at various levels of competition. For young people, there are multiple levels of participation in any number of sports which they can actively enjoy according to age, skill level and commitment. From after-school free play at home or at friends' houses, to semi-organized activities on playgrounds or in physical education classes, to local, regional, state, national and international competition—there is a place in athletics for everyone, at any age, to participate and enjoy.

Competition is not exclusive to organized athletics, although it becomes keener and more demanding on that level. Even at a very early age, children, without prodding, will challenge each other, whether at marbles, foursquare, tag or chase. Healthy competition builds confidence, allows children the opportunity to seek their limits and provides a feeling of belonging and involvement. Nearly everything we do in life has an element of competition built into it. This is true for the youngster as well. Whether on the playground at free play, or in the physical education class, and on upward, competition is involved to some degree.

Becoming a Spectator

There has been much criticism of pushing children to win, win, win. Some of this criticism is certainly well deserved; observations of its results on children support it. Expecting a young (or even older) person to always win and be the best, added to being disappointed when he or she doesn't meet these expectations, is not an attitude that promotes healthy competition, and can only be unproductive and destructive. No one denies that winning can be fun. But, when winning becomes the only reason for an activity, those involved have lost their perspective. With undue and unnecessary pressure, many children will eventually drop out of activities or be terribly disappointed and frustrated.

The fact is, as children grow older, competition naturally becomes keener and more sophisticated—because of the tendency of the developing youngster to want to excel and please others. The fact is, however, that not all can be the best. If winning, rather than the personal discipline, exhilaration and physical challenge of the activity, is the only motivating factor for participation, few will continue to be involved in competitive sports. Putting things into a sensible perspective will have a great deal to do with whether a child will stop being a participating athlete and join the ranks of the spectator.

John Wooden, the famous UCLA basketball coach whose teams won many national titles, has defined "the winner" as one who strives to do his best. That attitude no doubt had a great deal to do with the success of his teams. A similar attitude toward competition on the part of parents would be healthy and rewarding. (For more information concerning competitiveness, see Chapter 8.)

Types of Participation

Unorganized Sports

Children who are not interested in participating in organized sports should be encouraged to take an active part in playground activities, neighborhood play and physical education classes throughout their school years. The primary goals of such participation are to encourage physical activity and the give-and-take of interaction with other youngsters. Because many of these youngsters do not enjoy team sports, parents might consider directing them to activities which can be done in small groups or individually—swimming, tennis, gymnastics, skating and others in which they can maintain physical fitness, stay active and enjoy participation. Local youth centers, either city, county or privately-owned (such as the YMCA or YWCA) can offer facilities and other resources for a variety of activities. Keeping fit should become a lifelong habit. No youngster should miss the long-term benefits of fitness.

Youth Centers

Besides offering a variety of classes in athletic areas and excellent instruction and supervision in physical fitness activities, youth centers also provide organized spots at various levels of competition. The competition is usually based on a youngster's age, stage of growth and development, and/or skill level. Many centers offer participation in many sports, but emphasize "physical fitness" and "fun" first, with less focus on the competitive aspects of sports. Because of this alternative, youth centers are an excellent complement to the more organized outside-school sports. Youngsters of all ages, with varying skill levels, find a challenge in this kind of informal participation and competition.

Organized Non-Scholastic Athletics

Up to the junior high school level, a youngster may wish to be involved in outside-school organized sports such as youth baseball, football, soccer, softball, various gymnastic organizations, swim groups and many others. Such groups are directed by adults, who supervise and organize the athletic participation and competition. These groups may require a considerable amount of parental involvement and make heavy transportation demands.

Most of these leagues and organizations provide various levels of competition, again based upon the youngsters' skill, age or maturation. Youth baseball programs, for example, have programs for the young child, major and minor leagues based on age and ability, and programs for the adolescent participant. All-star teams are often chosen at the end of every season for competition on a regional level. In certain regions, winners progress to state championships, then to national championship play.

Some leagues and groups require try-outs and a sorting out process eliminates some hopeful participants, while in others, all who wish to participate are allowed to do so, with emphasis on fun and participation by all.

Junior High Sports

Many junior high schools have teams in various sports which play against teams of other local junior high schools. Others have intramural (inside the school) competition in which students at a certain grade level choose teams and form a "league." Not all 11- to 14-year-olds will choose to participate in this type of after-school activity, and some might be discouraged by not being chosen for the desired team. However, this is a level at which nearly anyone should be able to participate in some way and be encouraged to do so. The size and strength of athletes at this age vary a great deal. The youngster who matures later and has a delayed growth spurt might become discouraged at this age. It is for these youngsters that support and encouragement is often especially helpful. The late bloomer may find that just a few years make a great difference in athletic success.

High School Sports

Besides activities in physical education classes required in most states during high school, the young athlete may choose to take an active part in the high school athletic program. Depending upon the area of the country, a wide range of sports disciplines is available. Those most commonly offered are: football, basketball, baseball, track and field, cross country, tennis, golf, soccer, swimming, diving, volleyball, gymnastics, field hockey, wrestling and softball. Water polo, ice hockey, skiing, surfing and crew are offered in certain areas.

At the high school level, there will be a further sorting out of players, depending upon level of physical development and ability. Not all who wish to play will make the teams or squads. It is important for those who do not make the team (the relatively elite group which competes and represents the school), and wish to continue participation, to do so at a Youth Center or in intramural sports. For some youngsters, team participation in such positions as managers or trainers provides the contact with the sport that is desired, although physical activity and exercise should not be replaced with these positions.

By high school, many young people who wish to be active in

sports such as tennis, gymnastics, skating, swimming, running and others on a more competitive level will already have been involved with outside coaches and trainers for some time. In these individualized sports, it is rare that an athlete who starts late can catch up to the level of conditioning and expertise of the youngster whose skills and physical traits were nurtured at an earlier age with sophisticated training programs. But youngsters with exceptional natural ability and attributes are occasionally the exception.

Collegiate Competition

Many of those who were able to compete at the high school level will not be able to continue in organized competition at the collegiate level. However, most colleges and universities offer outstanding intramural athletics in almost every area of sports participation. This offers not only fun, but keeps the young people involved in sports and promotes fitness. Other young adults might choose participation and competition, either formal or informal, through community sports clubs and athletic centers.

Those interested in keener competition will by this time be immersed in and committed to their area of athletic interest and expertise. Indeed, in the traditionally American sports of football, baseball and basketball, collegiate participation may determine who will move on to the professional level. Those who want to be involved in the Winter or Summer Olympic sports will have been training with outside coaches and trainers for some time, even if they also participate in their sport as a representative of their school.

Fitness and Fine Performance Take Time

Making a champion requires that many things work hand in hand: a progression in the development of skills; a body type and physical traits particularly well suited to participation in one or more sports; early training with talented coaches; few significant injuries; and a commitment to spend the time and energy necessary to condition and to master the techniques required for a particular sport. Many aspiring athletes will be eliminated because of a lack or shortcoming in one of these areas. A few triumph in the face of poor odds—failure to start conditioning or participation at an early age; less than optimal body type; poor or nonexistent coaching; or serious injury. But none become champions without a commitment to sport-specific conditioning and training to fine-tune skills necessary for the sport.

For example, if you could take 50 children of equal ability and enthusiasm who are the same age and have similar physical characteristics, and start them at the same time in a summer swimming class, most likely the majority of them would do well and achieve a similar level of competence and skill by the end of the summer. If 25 of the children decide to continue swimming year-round, while the other equally skilled youngsters lay off until the next summer, chances are all will not compete at the same level again, even at the end of the next summer.

And, if 10 of the year-round swimmers begin two- or three-hour workouts three times a week, and the other 15 stay at a single two-hour workout session weekly, you'll see the 10 swimmers moving past the 15. Now, if 2 of the 10 begin specialized conditioning programs, with such things as specific endurance work and weight training, and have the additional benefit of outstanding coaching to aid in fine-tuning their swimming techniques, they will easily surpass all the others. The added ingredients of training, coaching and the time commitment spent in increasing endurance and perfecting skills will make the difference. A youngster's reaching higher levels of skill also requires parents or parent figures to provide transportation and support within the family structure necessary for this commitment.

One report states that competitive teenage swimmers spend an average of four hours in the water per day, and swim 60,000 yards a week. If this were done seven days a week, that would mean twenty-eight hours in the water and over 31 miles! Most youngsters will run some 60 to 70 miles a week to be able to compete in a marathon. Yet another study estimated that for a youngster to achieve reasonably high proficiency shooting baskets, it would take 1 million shots; pitching a baseball would require 1.6 million throws; and passing a football would need some 1.4 million passes. Gymnasts often spend three to four hours a day conditioning and perfecting skills—and the same is true for skaters, tennis players, runners and others. The time and effort needed to excel in these sports at a young age is staggering! When a youngster moves beyond the competition of the local club or league, the champion is often the one who invests the most.

International and Olympic Competition

An Avocation

Only very few of the children who want to be Olympic athletes, or whose parents wish them to be, will be able to reach this pinnacle of competition and level of performance. Only a handful of athletes will be able to compete in international competition in any one sport, out of thousands and thousands of talented and extremely successful young stars. Their years of work will be composed of thousands of grueling hours of conditioning, training and performing, and tremendous sacrifices in other aspects of life, particularly of the many social pleasures of early childhood and youth. Parents will have to spend a considerable amount of money on transportation, coaching and proper facilities. There will be sacrifices made changing the family lifestyle. A total commitment to training becomes a full-time job, one in addition to the youngster's schooling, and his or her social life.

Making a Decision

At some point, youngsters and their parents must decide mutually the extent of the young person's participation in athletic competition.

Youngsters often want to continue to higher levels of competition which parents feel aren't best for them. Parents may feel that money or time is a problem, or that the youth would be sacrificing too many other aspects of his or her life for the sport.

On the other hand, there may be young people who are not interested in competition at higher levels, but whose parents wish them to be because they are convinced the youngsters can succeed. These parents try to instill in the youngster the right amount and type of motivation to succeed (and indeed may be occasionally correct). But no one, particularly a youngster, should be forced into participation and competition beyond that which he or she desires.

Although both situations are problematic, the bottom line is clear: a youngster who is forced into a competitive level for which he or she is not fit, either physically or psychologically, will probably eventually feel like a failure, and may "burn out" or drop out. Often this selection process occurs without a conscious discussion or decision. The youngster loses interest and moves on to something else, or will continue to participate for the wrong reason: to please others at the expense of his or her own feelings and needs.

Success in athletics (regardless of level of competition) depends upon natural ability as well as conditioning and motivation. And it is only the youth who is happy—regardless of level of involvement—who will benefit from all that athletics can offer.

10.

The Physically and Mentally Handicapped Young Person and Sports

Programs for the Physically Disabled

In Georgia, more than 400 spectators crowd into a gym to cheer disabled youngsters playing basketball. In Boston, thousands watch 15-year-old John Rodolph compete in the most renowned marathon of them all. He trained 70 miles a week in his wheelchair. A young woman from Pennsylvania wins the mile and the hurdles at the 24th National Wheelchair Games. Skiers are frequently passed by those using a small ski for balance on the side where a leg has been amputated. Spectators line the shores as waterskiers move from their wheelchairs onto specially designed metal plates.

The list goes on and on, but the point remains: sports and physical activity have become a national pastime for the physically disabled.

Most non-disabled people are amazed at the ability of disabled youngsters and older people to participate and compete in sports. Much of the problem has been caused by a lack of understanding of what being physically disabled means in terms of limitations. But now there is increased focus on the disabled person's needs and wants.

Significant progress has been made in developing programs for the disabled of all ages in the last ten years. It wasn't until after World War II that the needs of the physically disabled were generally recognized. Even so, major steps were not taken until the 1960s and 1970s. This progress can be attributed to the persistence and hard work of disabled veterans and others who brought these issues to the nation's attention. Although much work remains to be done, great strides have been made in a variety of areas to allow the disabled to be more physically active. Special wheelchair designs, better technology and a greater understanding of the limits and "nonlimits" of various disabilities have helped promote more active participation in athletics for disabled people.

"The disabled person has finally made his or her presence known. These people are proving that they can be very active—want to be very active—not only in sports, but in all aspects of life," says Patrick J. Griffin.

Griffin is the director of the Recreation Therapy Department at Rancho Los Amigos Hospital, a widely recognized rehabilitation facility in Southern California. In the field of therapeutic recreation for 14 years, and as past-chairman of the Board of Registration for the National Therapeutic Recreation Society, he has great insight into the needs and rights of the physically disabled.

"Certainly what a young person can do depends on the injury or illness and the extent of the disability. But people tend to forget that disabled youngsters can do many of the same things normal kids can do. Parents and others need to be as creative as possible and look at each young person's 'ability,' instead of his or her disability. Based on that ability," Mr. Griffin explained, "these youngsters can be directed to many sports or become actively involved in some form of physical exercise."

Griffin points out that play is important to all children, and physical activity, participation and healthy competition are vital to good health and mental fitness whether a youngster is disabled or not.

Physically disabled young people should be encouraged and allowed to participate on the level at which they can be active and successful. Games and sports activities should be modified to meet the needs of these young people, and new games or activities can be creatively developed with a little ingenuity. Even at an early age, sports and other activities allow for the vital socialization that all youngsters need and desire.

"The point is, everyone in this world has problems of one sort or another. Some physically normal people can't play basketball very well, but do well at tennis. Others aren't as coordinated as some of their peers, but can develop their physical skills and strength, and find a sport or sports they enjoy. It isn't any different for physically disabled young people," Griffin noted. "Some will do better at one activity than another—some will be skilled and others will not. The important point is to let the young people try many physical activities until they find the ones best suited for them, and that they enjoy most."

The health benefits of being physically active cannot be overlooked either. With activity, blood circulation increases, the heart becomes a more efficient pump, and there is the added benefit of preventing pressure sores. Exercise strengthens muscles and tones them, and fluid intake vital in physical exertion helps in preventing bladder and kidney problems for those susceptible to them. Better coordination can be achieved and skills which help the disabled young person in everyday life can be acquired. Social interaction is an important benefit of participation, as is pure enjoyment.

Unfortunately for some disabled young people, sports and physical activity simply didn't exist in any organized fashion in this country—or elsewhere—until very recently. National attention focused on the disabled veteran during and after the Vietnam War and because they organized and developed support groups, things began to happen.

Because of more public awareness and the efforts of these groups, Public Law 94-142 was passed and took effect in 1978. The law states that all local school districts are obligated to provide disabled youngsters aged three to eighteen with "special educational services." Essentially, the young person is evaluated and if found eligible, *must* be placed (within the next school year after application) into a modified physical education program. This law was an important step in ensuring that the disabled youngster be given the opportunity to be physically active. Physical exercise on a routine basis is a vital part of any rehabilitation program. It enhances strength, fitness, functional skills, social skills, self-confidence, and the ability of disabled youngsters to better care for themselves (up to their ability level) as they grow older.

Any parent or guardian who has a youngster three to eighteen years of age who is physically handicapped and is not in a special program of physical education should contact the local school district to find out how to have the youngster assessed for eligibility in such a program.

Recreational Activities and Competitive Sports

Besides special physical education, the young (and older) disabled person can also take part in many organized recreational sports—and if desired, compete on one level or another. Cliff Crase, editor of *Sports 'N' Spokes*, himself disabled, has been covering recreational activities and competitive sports for a long time. He reports on and examines various recreational activities and competitive wheelchair sports year-round. The magazine is primarily for those afflicted with spinal-cord injuries, polio, amputations, and spina bifida (open spinal canal) and other congenital disorders. Published bimonthly, it contains special features for kids, provides coverage of major wheelchair events and recreational sports, provides an up-to-date calendar of events, reviews books, and publishes articles about new wheelchairs, wheelchair modifications and new technology.

"Recreational sports that disabled individuals are involved in are numerous," Mr. Crase explains. "There are golf, tennis, football, flying, skiing, kayaking, hunting and fishing, all-terrain vehicle driving, wilderness recreation, boating, water skiing, scuba diving, swimming, bowling, archery, basketball, volleyball, soccer, softball, table tennis, weight-lifting, marathon racing, and others. The competitive sports include track and field, basketball, marathon racing, pentathalon, softball, swimming, bowling, archery, table tennis and weight-lifting."

All sports in which disabled persons can compete have rules and regulations as well as qualifying standards—and all have various classifications depending on extent of disability. Various national associations, including the National Wheelchair Basketball Association, the National Foundation for Wheelchair Tennis, the American Wheelchair Pilots Association and many others, oversee competition or recreational activities.

"Certainly, the extent of your disability to some degree limits your ability to perform certain tasks or skills, but many people set their own limits on how physically active they want to be," Crase notes. "Because people have varying disabilities, there are seven classes (classifications) for competition to ensure fairness. These classifications are based on the degree of disability and are very specific, so you're not competing against someone in that sports area who can do things you really can't do, or who can perform them on a different level."

People who do not necessarily need to use a wheelchair every day, yet can't be physically active without it, are also eligible to compete in wheelchair competitions—in the category based on their degree of disability. Classification categories are regulated for both men and women. In most of these sports, competitors are 10 years old or older, and most range from 15 through the 30s. Anyone of any age can be involved in the spectrum of recreational activities, but there may be limits depending upon accessibility of sports programs and necessary special equipment.

Many organizations are helpful in directing parents, others who work with disabled young people, and the young people themselves in locating local, regional or state organizations which have sports programs for the disabled. Many local colleges and universities now have Disabled Student Services and usually have accessibility to sports program information, if not programs themselves. Many city and county recreation departments have special programs for physically disabled youngsters, and are an excellent place to start asking questions. Hospitals specializing in rehabilitation for the physically disabled also have information available, and some sponsor special leagues or programs for young people.

The National Wheelchair Athletic Association is yet another excellent resource. Anyone wishing information about recreational or competitive sports for the disabled in their area should write:

National Wheelchair Athletic Association
40–24 62nd Street
Woodside, New York 11377

Sports 'N' Spokes answers hundreds of questions weekly. Cliff Crase says they are always happy to help or refer people to the best other source of help. The subscription cost of the magazine is minimal, and its contents may be encouraging to many disabled youngsters interested in sports. For more information about recreational and/or competitive sports for the disabled, or a subscription to the magazine, write:

Sports 'N' Spokes
5201 North 19th Avenue, Suite 111
Phoenix, Arizona 85015

Another excellent source of information is the Paralyzed Veterans of America. They publish a very informative brochure which lists all the competitive sports areas available (with a brief description of each), the classifications based on disabilities, the most up-to-date qualifying standards for the various competitive sports, and a complete listing of associations (and their addresses) which are involved in competitive sports and recreational activities for the disabled. The brochure can be requested and other information obtained by writing:

Paralyzed Veterans of America
4350 East West Highway, Suite 900
Washington, D.C. 20014

Special Programs for the Blind

"Blind children can do many, many things given the right opportunities, a little creativity and appropriate supervision," says Norman Kaplan, Founder and Executive Director of the Foundation for the Junior Blind in Los Angeles, California. "We have an active sports program here, including baseball by sound, archery by sound, swimming, running, gymnastics, tumbling, basketball, bowling, bicycle riding, and rollerskating. We have a special summer camp which includes hiking, horseback riding, fishing, swimming, and almost anything you can think of. Although we are rather unique because we gear our programs around the things sighted children can do, I honestly believe and we have proven that the visually impaired can enjoy and be involved in those same activities—with a little modification to meet their needs."

Although the Foundation for the Junior Blind is a local non-profit organization, it is always happy to answer questions about the kinds of programs available to the blind across the country. Kaplan says the Foundation would be most happy to answer any inquiries about other organizations which might be of interest or help to those who request such information.

"Unfortunately, many people don't understand that a blind young person has great need for physical activity, as well as the socializing that sports participation has to offer. Youngsters need to express themselves and enjoy being active. It might take a little more creativity than with sighted youngsters, or, in some situations, more supervision, but the opportunities are there," Mr. Kaplan noted, "for parents of blind children to make their children's lives more fulfilling and healthfully active."

As with other types of physical disabilities, sports and physical activities are based on the young people's abilities, and games are modified to meet their physical limitations. But physical activities allow visually impaired youngsters to achieve physical fitness. And the opportunity to socialize and build self-confidence in their abilities and physical skills helps them become more self-reliant as they grow older.

Those interested in information about programs in their area can write:

> The Foundation for the Junior Blind
> Norman Kaplan, Executive Director
> 5300 Angeles Vista Blvd.
> Los Angeles, California 90043

For a complete listing of all agencies, nationwide, write:

> Directory of Agencies Serving the
> Visually Handicapped in the United States
> American Foundation for the Blind, Inc.
> 15 West 16th Street
> New York, New York 10011

For international information about agencies and organizations write:

> Directory of Agencies for the Blind
> Dept. of Health and Social Security
> Alexander Fleming House
> Elephant and Castle
> London SEI-6BY
> England

Programs for the Deaf (Hearing-Impaired) Youngster

Generally speaking, young people who are deaf or have degrees of hearing disability, can be actively involved in all sports, depending on their wants and needs. According to experts, there is very little reason for a deaf child not to be involved in sports. The major drawback seems to be that most deaf youngsters have not been encouraged to participate and are therefore less sophisticated in their skills than hearing youngsters.

Most schools where "mainstreaming" deaf youngsters takes place are open to the involvement and participation of deaf youngsters. Also, with Public Law 94-142, more deaf young people are becoming actively involved in sports at earlier ages.

It doesn't matter if it's just intramural activities or more advanced competitive sports, participation is vital for all young people; the hearing-impaired are no exception. School districts try to do all they can to encourage any amount of participation these young people desire. Most experts argue that we'll see more and more hearing-impaired youngsters involved in sports as they learn skills at younger ages and feel more confident about their participation. To their knowledge, there is really no reason to keep the children from participation, unless there is an additional handicap besides the deafness which would influence their ability to participate safely.

A story about the origins of the football huddle sheds light on the influence of the deaf on our national sports. It is said that the huddle was actually developed by a deaf football team who needed to use sign language to call plays, but at the same time obviously did not want their opponents to see what the next play was going to be. From there, others followed suit. Although the story may be apocryphal, almost all the experts mentioned it, noting that the deaf have a long tradition of athletic participation.

Gallaudet College in Washington, D.C. is the only college for the deaf or hearing-impaired in the United States. Their athletic departments (both men's and women's) encompass almost every sport now available at most other colleges and universities. Sports include: football, soccer, cross-country, baseball, track and field, tennis, softball, swimming, volleyball and so on. The men's teams are in Division III of the National Collegiate Athletic Association (NCAA) and the women play in the Association for Intercollegiate Athletics for Women (AIAW).

Signs are used for training; hand signals and the buddy system are utilized for officiating events. Gallaudet teams play colleges at which students have normal hearing, as well as those in special sports programs for the hearing-impaired. Men's Athletics Director, Joe Fritsch, says that in the nine years he's been at Gallaudet, he has seen little or no difference between the hearing college student in sports and the hearing-impaired. He does point out that the earlier the hearing-impaired are involved in sports, the more proficient they'll be in the area in which they choose to participate.

Gallaudet College personnel are happy to answer any questions about athletic participation and the hearing-impaired. They also offer information about the International Olympics for the Deaf which take place every two years. For more information about Gallaudet or the International Olympics for the Deaf, please write:

Jerry Jordon
Gallaudet College
Washington, D.C. 20002

Parents and others who wish to know more about the programs offered in public schools should contact their local school district. These people are very helpful and knowledgeable about various sports programs for the deaf in their areas.

The Special Olympics—A Special Program for the Mentally Handicapped

The Special Olympics were founded in 1968 by Eunice Kennedy Shriver, sister of the late President John F. Kennedy and Senator Robert F. Kennedy. Originally, the program was to be held under the auspices of the Joseph P. Kennedy, Jr. Foundation, a family Foundation established in 1946 in honor of young Joseph Kennedy, who was killed in World War II. The focus of the Foundation was and is to provide services to the mentally retarded (also known as the mentally handicapped), including research and rehabilitation. The Kennedy family has been especially concerned, compassionate and understanding of the needs of this special group of people because Rosemary Kennedy (the late President's sister) is mentally retarded.

Mrs. Shriver, Executive Vice President of the Foundation, had the idea of an Olympic-style event for the mentally handicapped, to be held in cooperation with the Chicago Park District. Up until that time, no one had ever attempted such an event, and many felt that it simply wouldn't work. Apprehensions were based on the fact that of the six million mentally retarded persons in this country at the time, fewer than 25 percent had experienced any kind of physical activity—and for even them, physical activity took place for one hour or less a week.

The first Special Olympics saw 1,000 mentally handicapped athletes, from 26 states in the United States, and as far away as France and Canada, compete in track and field and swimming. The program was so successful that a separate non-profit organization, The Special Olympics, Inc., was formed the next year.

Within two years, 250,000 Special Olympians competed. Ten years from its inception, the number soared to one million. Today, there are more than one million Special Olympians around the world—and the number is still growing. Certainly, no one could have imagined in 1968 that this unique idea would literally snowball into a well-established and highly acclaimed program in which 95 percent of all counties in every state of the Union, and 40 countries from every continent in the world, would enter participants.

The Special Olympics Program has been successful because there was so great a need for such a program. The mentally handicapped had been misunderstood for years, and their needs more often than not went unrecognized. The Special Olympics were instrumental in bringing attention to the many needs of the mentally handicapped, and helped families with these special children better understand them and their ability to be active and involved.

All children, young people and adults alike, need and enjoy physical activity whether or not they are mentally handicapped. Self-esteem and self-respect develop as a young person is given the opportunity to participate, achieve and excel. Physical activity, in general, also allows for a better and healthier life and provides many socializing benefits which may never be experienced otherwise. But the need for physical activity—a complement of better health and development of social skills—had generally been ignored for the mentally handicapped. Mental retardation carried a stigma, and most people thought such individuals could not be capable of intense sports participation, much less any form of competition—no matter how healthful it might be. The Special Olympics proved otherwise, and today physical activity and sports participation are encouraged as excellent therapeutic devices, as well as avenues to a happier life.

According to the American Academy of Pediatrics, in a policy statement regarding mental retardation and physical activities:

"Every retarded child needs a continuing program of physical maintenance with regular exercising and supervised athletic activities. If he (or she) is not able to participate in basketball, football, or baseball, he (or she) may be able to compete in track and field events, or playing catch. Swimming, hiking, camping, archery, soccer, trampoline jumping, tennis, bicycling, folk dancing, and boating are examples of athletic activities that can give a retarded youngster the satisfaction, the sense of participation, the social contacts, and the physical exercise that can be profitable for him (or her)."

The same official statement noted that, in general, mentally handicapped youngsters are obese, not physically fit and have poor coordination, all of which tends to get worse with age due to lack of physical and sports activities. Unfortunately, because of a misunderstanding of mental retardation, mentally handicapped youngsters are often excluded from physical and sports participation, and don't receive the benefits of exercise or personal experiences so badly needed. The American Academy of Pediatrics pointed out that often parents are unsure of the youngster's ability to participate, may be fearful he or she will get hurt or, on the other hand, push the youngster too hard, at a pace he or she cannot tolerate.

The Academy also recommends sports that require gross motor skills and not fine motor skills, and individualized sports instead of team sports. Competition among young people with like disabilities is also recommended, and participation in sports activities with youngsters of normal intelligence is good as long as it is non-competitive and not highly structured. Usually, competition among those of like abilities seems to be quite beneficial in motivating the youngsters to participate and in helping to encourage physical fitness, muscle development and better coordination.

One of the greatest benefits derived from the Special Olympics has been emphasis on and commitment to year-round sports training for the mentally handicapped. Their year-round programs teach and train participants through more than 17,000 Special Olympic programs, in 17 different sports. Every year, each State Chapter holds its games, which must include at least 6 sports areas. Then, every four years (like the Olympics) the grand finale Special Olympics (both winter and summer Games) are held in a different part of the country. Thirty-six states now offer winter sports such as alpine skiing, Nordic skiing, speed skating, and figure skating.

"What's really striking about the Special Olympics is that the mentally retarded people have demonstrated that they can do what others do," Herb Kramer of the Special Olympics explained. "The record for the mile run in the Special Olympics is 4 minutes and 24 seconds, which would have been more than enough for an Olympic medal some years ago. And there are other similar records that would make any athlete proud."

In the Special Olympics, every participant has a chance to win a medal, because those who compete do so against others of their own age and sex, with like abilities. Categories are determined ahead of time, making competition keen and very exciting for all participants. Essentially, everyone does well, but there are those who win and those who do not. Because each has done his or her best, Mr. Kramer noted, all are winners. Contrary to many people's expectations, the athletes understand victory and defeat, but have very healthy attitudes about both.

"The point is to get these people out, give them the opportunity to be active and interact with others, and let them enjoy themselves. Special Olympians do a great deal of sharing and enjoying, while reaping the benefits of physical activity. They know," Kramer said, "that what they are doing is significant, and that helps them feel good about themselves. Each shares in the others' victories and the others' defeats because it's a healthy and happy atmosphere."

Research done on the Special Olympics has shown that the program has contributed to decreasing the stigma of being mentally handicapped or having a mentally handicapped youngster. The program has had a tremendous value in strengthening the family and improving sibling relationships in households containing a mentally handicapped person. Participation has improved the self-image and self-esteem of those involved, and has proven the ability of the mentally handicapped to perform athletic tasks requiring coordination, strength, endurance and skill.

More than 350,000 volunteers work with Special Olympians to improve and teach sports skills and interaction, and encourage socializing. Emphasis is on skill, sharing, courage, the joy of participation, and physical fitness. Star athletes from a wide range of sports give freely of their time to help Special Olympians. For example, the National Basketball Association sponsors Special Olympics Basketball, and the North American Soccer League sponsors Special Olympic Soccer.

The point of the Special Olympics is well taken: all young people should be encouraged to be active and allowed to enjoy sports participation no matter what their intellectual level may be, and in a manner equivalent with their abilities and skills. Mental retardation in itself should not preclude a young person's participation in sports as long as ability level is taken into consideration, goals are reasonably set and supervision is adequate. Physical expression is an important form of communication and social interaction, and is the only way to improve physical fitness.

Qualification as a Special Olympian requires the person to fit the definition of mentally handicapped (retarded or mentally disabled), and live in a geographic area which supports a local program. In the United States, an IQ score of 75 or below meets the intelligence criterion. Those with multiple handicaps (such as amputees, the blind, those confined to wheelchairs) who are also mentally handicapped are encouraged to participate in the Special Olympics. Entrants with multiple handicaps are placed in categories with others of the same age and sex who have similar disabilities.

For more information about the Special Olympics or a local chapter in your area, write:

Eunice Kennedy Shriver
The Special Olympics
1701 K Street, N.W.
Washington, D.C. 20006

Further, the United States Department of Health and Human Services in Washington, D.C. offers information about recreation and physical education for the handicapped. Their information can be obtained by writing:

American Alliance for Health, Physical Education
and Recreation
1201 16th Street, N.W.
Washington, D.C. 20036

Sports Medicine and the Care of the Injured Athlete

11.
Sports Medicine—What Is It,
How Do I Find a Specialist,
and When Do I Take My Child?

SPORTS MEDICINE IS a relatively new field that has grown rapidly over the past few decades. America's boom in sports and athletic participation created a need for specialization in the care of the young athlete. But there have been many misconceptions as to what sports medicine is really all about.

The truth is, sports medicine is a unique specialty, a field that requires a multi-disciplinary approach to the care of the competitive athlete as well as the youngster and teenager (or adult) who merely wish to be physically fit and active.

How Sports Medicine Developed

People have been interested in the medical aspects and problems of athletes throughout history. But sports medicine attained a significant level of sophistication as a specialty in the United States after World War II. However, its greatest development in expertise and dissemination of information took place in the 1960s and 1970s. Before that, coaches, trainers, parents and others cared for the athlete most of the time, unless serious injury occurred. Doctors were reserved for serious problems, and were looked upon as last resort sources of information and help. Physicians usually did not get very involved, and the idea of total care of the athlete or active individual was unheard of. Sports medicine professionals who play such a major role today did not exist as a group thirty years ago.

Folklore was abundant and many non-professionals gave advice on injuries and training. For example, the idea that water and other liquids be restricted during competition and training was one such old wives' tale. The true athlete, it was said, was one who had stamina; it was "macho" not to replenish fluids. Many believed fluid intake during participation would make the athlete sick or give him or her stomach cramps. Some serious muscle, tendon, and joint injuries went unattended, because the "true" athlete was inspired to play in spite of pain and "work off" or "walk off" the problems. Little was known about the effects of exercise on the cardiovascular system or pulmonary function. Information on alcohol, drugs, stimulants and hormones was limited, and the idea of conditioning as we know it today was still in its infancy. Little information was available about the activity or participation of youngsters, and misconceptions abounded when it came to the female and sports.

With the tremendous surge in sports participation, more research was done and the results widely published. Together with an increasing interest in the unique needs of the athlete by physicians and other professionals, the idea of "total care" of the athlete or active youngster and adult emerged. Although some coaches, parents and others still resort to inappropriate medical self-care, many more have realized that in certain situations, doctors and medical paraprofessionals should be consulted about conditioning methods, dietary needs, ways to improve performance, means of prevention, as well as treatment of, injuries.

Where Has This Information Come from?

This great leap forward in sports medicine was the result of years of diligent work and investigation by many medical specialists: orthopedic surgeons, family practice physicians, pediatricians, internists, cardiologists, exercise physiologists, psychiatrists and psychologists, sports sociologists, physical educators, athletic trainers, biomedical engineers, chemists, biomechanics experts, coaches—and the athletes themselves. Experts in other areas of medical specialization have made major contributions to the field of sports medicine too: nose and throat specialists, neurologists and neurosurgeons, gynecologists, urologists, and ophthalmologists.

Exercise physiologists, in particular, have made a tremendous impact on athletics and fitness. These M.D.s and PhD.s, working in human performance laboratories, have brought a vast knowledge and scientific approach to athletics and performance. Their contributions have resulted in improved training techniques, more information about the response of the human body to physical stresses and training, new knowledge about prevention and prediction of injuries, the advent of innovative ways to aid in the achievement of goals, and the establishment of sophisticated rehabilitation techniques. Although they are not directly involved with the medical care of the athlete, their impact on care has been vital and long-lasting. Others—dentists, optometrists, chiropractors, podiatrists, osteopathic physicians and brace technicians—have also had a great influence on the care of athletes, young and old.

Add up all these specialty areas and you see the need for an individual who can coordinate all the information and disciplines required into a new multi-disciplinary specialty—sports medicine.

The Sports Medicine Specialist Today

The orthopedic surgeon who specializes in the care of athletic injuries is often seen as a sports medicine specialist. But he is really a sports traumatologist, an expert who specializes in the care of injury to the musculoskeletal system. The specialist in sports medicine may indeed be an orthopedic surgeon, but his or her area of expertise would extend beyond sports traumatology into total care of the athlete. Total care would include conditioning and training, prevention as well as treatment of injuries, rehabilitation, nutrition, and a desire to promote and enhance performance and fitness. This specialist would be involved in bringing all medical and scientific data available today to the aid of the athlete as a complement to the athlete's achieving his or her goals. The physician would also be interested in the health benefits of sports and fitness as well as in performance.

This means, too, that a family practice physician or a pediatrician with interest and expertise in the field could be a sports medicine specialist. Or an internist might bring his or her expertise in such areas as the care of athletes with diabetes, epilepsy, heart problems, kidney problems, asthma, and others to the specialty of sports medicine. Many of these physician-specialists will perform detailed pre-participation physical examinations, screen injuries and make referrals to orthopedic surgeons or other experts if the injury warrants it.

They will be able to discuss and recommend conditioning regimes, injury prevention procedures, nutritional guidelines, rehabilitation techniques and management and, generally, they will be able to care for the athlete's overall needs.

Sports Medicine Helps Everyone

The health benefits of athletic participation and conditioning to achieve fitness should be life-long—and should benefit all age groups. While sports medicine helps young athletes striving toward greater and greater levels of performance, it has as much to offer to leisure-time players who are interested in fitness, fun and fine-tuning their bodies toward the highest level of physical performance for the sake of good health.

Gone are the days when a youngster arrived at a physician's office and said, "When I run five miles, my legs hurt," only to be told "Don't run!" People want a more helpful answer than that and deserve it. Today, the specialist in sports medicine would evaluate the youngster, explain the problem(s), discuss the way(s) to solve the problem, and note the potential consequence(s) of doing so. The specialist would be able to tell the young person and the parents what steps could be taken to make participation less painful.

For example, following a significant injury to the knee, running may be detrimental until rehabilitation has progressed somewhat. The physician may suggest that the youngster switch to swimming or cycling—non-weight-bearing sports—for a period of time. This would provide the young athlete with the health benefits of physical challenge, while at the same time diminishing stress on the painful joint and allowing the injury to heal. If, on the other hand, the young athlete insisted on playing the desired sport, he or she would at least know the possible long-range consequences of that decision.

Therefore, sports medicine deals not only with healing the young person's sports-related injuries, but includes preventing them and protecting the athlete from problems, while still emphasizing the best ways to stay fit and active. For those involved at high levels of competition, another goal of the sports medicine specialist is to help the athlete get back into competition as soon as possible after an injury, at the same level of performance—as long as it is consistent with safety and good health principles.

Finding a Sports Medicine Specialist

American Orthopedic Society of Sports Medicine

The majority of clinicians practicing as sports medicine specialists today are orthopedic surgeons. About ten years ago, the American Orthopedic Society of Sports Medicine was founded for the purpose of exchanging ideas about the care of the athlete or active individual who has special needs. And the society is committed to education and research, with the purpose of informing the public about sports medicine. Members are found in all major cities and in larger communities.

All Board-certified orthopedic surgeons have expertise in dealing with basic athletic injuries, but the members of this Society are encouraged to specialize in sports medicine in addition to sports traumatology. So, when injury occurs, finding an orthopedist who belongs to this society will be helpful.

American College of Sports Medicine

This group is made up primarily of exercise physiologists, sports psychologists, nutritionists, kinesiologists, sports sociologists, physical educators, podiatrists, osteopaths, chiropractors, physicians and others interested in the study of human performance, medicine and science in sports.

Other Sports Medicine Societies

The National Athletic Trainers Association (NATA) is composed of certified athletic trainers. It would be ideal to have them in every high school for injury prevention, recognition, first aid and rehabilitation.

The American Physical Therapy Association (APTA) has a sports medicine section. Their work involves rehabilitation and conditioning of athletes.

Many other specialty areas in medicine have sports medicine societies. These include podiatry, chiropractics, osteopathic medicine, and others. Local, regional, national and international societies all contribute to the field of sports medicine.

Sports Medicine Clinics and Centers

A guide to sports medicine clinics and centers, updated yearly, can be purchased at a low price from the magazine, *The Physician and Sports Medicine*. Write:

> *The Physician and Sports Medicine*
> 4530 West 77th Street
> Edina, Minnesota 55435

Choosing a Sports Medicine Specialist

Unlike pediatrics, family practice, orthopedics, and so forth, the specialty of sports medicine has not yet been standardized. Standardization means that an accrediting board is formed to formulate and judge post-graduate training (work beyond medical school) and mandate the level of proficiency (through testing and experience) required for accreditation. Presently, there is a movement to institute such an accreditation board so that those meeting the standards would be Board-certified in the field of sports medicine as physicians are certified in other specialties.

But until standardization of the specialty occurs, physicians will continue to be chosen to care for the young and older athlete according to reputation, experience and recognition by his or her peers and even on the basis of the calibre of athletes under their care or management. Today, there is simply no specific place where a parent, coach, teacher, or school nurse can check on the credentials of a sports medicine specialist. You can get some idea as to who should see the young athlete by inquiring at your local medical society, which might have a referral list of specialties. Also, local junior high and high school teams and the nearest college or university teams usually have sports medicine specialists as consultants to their athletes, so they would be a good source of information. The family doctor or pediatrician is usually an excellent resource and can make an appropriate referral, if necessary.

Who Should Be the Youngster's Primary Physician?

It is important, then, that the family doctor or pediatrician be the primary physician during the growing years until the early twenties. You may wish to discuss the youngster's interest in greater and greater participation in athletics to learn if the doctor feels specialized management is indicated or warranted. You may find that the family doctor or pediatrician has a special interest in sports medicine, which would make him or her an even more ideal primary-care physician and an excellent resource if specialized care due to injury was necessary. If the physician is not particularly interested in or aware of sports medicine or the special needs of the athlete, he or she may wish to refer the youngster to a specialist who is. This judgment is generally based on the youngster's needs, extent of participation, age, level of competition and long-range goals.

When Injury Occurs

Ideally, when a problem or injury occurs, the youngster should first be seen by his or her family physician or pediatrician for evaluation. Obviously, this does not apply to emergencies for which immediate intervention by paramedics or emergency-care specialists at a nearby emergency-care center is necessary. The young person should be seen by a sports medicine specialist if the primary physician makes the referral. If the young athlete experiences persistent pain or restricted function of a limb, joint or other part of the body, it is best to seek out a specialist in these kinds of injuries or problems. Further, if a parent perceives any deviation from the norm with the youngster, it is advisable to seek a medical evaluation first from the primary physician, then referral to a specialist if required. And if a second opinion is desired, it is a good idea to have that second opinion come from a specialist who is recommended as being familiar with the type of injury, problem or treatment thought necessary.

12.

Important Medical and Orthopedic Considerations in Sports Participation

CERTAIN MEDICAL AND orthopedic conditions should be considered when a youngster takes an interest in sports activity. The type of sports activities a child engages in must be based on what is healthy and safe for that particular youngster. Some conditions will have very little impact on participation, while others will dictate the extent and type of activity in which the young person can safely be involved.

These medical or orthopedic conditions should be identified in a complete physical examination prior to serious conditioning or athletic participation. Identifying health problems will make it easier for parents and others to know the child's limitations and to direct the youngster into areas of activity which will provide the most enjoyment and greatest benefit.

Physical Examinations

In most cases (although there are exceptions), children with very serious health problems have been identified at an earlier age through routine examinations by the pediatrician or family doctor. The majority of children with significant cardiac (heart) problems are usually identified during early childhood. However, some problems, such as diabetes, asthma, epilepsy and others, may appear in later childhood, adolescence or afterward so thorough physical evaluation to detect significant and/or manageable problems is a vital part of preparing for athletics and physical activity.

Ideally, the young person's family doctor or pediatrician should perform the in-depth pre-participation physical examination. This physician is familiar with the young athlete's medical and family history, and has followed the youngster's physical status over the years.

Unfortunately, either because of economic reasons or misinformation, many young people do not receive a thorough pre-participation physical, and must rely on the yearly pre-season general screening in hopes that any significant problems will be identified. The pre-participation physical should include two areas: medical considerations and orthopedic considerations. The medical evaluation may include:

History and examination
Blood test for anemia
Urine analysis
Blood pressure and pulse
TB test
Sight and hearing examinations
Growth and development assessment

The orthopedic considerations (structural factors which may or may not limit the amount or kind of sports participation) are discussed later in this chapter.

The more extensive examination is not necessary yearly but the pre-participation screenings should take place each year.

Pre-Participation Screenings

Usually, pre-participation screenings, done before a sports season begins, are carried out in large rooms with the youngsters lined up, military-style. Because of the numbers of children and the time limitations, these young athletes are seen quickly and in a cursory manner despite good intentions. In this situation, physicians can still detect such things as irregular heart beat, heart murmurs, growth and development irregularities, asthma, ruptured ear drums, and undescended testicles in the male. However, because these screenings are done so rapidly and in such a difficult environment, many things may be overlooked.

Clifton Rose, M.D., team physician at Long Beach State University in California, offers very specific guidelines when it comes to the evaluation of the athlete before participation begins. A pediatrician by training, Dr. Rose has also been a team doctor for pre-adolescent and high school teams.

"Today there is greater emphasis on more careful evaluations of the young athlete than ever before. On the whole, we're seeing better and better screening of the young people who are going out for teams, but there is still some concern that in the younger child, as well as those at the high school level, screening is done much too quickly. This situation has been helped by family practice physicians and pediatricians who are getting involved more directly in the screening process and setting up the guidelines of the evaluation," he says.

Dr. Rose and others involved in the evaluation of athletes recommend an in-depth physical examination at age six or seven when the child first enters school and begins physical activity; another upon entering high school; and yet another at the beginning of college. In between these more extensive physical examinations are the yearly pre-participation screenings. For those with known problems or previous injuries, a more in-depth evaluation should be completed routinely to ensure the young athlete's safety during participation.

"Although most young people who are active and want to participate in sports are in good health, such careful evaluations may detect not only conditions which impact the youngster's performance or participation, but can have implications for long term health and therefore should be identified," he notes. Most young people will not jeopardize their own health or well-being if something is wrong; generally, they let you know and won't participate if they are feeling bad—unless they are being pushed.

Parents must realize that, in most cases, a pre-participation screening is *not* a physical examination and should not be substituted for one. Although most colleges perform extensive physical examinations on their entering athletes, this kind of complete physical is not commonplace for other pre-participation screenings. Parents should find out the extent of any pre-participation examination. Often the permission authorizing the physical will ask medical history questions and explain the extent of the physical examination which will take place. With the younger child, the parent may be present and can see what is done. The parent can ask the older child what tests and procedures were completed. In some cases, schools give parents the option of having the child or young person seen by his or her own family doctor.

Medical Considerations

Conditions That Should Be Evaluated
before Participation

Heart conditions of certain kinds will preclude a youngster from participation in athletics. In many cases, these conditions were identified at birth or during a routine examination in early childhood. The youngster's doctor is the best judge as to the level of activity safe for a child with a cardiac problem. But the presence of a heart murmur does not necessarily mean heart disease. A heart murmur is an extra noise heard during heart action and may be loud or soft, significant or insignificant. At some time in their lives, many children will show evidence of a heart murmur. Evaluation by the family physician or pediatrician will determine if there is any reason to limit physical activity or if more specialized evaluations are indicated. Take care not to overreact to a heart murmur—ask questions and follow the physician's recommendation as it applies to the individual child.

The majority of significant problems involving the heart are identified very early, but on very rare occasions, some cardiac conditions (such as some rhythm disorders or conditions in which some blood vessels are too narrow) which can only be detected by very sophisticated testing go unidentified. Deaths associated with these unusual unidentified situations are unpredictable. These are very unfortunate and tragic situations, but they are also very, very rare.

Diabetes mellitus should not exclude a youngster from rigorous participation in athletics as long as the disease is under control. The young diabetic does have special needs—special diet and insulin requirements—and should be under the care of a physician who knows the child wishes to participate in sports, and the type of sport the child prefers. Changes in a youngster's activity require adjustments in diet and insulin dose, which the physician can help supervise. Many experts agree that exercise is helpful in controlling diabetes and should be included in the youngster's overall health program, but only under a doctor's supervision.

Asthma used to preclude a child from athletic participation because of serious concern for his or her safety and well-being. Yet recent research has shown that most children with asthma and allergies do well in physical activity, although certain asthmatic children may have to keep the exertion to under-five-minute intervals. After five minutes of strenuous exercise, some youngsters with asthma may experience bronchospasm, the characteristic wheezing associated with the disorder. Pulmonary function may be improved and a high rate of physical exertion may be achieved by a graduated program. But these techniques should be directed by specialists in cases concerning youngsters with severe asthma.

Medications prescribed by the young person's physician should always be at hand, and coaches and others must be made aware of the youngster's condition, and told the steps to be taken should a problem arise. Most schools and other sports programs require a note from the young athlete's doctor to allow participation. Although most children with asthma find few restriction in sports, the young person should always be under the care of a physician and his athletic program supervised as the doctor recommends.

Seizure disorders or other conditions which result in loss of consciousness should be evaluated carefully in young athletes. Their participation in sports and athletic activities might not need limitation if their conditions are under good medical control. However, when there is a question about how well controlled the problem is, the youngster's potential for probable injury must be considered. Sports which might result in serious injury if loss of consciousness occurred while the youngster was participating should probably be excluded. These might include such sports as diving, competitive downhill skiing, and most of the strenuous contact sports. Swimming should be performed under supervision but it does not necessarily need to be omitted from the "can do" activities. The level of impairment of a child's judgment due to prescribed medications must also be taken into consideration when making a decision about his or her participation in various sports.

Sickle cell anemia or *sickle cell trait*, and other forms of *anemia* might be conditions that would preclude a youngster's participation in some sports. Sickle cell problems are chronic hereditary anemias which are most often found in black youngsters, and have an impact to a greater or lesser degree on health and activity. (Anemia is a condition in which there are fewer than the normal, or healthy, number of red blood cells.) Anemia, in general, causes a reduction in a youngster's exercise tolerance and stamina. Without a normal level of red blood cells that carry oxygen and nutrients to all areas of the body, the young person is more easily fatigued than other youngsters. Sickle cell *disease* is often so serious that the youngster cannot tolerate strenuous activity, even with a good conditioning program. Those with sickle cell *trait*, however, are usually able to participate even in very strenuous activity without problems. Other forms of anemia can also limit participation depending upon their severity and the amount of exertion required for the specific sport. A special warning with sickle cell disease—the activities which involve a significant amount of anaerobic metabolism might cause a sickle cell crisis because of relative lack of oxygen to tissues of the body. This can also be accentuated by activity at high altitudes, and by changes in body temperature, rapid cooling in particular. A sickle cell screening test can be performed for the black athlete if sickle cell status is in question.

Chronic pulmonary (lung) problems and the respiratory changes in *cystic fibrosis* might limit the kind of physical activity a youngster can tolerate without serious compromise of his or her respiratory system, but should not exclude all activity. Careful medical evaluation, with assessment of pulmonary function, is important in determining what level of activity is safe. In general, these youngsters are not able to perform in the very strenuous sports, whether contact or not, because they are unable to tolerate the demands on their pulmonary function.

Although there is some controversy, most people would agree that contact sports should not be part of the activity of youngsters who have only *one functioning eye* or *one functioning kidney*. Even with appropriate protective wear, there is enough potential risk to the remaining vital organ that it would seem prudent to try to steer a young person to another area of participation.

Boys who have an *undescended testicle* and one functioning testicle must wear appropriate protective cups when participating in contact sports, and some experts would recommend that they not participate in such sports at all. Decisions in these matters involve making available the best medical advice and the assessment of risk factors for the individual young athlete.

Acute illness is a reason for temporary non-participation in most organized athletic events. The young person is not at peak performance capability during this time, judgment is askew, and stamina is usually limited. This means that the danger of injury is greater, and the risk for transmission of the illness to other athletes, especially infections, is a real one. Even an active herpes lesion (cold sore) can be a problem in infection control, especially in a sport such as wrestling.

An *enlarged liver* or *spleen*, or both, is a good reason for a youngster not to take part in contact sports. There is a real risk of rupture of the enlarged organ which can lead to death. Such enlargement might be a result of an acute infection such as infectious mononucleosis, or hepatitis, or of some chronic problem. In acute conditions, participation is permissible once the enlarged organ is back to normal size, the youngster has recovered, and his or her doctor has approved participation again.

Hypertension (high blood pressure), when not under control through diet or medication, might limit the youngster's participation to less strenuous athletics. High blood pressure can be made worse by strenuous physical exertion, but conditioning slowly can be a successful way, in some cases, to make it safe for these youngsters to participate.

The youngster who has had *repeated concussions* or head injuries, especially those which resulted in loss of consciousness, should be evaluated carefully before being allowed to participate further in sports. Obviously, the danger to the youngster of subsequent injury in a sport in which he or she is interested should be considered. This is particularly true of contact sports and others in which head injuries occur frequently. No one knows exactly how many times are too many when it comes to these head injuries. For the long-term health and well-being of the youngster, it is best to reduce the risk, if possible. In deciding whether or not a youngster with past repeated head injuries should be allowed to participate in high-risk sports, the severity of the past injury or injuries must be considered carefully. A physician may suggest substituting an athletic area in which the young person would not be so susceptible to further injury.

A *hernia* or *rupture* is an abnormal protrusion of body tissues from one area into another. Although the number of youngsters who have or will develop a hernia is great, the number who will have symptoms or require surgery to repair a rupture is small. In general, concern expressed by parents and others is often greatly out of proportion to the problem. Hernias do not cause sterility or sexual dysfunction, as has wrongly but frequently been attributed to them because people do not know what they really are.

Although hernias in the groin (called inguinal hernias) are the most common type seen in athletes, others such as muscle hernias, ruptures of knee structures (synovial hernias) and bulges in the umbilical area (umbilical hernias) also occur. A rupture (hernia) may be large or small, and may or may not be difficult to reduce (put back into place). Several forms of treatment are possible.

The most common hernia, the inguinal hernia, is usually discovered by a youngster or parent who notices a bulge or lump in the groin area. The bulge is usually without symptoms, but occasionally the youngster experiences a "dragging" sensation or some discomfort. At times the bulge will extend all the way into the scrotum in boys. A thorough evaluation by a physician is necessary with any possible hernia, so that an appropriate form of treatment can be determined. Such an evaluation will also differentiate between a simple hernia and other possible causes of groin bulges, such as an undescended testicle or hydrocele (collection of fluid around the testicle).

With most hernias, the tissue of the rupture slips easily in and out of the hernia sac, without getting stuck. In some situations, there is risk for the hernia contents to be trapped (incarcerated) and unable to be reduced (returned to normal position). This may lead to loss of blood supply (strangulation) of the contents of the hernia sac, and resultant damage to the cells of the trapped tissue.

Some very small hernias require no treatment at all. Others, especially those which are large and where the contents slip in and out, may be helped by the use of a truss or pad to hold the hernia in place. Still others, especially groin hernias which have a risk for incarceration and strangulation, will require surgical treatment. A physician will be able to make an accurate diagnosis and recommend the most appropriate treatment. Most hernia surgeries are very successful and without serious complications. A few youngsters, however, may develop another hernia in the same place even after surgical repair.

Orthopedic Considerations

In evaluating a youngster's ability to participate in any athletic or conditioning program, it is important to consider whether or not there are specific problems with the musculoskeletal system that might limit his or her ability to actually perform the tasks required—or those which would increase the risk for creating problems. Pre-participation examinations and physical assessments should be designed with careful attention to detecting conditions of the bones, joints and muscles which might limit or eliminate a young person's participation. These conditions might be new or old, inherited or the result of illness or injury.

The doctor screening the youngster looks specifically at how the young person moves, and whether or not there are any obvious deformities. Pain or limitation of motion in a joint or extremity, or decreased strength in a specific muscle group, should be evaluated further. It is important to have no restrictions in bending and twisting of the neck and back, as well as to have the full movements of each extremity. These evaluations can identify abnormalities that might cause problems, especially in strenuous activities and contact sports. An assessment of general fitness and strength is also part of a pre-participation musculoskeletal evaluation.

The goal of recognition of orthopedic problems is to prevent repeated injury and potential long-term disability. If a problem is found it can, in many cases, be treated. In those circumstances, the youngster might be guided to another area of participation temporarily, while treatment or correction takes place through a specific conditioning program. It is not worth the chance of premature arthritis or increasing handicap in order to play for one season. If the problem is serious, the youngster may be permanently barred from that sport if there are no means to alter the deformity. In either case, most youngsters can be directed to another sports area where participation is safer for them based on their specific physical problems.

Let's take a closer look at some common orthopedic problems that might limit participation or, when present, deserve evaluation.

Problems of the growth plate (damage to the area of the bone where growth takes place during the growing years) often require individual evaluation and recommendation by a physician. The influence of growth-plate injuries on sports participation depends on the type of growth-plate injury and its severity. Some will dictate that a youngster limit or modify participation in order to prevent further injury, while others will be of concern only in that they cause the young person discomfort, but not permanent disability. (For a detailed discussion of the growth plate and its potential problems, see Chapter 15.)

Osgood-Schlatter disease is a common growth-plate problem of the knee. Pain and tenderness at the upper part of the shin (tibia) just below the knee occur because there is a problem with the growth center and the tendon attachment of the quadriceps muscles (large muscles of the thigh). A youngster with this condition will most likely experience discomfort or pain in running, jumping and other activities which require repeated forceful bending and straightening of the knee. Usually this problem improves with rest, and the youngster's participation in athletics is limited solely by pain. Participation should not be allowed to continue to the point of severe pain, and a protective pad may be worn over the tender area of the shin.

The symptoms may increase during a growth spurt, with the onset of new strenuous activity—or even with no apparent relation to either. It may subside in a few weeks or may recur on and off throughout the years of growth.

Growth-plate problems in the heel (such as Sever's Disease) cause heel pain, and may also limit the amount or type of participation in sports. For some young people, the simple addition of a heel lift, or orthotic, will allow full activity without pain or discomfort, while for others, more extensive rest may be required to diminish or eliminate the problem.

Youngsters with *hip problems,* restricted motion and altered structure, such as slipped capital femoral epiphysis and Legg-Perthes disease (see Chapter 15 for further details) should not participate in strenuous sports unless approved by an orthopedic physician. Hip pain should always be evaluated carefully, and never ignored.

Back problems (round back, curvature, and congenital abnormalities), *back pain* and *injuries* are special considerations. Although they are relatively unusual in athletic young children, conditions of the back which cause pain or limited movement should be evaluated carefully. Some of these are a result of activity and will resolve with rest. Others are so serious that no participation should be allowed during periods of treatment. Again, keep in mind the long-term effects of participating in the face of a potentially life-long problem. *Scoliosis* is a condition which most commonly affects adolescent girls and results in curvature of the spine. Usually, mild degrees of scoliosis should not limit sports activity. In fact, even moderate degrees of curvature do not usually affect performance or stamina. It is, however, important that this condition be detected, evaluated and followed by an orthopedic surgeon who is quite familiar with its natural course and potential problems. The spine deformity may increase rapidly in association with growth. However, once growth is complete, the condition stabilizes.

Positional abnormalities of the legs and feet, such as in-toeing and out-toeing, knock-knees and bowlegs, often cause undue concern. Better knowledge of the usual development of the leg and foot and of minor variations from the norm may help to allay anxiety.

At birth, the newborn is usually bowlegged. As a result of a baby's usual position in the uterus, the legs look as if they are turned in. Over the first year or two of life (modified by the stresses of starting to walk and run), the toddler looks duck-footed and bowlegged, but gradually the legs straighten. By the age of three, many youngsters are actually knock-kneed, which gradually changes to the normal leg position by adolescence. But variations from these general progressions are common, and should not cause undue concern.

Youngsters at any age can be pigeon-toed because of difficulties in the foot, in the lower leg, or at the hip. In general, coordination and performance are not significantly influenced by this leg position, and its presence should not limit activity in any way. If a youngster has enough toeing-in to cause tripping, (especially when running), a more detailed evaluation may be needed. Generally, use of special shoes or lifts in shoes does not *correct* the problem, but may alter the way the child walks or runs. Correction is usually spontaneous over several years without treatment.

As with pigeon-toed posture, the duck-footed or turned-out position is a common variant of normal positioning. Here again, the youngster rarely experiences a problem with pain or injury as a result of activity or exercise. Repeated activity and the stresses associated with them, along with growth, may remodel and alter the position of the legs and feet.

Knock-knees and bowlegs are a common cause for some parental concern. However, neither of these conditions normally results in limitations in athletic participation, nor are they usually associated with pain or injury during childhood. The severely knock-kneed or bowlegged youngster may be helped with special shoes, braces and even surgery but require special evaluation and assessment.

Flat-foot deformity has long been the source for many old wives' tales about foot problems and a variety of other aches and pains. Much of the worry about being flat-footed is unwarranted. Prior to World War II, prospective military recruits could be refused entry into the military service if they had flat feet. After the war, and with a better understanding of flat-foot deformity, it was obvious that recruits with flat feet had no more foot problems (or foot pain) than those without flat feet. This restriction was then dropped.

Two other separate conditions look like the common type of flat foot and are confused with it. In the "normal" flat foot, the arch of the foot is actually flexible, and the foot tends to collapse when weight is placed on it. This may put additional stresses on the muscles of the legs, but with proper footgear and conditioning does not limit participation, and does not cause discomfort. On the other hand, in a foot which is flat because of abnormalities of the bones themselves, or because of tight muscles (a spastic flat foot) the problem can be more serious. This kind of flat foot is rigid and inflexible. The difference is noticeable to a physician, who will be able to determine whether further intervention is necessary. (An infant's or toddler's foot looks flat because of excessive fat in the arch, in comparison to the older child's. This is not a flat foot, but rather a fat foot.)

A *high-arched foot* may cause a problem for an active youngster because of difficulties in fitting footwear properly and in providing enough support under the arch during vigorous jumping and contact of the foot with the ground. A high-arched foot provides an altered area for contact with the ground, and may be associated with the development of calluses and pressure points over the bones (sole) of the foot.

Growing pains is a designation commonly given to the recurrent achy or crampy pains about which youngsters generally complain. Typically, the growing youngster (between four and ten years old) wakes up at night complaining of aches in the lower legs, and may describe cramps in the calves of the legs. Examination by a doctor shows no abnormalities. The young person has usually started a new activity or has been extremely active on the day before this occurs. As long as these problems don't persist, and seem to occur after activity, there is rarely a reason for concern. If, however, limping is observed, or other signs that the discomfort is limiting normal functions are seen, the young person should be evaluated by a physician. Even though it is usually not a problem, night pain that persists should be evaluated by a physician. Although bone tumors are very rare in children, night pain may indicate their presence.

Chondromalacia is a condition of the cartilage in which it becomes worn and irregular because of repeated stresses, injuries, and improper alignment. Such a degenerative problem can affect many areas of the body, but is most common under the kneecap, particularly in athletes. One of the most frustrating orthopedic conditions is chondromalacia of the patella (the abnormal wearing of the undersurface of the kneecap). This may result from repeated injury during sports which involve a great deal of jumping, such as volleyball and basketball. When pain or discomfort is severe, a limitation of activity is sometimes necessary, but solely because of the pain. For this problem, the orthopedist or sports medicine specialist may recommend special exercises to strengthen certain muscles. The youngster who wishes to continue to participate in a sport requiring a lot of jumping and strenuous use of the knee may be limited for a while. Although usually it is a recurring problem that is not disabling, on occasion surgery is a consideration.

Repeated *shoulder dislocations* and *shoulder subluxations* can plague some athletes, and may be causes of limited participation. When these conditions become severe, surgical correction may be the only solution to control the problem so participation can resume. (For more information on dislocations, see Chapter 16.)

Repeated *dislocations of the patella* (kneecap), on the other hand, cause less of a problem in most cases, and can be categorized as a nuisance for most who suffer from them. Usually the slippage of the kneecap is minor, and does not cause persistent pain or deformity. Exercises which strengthen the quadriceps may help make this condition less problematical. When serious dislocation occurs and pain and swelling result repeatedly, surgical correction may be recommended.

The evaluation of the young athlete with a previous repeated injury or injuries presents a special problem. The goal of the pre-participation assessment is to determine what factors might warrant limitation or modification of activity in order to prevent further injury or damage, or to lessen the chance of a possible life-long disability. When a previous orthopedic injury (or injuries) has been severe, and the risk for further, repeated injury is high, it may be wise to consider a change in sports area or limitation of the activity in order to preserve a young person's long-term health and ability to function. This kind of consideration is especially important when repeated head injury is involved, and may apply to situations with constant injury to the knee, hip, elbow, ankle, back or neck.

Each athlete and his or her family must make this decision in conjunction with a knowledgeable sports medicine expert or family doctor who is aware of the requirements and demands of the sports area the young person is involved in, as well as the present and potential problems that may result from further participation.

13.
Predicting and Preventing Injuries

WITH HALF THE YOUNG male and a fourth of the female population (14 to 17 years of age) involved in organized, competitive sports, and more than 33 million youngsters from 5 to 13 years of age involved in sports activities, prediction and prevention of injuries have become an important area of sports medicine.

A study from HEW showed that more than half a million high school students suffered sports-related injuries during 1975–1976. In 1977, a group of 3,049 students participating in 19 different sports showed injury rates as high as 85 injuries per 100 participants for high school boys playing football, and as low as 2 to 3 injuries per 100 participants in swimming. Boys and girls playing the same sport had slightly different rates of injury, but the average number of injuries was 39 for each 100 participants. Nearly two-thirds of the injuries were strains and sprains, and most of these involved the legs.

Greater numbers of young people are beginning to participate in sports, partly because of increasing emphasis placed on sports and physical fitness, and because more leisure time seems to be available. This increase in activity has produced an increase in the number of injuries.

But the fact that more and more young people are engaged in sports accounts for only a part of the injury rate, and reliance on this factor as a sole explanation could be an oversimplication of the issues. Another aspect to consider is the teaching of injury prevention to all physically active people, so that their participation can be safer and the risk of injury reduced.

A third component—injury prediction—is still new and few concrete facts have been widely accepted. Injury prediction is based on an analysis of multiple physiolial and psychological traits of participants, as well as environmental factors.

Injury Prediction

Many experts have studied, and are continuing to study, possible physical and/or psychological traits which might predispose an athlete to certain kinds of injuries, or to be injury-prone in a particular sport. This kind of information will prove to be invaluable in directing youngsters into sports areas in which they will more likely suffer few injuries. With fewer injuries, athletes will be able to maintain their conditioning level and continue participation without being slowed down.

Many dedicated athletes, both competitive and non-competitive, are hindered or even eliminated from top-level competition by a serious injury or by less severe recurrent injuries. Often an injury can become a problem due to inadequate treatment. At times, an athlete may have to change sports in order to participate at all and be active without aggravating an underlying abnormality and prolonging time spent on the mend.

Often it is difficult to put the problem of long-term effects of injury into perspective. Sustaining an injury, no matter what the level of athletic participation, can be a frustrating experience for any athlete. To have to live with the adverse effects of such an injury for a lifetime, without continued participation, or with a modified ability to be active in sports, is even worse. You've heard of the 40-year-old who, because of chronic knee injuries from high school football suffers pain when running or even walking up stairs. Or the tennis player with such bad elbow problems that he or she can no longer play without pain, and must give up the sport. Or the runner who, when young, sustained repeated ankle injuries, and is no longer able to enjoy running during adulthood.

Many, many injuries are purely accidental. Sometimes a young athlete is simply at the wrong place at the wrong time. This may occur even if the athlete has followed a graduated, progressive conditioning program, is careful to warm up and cool down, and essentially does all the right things. But they should be the cause of the minimum number of mishaps for a given sport.

The idea of injury prediction in athletics is not new, but research as a serious, concerted effort is in its infancy. Experts are evaluating body composition (lean body weight and percentage of body fat); strength, power and endurance of specific muscle groups; metabolic tests (stress testing/stationary bicycle or treadmill); performance tests; psychological tests; flexibility measures; joint flexibility and power tests.

The hypothesis is that injury occurs as the result of a "summation of variables" that interact at a given point in time. Therefore, such factors as the type of sport, the level of competitive participation, experience, playing conditions, equipment used and coaching techniques will all interact with the athlete's physical characteristics, such as speed, strength, size, coordination, agility, flexibility, physical fitness, ligamentous laxity and personality traits. The problem is that the physical and personality variables, in their interaction and combination, vary significantly with every athlete.

Considering all the possible variations and the magnitude of the undertaking, it is difficult (from what is known now) to develop an easy, consistent formula for injury prediction.

"As you can imagine, it is most important for us to be able to identify various traits for injury proneness in specific sports. The more we know, the better we can direct young athletes into areas where there is less potential for them to be injured," James Nicholas, M.D., notes. Dr. Nicholas is director of the Institute of Sports Medicine and Athletic Trauma at Lenox Hill Hospital in New York City. He is now involved in a long-term study to determine the relationships between leg and arm strength, cardiac function and sports. The joint project carried out by the Departments of Orthopedic Surgery (of which Nicholas is director), Cardiology, Psychiatry and Nephrology at Lenox Hill hopes to analyze body composition studies, performance tests, the quality of strength and muscle balance in specific areas to formulate a better theory of injury prediction.

The problem with injury prediction is in the number of variables involved. So far, one study tends to contradict another. Until more research is done, injury prediction can be discussed only in general terms. It would be premature at this point, without specific, well-documented predictors and their associated variables, to counsel youngsters extensively.

In a study of 3,072 athletes (2,817 West Point cadets, 108 high school football players and 147 female gymnasts) joint flexibility was studied. Although flexibility had received great attention over the years, among the 2,817 West Point cadets included in the study, there seemed to be no relation between joint differences and joint injuries sustained in athletic participation.

Other studies involving the NCAA and a high school football team again produced no significant findings. These studies by Jackson, Jarrett, Bailey, Kausek, Swanson and Powell, (Injury Prediction in the Young Athlete), noted that Cattell's Sixteen Personality Factor Questionnaire (also part of the study) had some potential for predicting football injuries. The test indicated that dependent, overprotected, sensitive players are more likely (on the average) to be injured than those players who are tough-minded, self-reliant, and "no-nonsense" individuals. Interestingly, the study also showed that offensive players tend to be more sensitive than the defensive players, and more injuries were attributed to offensive players than to defensive players.

This study also stated that part of the problem of evaluation is that, undoubtedly, many youngsters are eliminated from athletic competition long before they reach the high school level because of physical or psychological factors or both. That makes determinations that might be significant to standardizing an injury profile assessment even more difficult. For example, youngsters with marked flexibility and laxity tend not to be found in the athletic groups studied—which means they are usually eliminated early. They meet frustration in coordination events and by choice drop out. This is a "survival of the fittest" seen in athletes.

When athletes who had sustained multiple joint injuries were studied and followed because they were thought to be injury-prone, no specific personality or physical traits seemed to be common among them.

Also problematical is that experts are not in agreement about the definition of an injury: Is it to be classified as an injury whenever a young athlete sees a doctor? When he or she can't finish the game? When the youngster misses a practice? Or only when a game or entire season is missed? Or when surgery is necessary? Obviously, there are degrees of severity of injury. Some youngsters will continue to play with a problem or injury that would take another youngster out of the game. One doctor will suggest surgery for a specific injury, while another will not. All of these factors make comparisons in injury studies difficult.

Studies now in progress at the U.S. Olympic Training Center in Colorado Springs may be helpful in the advancement of knowledge in this area. Gene Hagerman, Ph.D., an exercise physiologist who is part of a team of specialists which has evaluated three to four thousand top-notch athletes agrees that while the field of injury prediction is still new, more information will be forthcoming in the next few years. A few things, however, are already certain.

"We know that a pretty good predictor of injury is an unbalance of strength in the legs, either due to weakness or injury. Unless this unbalance is alleviated, you have a good chance for an injury somewhere down the road," Dr. Hagerman notes. "We're also looking at the major muscle groups. It is possible that weakness in one group might possibly predispose an athlete to injury in that area, but not enough is known as yet to verify that."

In Russia and other Communist-bloc countries, where athletes are identified, nurtured and followed carefully from a very early age, a great deal of research is being done—not only on injury prediction in sports, but in sports/athlete profiling. In this country, Dr. Hagerman notes, such studies are almost impossible and would require enormous amounts of money.

"We're really talking about a system which 'raises' its athletes, controlling their environment and accessibility," Dr. Hagerman explained. "This kind of research (both profiling for traits by sport, and injury prediction) has to begin at an earlier age, with a careful evaluation as the young athlete matures. Maybe then, certain specific, identifiable and repeatable traits can be identified. There is a difference if you want to know how to pick very young athletes who will be world-class competitors someday, and who will not be plagued by injury which would hamper this performance.

"In the United States, on the other hand, we would like to be able to direct young people into areas where they will not experience injuries because of predisposing physical and/or psychological attributes. Obviously, if this were accomplished, our athletes would also be in sports for which they were best suited, and less prone to injury related specifically to that sport. So, that kind of information would have benefits for everyone if utilized wisely and not abused."

Injury Prevention

As long as there are no hard, cold facts about specific injury prediction traits by sport, the obvious and logical solution right now would be to identify the ways in which an athlete could prevent injuries from occurring. Although injury prevention has many facets, a general knowledge of each factor will better enable parents, others who work with youngsters, and the young athletes themselves to ensure that all precautions are taken for safer and more enjoyable athletic participation.

Warming up and Cooling down

Stretching exercises are important in preventing injury. With adequate muscle stretching, the blood supply to the muscles will increase significantly and the temperature rise in them will make them more flexible and therefore less injury-prone. The point of a good warm-up is to gradually increase the intensity of the workout so the muscles have time to adequately adjust to the demands of exercise. Warm-up is different for each sport, and is based on the specific physical demands of the sport. The best way for a parent or young athlete to determine a good warm-up routine is by arriving early to watch the local college or university team go through their routine before competition in the desired sport, or by watching the warm-up at the beginning of a practice session.

Just as warm-up before participation or practice of a sport is important, so is a cool-down session at the end of activity. Such a gradual slowing of exertion allows the muscles to cool off gradually, by gradually reducing their blood flow, and allowing heat to dissipate. This tends to minimize the stiffness and aching following strenuous participation.

Conditioning and Training

Many of the athletic injuries which take place occur in the "weekend athlete" (whether young or older) who is not involved in a consistent, appropriate conditioning/training program. Conditioning, as stated before, is vital to establishing physical fitness and the associated health benefits. And without a consistent, well-rounded conditioning program, those young people who wish to excel in a sport will probably be unable to achieve a high level of expertise. "Conditioning" means what it says—to condition or train the body to meet the increased demands placed on it. With an adequate program, fewer injuries will occur.

Overtraining, on the other hand, is as potentially harmful as undertraining or lack of training. Too strenuous workouts, which place too many demands on the body, can result in muscle, tendon, ligament, joint or bone injury. Training and conditioning with pain is totally inappropriate for the young athlete. Good conditioning programs contain hard and easy days, and also include days of rest. Increasing speed, and building endurance, agility or strength are gradual processes. Adding new skills or additional routines to conditioning/training programs also takes time and needs to be integrated into the plan slowly. If the young person attempts to side-step this gradual process or overextends his or her body, injury may occur.

Specific sports-skills training is also important in decreasing the potential for injury. As the body adjusts to certain motions, stresses and demands placed upon it by training for the specific sport, the skill level can be increased gradually without unnecessary risk of injury.

(For more conditioning and training information, see Chapter 4.)

Proper Supervision

Coaches or teachers, officials and parents all have important roles in supervision.

Parents need to encourage healthy attitudes about participation, so that youngsters do not become so overzealous about winning that they become destructively aggressive, injuring themselves or others. They as well as the coach (whether he or she is a parent assigned the job, a school representative or a professional) must make sure the young people know the rules and participate with sportsmanlike conduct.

Coaches are responsible for eliminating any potential hazard or risk to the young athlete by directing proper warm-ups, carrying out a conditioning and training program, displaying an exemplary attitude about the game and the opponent, and enforcing the use of proper and safe equipment. Playing areas should be checked for hazards and any potential dangers eliminated before participation begins. Youngsters should be removed from games as they tire; fatigue may precipitate injury. Plentiful water should be available throughout participation, and youngsters should be encouraged to drink as often as necessary. Lack of adequate fluids may result in dehydration and various degrees of heat exhaustion.

Officials who know and properly enforce the rules of the sport are invaluable in reducing the number of injuries. Without adequate officiating, many liberties (which result in injury) could take place. For example, if someone is clipped in football, there is a penalty. A penalty hurts the team, and the player will be more cautious about doing this again. In this respect, dangerous behavior with potential for causing damage is discouraged through simple enforcement of the rules. Rules also foster a sense of fair play. Modifications in rules and regulations for certain sports, especially for younger athletes, will continue to occur as data on sports injuries accumulates.

Using Safety Equipment, Proper Equipment and Wearing Appropriate Clothing

Many sports depend on safety equipment in order to lessen the risk for injury to players. Football players wear helmets and a variety of protective pads. Catchers wear masks, helmets, shin guards and chest protectors. Males wear protective cups in their athletic supporters. Soccer players wear shin guards, while volleyball and basketball players often wear knee and elbow pads. Some swimmers need ear or nose plugs. Hockey players wear shin guards, helmets, and a variety of pads, and the goalie wears a special mask and a chest protector. Protective safety equipment has been developed over the years to meet the needs of each sport. But, to be effective, the equipment must fit properly and, above all, must be worn.

Proper equipment means that it isn't so old that it is hazardous. Worn-out, dilapidated shoulder pads won't do the protective job they're supposed to do. This is also true of shin guards that have missing straps and slide around, helmets with worn-out interiors or cracked exteriors, and badly damaged hockey sticks, baseball mitts, bats, vaulting poles and tennis rackets, to name just a few.

Proper clothing is also essential. Adequately padded and supportive footwear is a must for sports where running, stop-and-go movements and jumping are involved. Warm-up suits are beneficial, particularly in cooler weather or until the young athlete has warmed up. Loose-fitting shorts and tops worn during vigorous play or in hot weather reduce the potential for heat stroke and heat exhaustion, and allow muscles to move freely without binding. Wearing sweatpants and sweatshirts in warm weather, on the other hand, increases the risk of heat injury. In those sports which require long pants and/or sox for protection of legs and knees (baseball, football, skiing, equestrian events, etc.), clothes should be made of a material appropriate for the weather and which absorbs sweat well.

Matching Levels of Growth and Development

When a 150-pound 13-year-old is pitted against a 100-pound 13-year-old, the chances of a mismatch obviously increase. In the spirit of fair play—and safety—young people should be matched according to size, maturation and skill level. Parents and coaches should ensure that young people are placed in a category, league or division best suited to them. Then the youngster will be able to excel in and enjoy participation, and the risk of unnecessary injury is diminished.

Playing with Pain

No young athlete should be encouraged or taught to play with pain. Pain is the body's way of warning that something is wrong. The young athlete who complains of pain should be removed from participation to rest, and be evaluated carefully by a physician if the pain persists or is severe. Minor injuries or irritations often become a more significant problem if the "pain warning" is ignored and the youngster participates nonetheless.

14.

Common Injuries of the Young Athlete

WHEN YOU CONSIDER the great number of youngsters playing organized and free-play sports every day, it's obvious that all will at some time experience some minor type of injury in the course of participation. Indeed, when it comes to such things as bruises, sprains, strains, lacerations and abrasions, children and adults alike experience these things, athletes aside, during everyday life. People twist ankles, scrape knees, lacerate faces and strain muscles doing simple things from stepping off a curb or going downstairs.

Bruises

A bruise is an injury to a body tissue caused by external force applied to the body.

One of the most common injuries sustained by athletes, regardless of a particular sport, is a contusion, commonly called a bruise. Although a bruise can occur to the skin, to the subcutaneous tissue, or to the bone, in athletics the term bruise usually means an injury to the muscle. Essentially, the muscle bruise is tissue damage caused by an external force applied to the muscle or sustained when the body strikes an external object. In other words, either the body is struck by an object (another person, a racket, a ball, a club), or the body runs into or falls onto something like a pole, the ground, a bench, etc.

Unknown to most, an interesting bit of folklore is nevertheless associated with the muscle bruise. In the 1890s, a white horse named Charley pulled a leveling device on the infield of a Sioux City, Iowa, baseball field. Poor Charley had a characteristic limp and the players used to say "Here comes Charley Horse." As time passed, an injured player who limped out onto the field was likely to be greeted with "Here Comes Charleyhorse." The saying caught on, and its use spread to many other athletic circles, then into common usage, and a

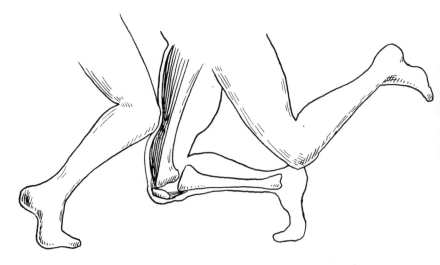

ABOVE.
*Contact such as this can result in a
contusion (bruise) of the muscle.*
RIGHT.
*Arrow points to muscle bruise on
the thigh.*

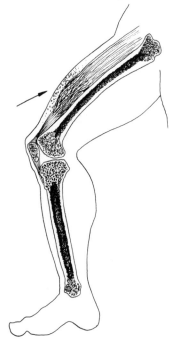

muscle bruise came to be known as a "charleyhorse." Although the term is occasionally used incorrectly to mean a muscle cramp, it really refers to a muscle bruise or contusion of the muscle on the front of the thigh.

With a muscle bruise, the damage to the muscle itself, although potentially disabling for a short time, is usually temporary. There is usually local bleeding associated with this type of injury, which is the cause of the almost immediate swelling and discomfort. The bleeding can continue oozing until there is enough pressure built up in the area of the muscle to stop it. The bleeding may work its way to the surface or, if the insult is near the surface of the skin, a bluish discoloration, called an ecchymosis (the typical "black and blue mark"), may result. However, a deep muscle bruise can be present even if there is no visible discoloration.

The disability resulting from a bruise is directly related to the amount of actual muscle and tissue damage, and the amount of bleeding that results. The more extensive the bleeding and swelling, the longer the recovery period will be. Although we know a bruise will heal even if nothing is done to treat it, when athletic participation or competition is involved, it is usually important to the young athlete to minimize the effects of such an injury and hasten the recovery period where possible.

The best way to diminish the extent of disability related to a muscle bruise is to control the bleeding and swelling when the damage occurs. Apply ice to the area of the bruise as quickly as possible. A compression dressing such as an elastic wrap, and elevation of the injured part, will also help. Resting the injured muscle initially is very important for recovery and tends to shorten the period of disability.

To be sure a muscle bruise or charleyhorse has healed, be sure that muscle function and strength have been re-established before the child returns to play. There must be a return of the full range of motion in joints adjacent to the bruised area with muscle function restored in the entire extremity. The surface discoloration (black and blue mark) may take some time to resolve but its presence does not preclude the youngster from returning to participation.

A special complication of a muscle bruise is a condition called myositis ossificans. An occasional athlete will experience a muscle contusion so severe that the healing process is disturbed and the body begins to deposit bone in the area of the bruise in reaction to the severe inflammation and damage to the muscle cells and surrounding tissue.

Myositis ossificans is most likely to occur in large muscles such as the thigh muscle (quadriceps) and in the muscle on the front of the upper arm (brachialis). There is significant swelling and inflammation when this process occurs. This abnormal bone formation caused by injury is, on occasion, confused with a malignant tumor. Parents should remember that myositis ossificans is *not* a form of cancer and does not change into cancer with time. There is usually no specific treatment for the problem of myositis ossificans, once the abnormal deposit of bone has taken place. On occasion, where the bony tissue interferes with muscle function, it may be removed surgically.

Prevention of muscle bruising is sometimes possible. The use of special pads or guards has resulted from past experience with repeated bruising of athletes in many sports. For example, in soccer the shins are very vulnerable to being kicked and shinguards are used. In football, where the thigh muscles are vulnerable, players wear thigh pads for protection. The list goes on and on, but the principle is the same—the value of protective equipment should not be underestimated, and young athletes should be encouraged or required to wear it whenever playing.

A young athlete who suffers injury severe enough to produce great swelling, pain and limitation of motion of an adjacent joint should be evaluated by a physician who is knowledgeable about sports injuries, to be sure the damage is to the muscle alone, and not to the bone itself, the growth plate or the ligaments of the adjacent joint.

Sprains

A sprain is an injury to a ligament.

A ligament is a strong and durable bond of fibrous tissue with some elastic properties. It connects bone to bone, provides stability to the joints of the body, and reinforces the joint capsule. With extensive ligament damage, the joints become loose and unstable, and may collapse unexpectedly when the athlete changes directions or speed. See how ligaments stabilize the knee joint in the illustrations on page 180.

A simple way of looking at the ligament is to compare it to a rope, which, when stretched beyond its point of endurance, will break.

When a ligament is stretched beyond its resting length, it is susceptible to injury, and with severe enough force, it may be torn apart.

Ligament injuries, or sprains, can be graded in terms of severity. A Grade I sprain is mild and does not permanently alter the function of the ligament. Recuperation involves allowing the swelling and inflammation associated with the injury to subside, at which point athletic participation can be resumed safely.

A Grade II injury results in stretching of the ligament, leaving it longer than it was before the injury. Note the illustration on page 180 as an example. Some permanent instability of the joint may result because the ligament never returns to its pre-injury tightness.

This type of moderate sprain usually requires a two- to six-week recovery period before the youngster can return to his or her previous activity level, and may require special training to overcome or adapt to the looseness of the joint. On occasion a brace may be beneficial. Rarely is surgery necessary, but it may be in cases involving re-injury and incomplete recovery.

A Grade III sprain is more severe still, and involves a rupture of the ligament. Essentially, the integrity of the ligament is lost and the joint is often unstable—it gives way when certain forces of weight are applied to it. Note the ruptured ligament in the illustration on page 180. Many Grade III sprains require surgery in an attempt to repair the damaged ligament. Fortunately, though, when this kind of severe sprain occurs in a joint such as the ankle, where there are many ligaments, a complete rupture of one or even two ligaments may not result in complete joint instability, and surgery might be avoidable. This type of severe sprain requires prolonged rest and often casting if surgery is not needed.

The degree of severity of a sprain can usually be gauged by the amount of disability associated with the injury. Swelling and inflammation result from tearing of blood vessels and tissues around the ligament and joint, and by bleeding in and around the joint. This swelling usually reaches its peak within 24 to 48 hours of the injury, then gradually subsides over the next few weeks. In fact, many people who have suffered a sprain are confused because they have more pain from the injury when they awaken the next morning than they were aware of at the time of the injury. This is a direct result of this gradual bleeding and swelling.

Not surprisingly, the most common sprain sustained in all athletic

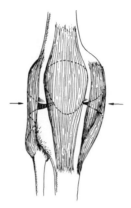

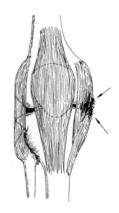

ABOVE LEFT.
The ligaments give stability to a joint, shown in the knee.
ABOVE RIGHT.
A Grade II sprain stretches the fibers of the ligament.
BELOW RIGHT.
Grade III sprains involve an actual rupture of the ligament, seen here in the knee.

participation is the sprained ankle—the common "twisted ankle." Wrist injuries are also common. Keep in mind that sprains are more easily diagnosed in the older athlete than in the younger one, and growth-plate injuries that occur in the younger child may be confused with a sprain. This possibility must be considered when an injury in a young child looks like a sprain. (For more information on growth plate injuries see Chapter 15.)

Some guidelines for estimating the severity of a sprain might be useful. It is most accurately judged 24 to 48 hours following injury when swelling has stabilized. If a young athlete can walk without a limp and can rise up on the toes, or use and bear weight with an injured arm, he or she will usually recover within seven to ten days. If, on the other hand, the youngster has difficulty putting weight on the injured part, the injury is moderate and recovery can take from two to three weeks. If the injured athlete cannot put any weight on the injured part, the injury is likely to be severe and merits special attention and evaluation, including X rays. X rays of the less severe sprains in children are often necessary to rule out an associated growth-plate injury.

The treatment for sprains is much the same as for bruises. Ice application limits the amount of bleeding and swelling, as do elevation and a compression wrap. Use of crutches to promote rest of an injured leg reduces pain and may promote earlier recovery.

Recovery from a sprain is complete when all swelling of the joint is gone and there is no pain. The joint motion should be complete, and strength of the muscle controlling the joint should be normal with no abnormal ligament instability of that joint. When recovery is complete, it is safe for the athlete to return to participation in sports.

Strain

A strain is an injury to a muscle-tendon unit.

A muscle-tendon unit provides power and strength resulting in movement of the joints. Injury to any part of this unit is called a strain, and should be differentiated from the sprain or ligament injury.

The fibers of a muscle contract or shorten, causing the movement of the joint. The size, strength and condition of the muscle determine the force transmitted through the tendon. The tendon attaches the muscle to the bone and is tough, fibrous and usually resistant to tearing. Muscles produce the power and tendons transmit it to the bone, resulting in joint motion, or body movement.

The muscle-tendon unit can be injured several ways. Tears in the muscle fibers themselves are common, and the resulting injury is called a muscle strain. Tearing of the tendon fibers at the junction with the muscle, or in the substance of the tendon itself, or at the tendon attachment to bone, are called tendon strains. Although it is possible to injure both ligaments and muscle-tendon units at the same time, this is a less common, very severe injury. More commonly, the injury involves one or the other—not both—especially in the youngster.

Like sprains, strains are graded as to severity. A mild strain in which fibers of the muscle-tendon unit are damaged but not torn is a Grade I strain. The swelling and discomfort from this injury may take five to ten days to resolve.

A Grade II strain involves tearing of either the muscle or tendon fibers, and will take two to three weeks to heal. The injured part requires protection from further injury and rest during this time, and may require rehabilitation to re-establish full muscle function.

A Grade III strain is much more serious and involves a complete rupture of the muscle or tendon unit. Although this type of injury is rare in the growing youngster, it can occur. Note the rupture shown in illustration seven.

This type of injury to the tendon usually requires surgery to repair the tendon, although occasionally splinting alone may suffice if it is the muscle that ruptures.

A "pulled muscle" is the common term for a muscle strain, and a hamstring pull (the hamstring muscles are those on the back part of the thigh) is one of the more common strains. As with other injuries

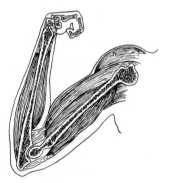

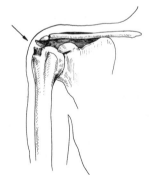

A normal muscle-tendon unit provides power and strength to the joint resulting in movement.

A Grade III strain involves a complete rupture of the muscle-tendon unit, as noted in the shoulder.

around or near a joint, the possibility of a growth-plate injury must be considered if pain or disability is severe or prolonged. Careful evaluation by a physician knowledgeable in diagnosis and treatment of this type of injury is important. (For more information about the growth plate see Chapter 15.)

Again, ice, compression, elevation and rest help to limit and resolve the swelling and bleeding associated with muscle-tendon strains. Crutches may help to reduce use of the injured area or splinting, bracing or casting may be needed, depending upon the severity of the injury.

Full recovery from a strain requires an adequate period of time for the muscle-tendon unit to heal, and assurance that the unit has returned to its previous strength. Rehabilitation may include muscle strengthening exercises prescribed by a physician, sometimes under the supervision of a physical therapist.

Lacerations

A laceration is a wound in which both the skin and the underlying tissue are damaged and there is a gap or "cut."

Lacerations or cuts in the skin and tissues are common injuries, both in athletics and other activities of living.

Lacerations can be very superficial, not much deeper than the skin itself, or can extend through the subcutaneous tissue and fat, down to muscle, tendon, ligament, nerves, arteries, and bone. The deeper and more extensive the laceration, the more dangerous the cut is, both immediately and for causing long-term disability.

The most immediately obvious result of a laceration is bleeding— blood vessels are cut during the injury. With all lacerations, control of bleeding should be the first priority. First apply direct pressure to the wound (with as clean a cloth as possible or with your hand when necessary) and continue the pressure until bleeding stops, or until help arrives and the youngster can be moved to an emergency facility for repair of the cut. If the bleeding is not controlled by steady direct pressure, suspect that an artery has been cut, and apply pressure over the arterial "pressure point" nearest the injury (found in the groin or inside upper arm for instance). Use a tourniquet only as a last resort. With bleeding this severe, transportation to the closest emergency facility is of paramount importance. Remember, direct pressure will control the vast majority of lacerations sustained in sports participation.

Deep lacerations require careful evaluation and repair. If a cut extends into a joint, surgical repair and careful management are necessary. If a large nerve has been lacerated it will require specialized surgical attention.

Some serious lacerations may require suturing (sewing) in order to promote faster or better healing, while others might heal without suturing. The wound and its treatment are shown in the illustrations on the next page.

Whenever there is a question, the laceration should be evaluated by a physician, who can best determine whether closure of the laceration would be beneficial. If sutures are needed, they are removed once the laceration has healed to the point where the wound remains closed by itself. Minor and moderate lacerations usually heal by themselves in one to two weeks, depending on their location and extent, as well as the blood supply to the area.

If a laceration has been sutured, care should be taken to keep it clean and dry while the sutures are in, and to have the stitches removed when recommended to prevent excessive scar formation. With some lacerations located on low-stress areas, the young athlete may continue to participate in sports after a few days, while in others, this is not recommended. Ask the doctor about returning to sports after such injuries, especially if they required extensive repair.

Special care is warranted, too, with lacerations of the hands and fingers. In this location, what appears to be a minor laceration can be a serious injury. Be sure that a child with a laceration of the finger or hand has *full function* of all parts of the hand before dismissing an injury as insignificant. Assure yourself that the youngster has feeling in all parts of the finger and hand, and can move the fingers fully in all directions. If there is any question, obtain a professional evaluation.

Head and neck lacerations require different management and will be discussed in Chapter 17.

On occasion a laceration, whether sutured or not, may get infected. The best treatment for this is prevention, by assuring that the injury is kept clean and dry. However, if purulence (pus) is seen around sutures, or if drainage, tenderness, redness and swelling de-

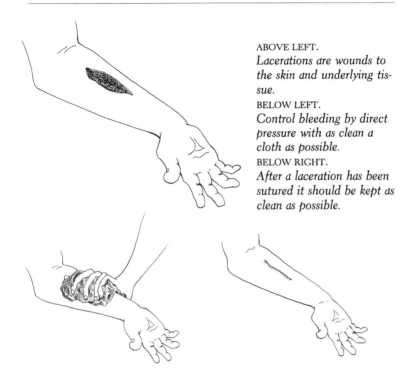

ABOVE LEFT.
*Lacerations are wounds to
the skin and underlying tissue.*
BELOW LEFT.
*Control bleeding by direct
pressure with as clean a
cloth as possible.*
BELOW RIGHT.
*After a laceration has been
sutured it should be kept as
clean as possible.*

velop around the cut, it should be evaluated and treated by a physician. This may require special local care and antibiotics.

Abrasions

An abrasion is a superficial scraping damage to the skin and underlying tissue, usually caused by sliding or falling.

Abrasions are very common in the young athlete, and usually cause no trouble other than minor discomfort and distress. Although the skin itself is disrupted, there is no serious damage to the underlying tissues.

Most abrasions result from skidding, sliding or falling on grass, dirt, cement or gym floors. Such injuries result in variable amounts of swelling, redness, heat and pain. These injuries may be called "strawberries," "raspberries," "grass burns," "road rash," or "floor burns," and happen in every sport in which a person might slide or fall.

Abrasions can usually be treated by the athlete, the parent or the coach by simply washing the area well with soap and water, and keeping it as clean as possible until it heals. The scrape should be checked carefully for dirt, pebbles or pieces of clothing that may have been embedded in the abrasion. If such particles are found they should be gently washed out immediately after the injury, in order to prevent infection and minimize permanent discoloration or "tattooing," of the skin. If this seems too cruel for you to do, do not hesitate to have a professional do it—the immediate pain is less a problem than the long-term scarring that can result.

Muscle Cramps

A muscle cramp or spasm can be very painful and may take place in any muscle of the body, but most frequently occurs in the legs, arms, neck and back. Commonly, the muscle cramp is experienced in the leg, its onset quite sudden and the pain momentarily debilitating. Muscle cramps have many causes: they may occur in the young athlete who is not very flexible and has not been stretching; they can be caused by the inability of the heart and lungs to sustain the desired level of muscle activity (incomplete conditioning); muscle fatigue may be the culprit; or too tight taping or wearing binding clothing around the muscle may also result in a muscle cramp; disturbance in the salt concentration in the blood may be involved; muscle injury or even increased nerve irritability may be to blame.

Muscle cramp pain can usually be alleviated very quickly, particularly in the muscles at the back of the leg (calf muscles). The discomfort will subside by simply grabbing the front part of the foot (including the toes) and pulling the foot up toward the body. This pulls the shortened muscle in a direction opposite to that of the muscle contraction, relieving the cramp. Standing with the feet flat and the knees straight similarly stretches the contracted muscle. What shouldn't be done is to shorten the muscle further.

Once the pain subsides, activity can begin again. If, however, recurrences of the cramping persist or the cramps worsen, the cramping muscle should be rested. Ice is helpful in minimizing swelling, decreasing the irritability of the muscle and the soreness that follow severe cramping. If after rest and icing there is no marked improvement, the young athlete should be seen by a physician to determine if some other type of muscle injury occurred or some underlying cause needs to be corrected.

Shin Splints

When it comes to shin splints, race horses, greyhounds and humans have something in common. They are the only animals to experience the problem of shin splints to any significant degree. There is still a general lack of agreement among professionals as to the precise definition of a shin splint, in terms of the exact cause and location on the leg. This has resulted in a great deal of confusion among athletes, coaches and parents. The shin, however, is the front part of the leg between the ankle and the knee. Sometimes muscle injuries or swelling, tendon inflammation and stress fractures (fatigue fractures) are referred to as shin splints, and require a specific evaluation and treatment.

Shin splints have been associated with running on hard surfaces, poor or improper warm-up before running, or excessively heavy, early training. Improperly fitting and poorly cushioned shoes have also been associated with a greater risk of shin splints. Leg pain and shin splints can best be prevented, and other problems with pain and discomfort due to running and jumping limited, if the young athlete has properly fitted and well-cushioned shoes; is careful to warm up properly; follows a reasonable conditioning program which slowly increases running distance; allows time for the body to adjust when changing to a different type of running surface; and, in some cases, makes adjustments in running style.

Overuse Syndrome

Overuse syndrome means exactly what it says—the overuse of joints, muscles, tendons, ligaments, and bursae in various areas of the body. Overuse syndrome can occur in any joint, but occurs most often in the shoulder, elbow, ankle, and knee. It can be associated with discomfort of muscles, tendons, ligaments or joints, but again, most often with those of the legs, arms, shoulder, neck and back. The pain is usually relieved by a period of rest from the aggravating activity.

Sometimes icing the area also helps if pain, swelling or inflammation is present.

Overuse syndrome is frequently associated with too strenuous and rapidly increased conditioning and training programs. For example, if running is involved, the young athlete may experience leg pain. A careful look at the training program may reveal that the young person did not properly condition for the distance being run. By first resting the legs until pain has subsided, then slowly working up (over weeks or months) to the desired distance and speed, the young person will more than likely not experience overuse syndrome.

Overuse syndrome can be experienced in any sports activity and can take place in any area of the body, and sudden overuse can turn into actual tissue damage to joints, muscles, ligaments or tendons. This is why resting adequately is important if pain is experienced following an overly strenuous activity. Rest allows the overused area to return to normal, and happens particularly rapidly in the young athlete.

If pain is ignored and activity continued, the potential exists for serious injury or permanent disability. At this point, overuse turns into abuse of an area and may override the body's ability for restoration of damaged tissue. The young athlete will then be forced to "live with" a painful joint or body part for the rest of his or her life. This type of unfortunate situation could easily have been prevented. Most often, young people will not continue to participate when they are in pain—unless a parent or coach encourages them.

Parents, coaches and young athletes should be aware of the risk of playing with pain, and allow proper rest with appropriate reconditioning before play is resumed. The benefits of physical activity can be defeated if a chronic problem results from repeated overuse and abuse, and the youngster may be plagued with a lifelong problem which may even remove him or her from certain sports participation or participation at any significant level at all.

If a young person experiences overuse syndrome with pain persisting after adequate rest, he or she should be seen by a physician; in some cases greater injury has occurred and must be evaluated. If overuse syndrome becomes a frequent or repetitive problem, the youngster should also be seen to find a way to manage the problem by specific strengthening exercises, change in routine or adjustments in style. If a problem is caught early, usually it can be managed or totally alleviated with proper care and conditioning. Youngsters who experience persistent joint pain, limping and swelling should be evaluated by a physician to ensure that a growth plate injury or an underlying destructive process has not developed—which might require special management to guarantee normal growth and function.

Heat Exhaustion

During exercise, the body regulates its temperature by sweating, which allows the body to expel heat to the outside by evaporation. Each individual has a slightly different response to exercise, but in all, the more vigorous the exercise, the more sweating occurs. As exercise is prolonged, sweating results in increasing loss of both water and body salts, and a pronounced loss of fluid (dehydration) may result in a serious problem for the young athlete.

The first symptoms of heat exhaustion are usually extreme weakness and fatigue which come on over hours or even days. Heat exhaustion should especially be suspected when the outside temperature is high and the young athlete has been increasing the amount and duration of exercise without adequate intake of fluids. In addition to loss of water, there may also be excessive loss of salt, and a resulting lack of enough salt in the blood. This problem can only be detected through a blood test, but can be suspected when other heat exhaustion symptoms are present.

The best treatment for heat exhaustion is prevention. Prevention is best accomplished by having enough water available to the active youngster, and encouraging him or her to drink when thirsty. Cool water (or even fruit juices or some drinks containing sugar) are better than very cold liquids. Water is probably the best liquid for this purpose because most of the symptoms attributed to heat arise from water loss. Some believe that juices, "ades" and the commercially available electrolyte solutions (such as Gatorade®) are helpful in replenishing salt and fluids. Liquids containing sugar remain somewhat controversial and may make an athlete more thirsty and raise the blood sugar level which then plunges rapidly, sometimes resulting in greater fatigue.

Use of salt tablets to replace salt lost during exercise is hazardous and not recommended for the young athlete. Although salt tablets are a good source of salt, they may overload the normal body mechanisms for control of salt intake. While the taste buds of the mouth usually prevent a person from taking in too much salt, this mechanism is non-functional when a tablet is swallowed. Taking too much salt with too little water can lead to a different kind of dehydration and cause serious damage to the tissues of the body. Appropriate clothing to allow ventilation and evaporation is desirable. Water should always be available to the young athlete, whose own thirst should be the guide for how much water intake is enough. Young people should be encouraged to drink as much water as they want throughout all workouts. If fatigue occurs during activity in warm weather, the athlete should rest and be given water to drink.

Heat Stroke

Heat stroke is a serious, life-threatening emergency in which the body's temperature regulation mechanism fails to work. Instead of sweating, thereby releasing heat from the body, the young person stops sweating and the internal temperature rises to dangerous levels. If this process is not stopped, serious tissue and brain damage and even death may result. (For more information on heat stroke see Chapter 17.)

Sunburn and Exposure

Exposure to the sun results in skin injury which can be at best annoying, and at worst, a real problem. The ultraviolet rays of the sun burn the layers of the skin increasingly with more exposure. With increased exposure, the skin becomes red, then may blister. Sometimes the internal body temperature rises also, and the person may feel hot, sickish, nauseated and shivery. It is important to remember that damage from the sun can occur even in overcast weather, and that increased altitude and wind are associated with greater risk for skin damage to exposed areas.

Dryness and cracking of the skin, including the lips, is a common problem, but a good protective lubricant (many are available) will help to some degree. Use of tanning preparations and sunscreens is recommended for anyone who will experience excessive exposure or who is susceptible to excessive burning (those with fair skin). Sunscreens, to be effective, must be reapplied whenever they have been washed off by water and sweat. It is best to reapply a sunscreen frequently. All sunscreens and tanning lotions are required to state the degree of screening protection they provide, so it's best to check labels to ensure the one purchased will give the kind of protection desired. Appropriate protective clothing light- or heavy-weight, long-sleeved apparel, hats, and long pants are helpful.

Some young people are plagued with unusual reactions to the sun. These are best recognized and prevented rather than treated after the fact. Youngsters susceptible to herpes lip infections (called "fever blisters," or "cold sores") may develop a new blister with exposure to the sun. Use of a good sun blocker such as zinc oxide might be of some help but is not a sure thing. Some medications, such as some antibiotics and tranquilizers, may increase the risk for sunburn or reactions to the sun. Young people taking prescribed medications who experience problems when exposed to the sun's rays, should check with their doctors about possible substitution of other medications if they must be in the sun, or use protective clothing and sunscreens if this is not possible.

Snow Blindness

Snow blindness is a problem which results from damage to the cornea (front clear membrane over the eye) and the retina (the innermost layer of cells sensitive to light) because of the ultraviolet rays and excessive light. Although usually a temporary problem, it is quite frightening. Blurred vision, and even loss of vision, result. Obviously if a young person is having trouble seeing or totally loses his or her sight the danger of serious injury is great.

This problem is seen not only in the snow, where the whiteness contributes to intensifying the rays of the sun, but in water sports where the sun is reflected off the water or other surfaces, and in situations which involve reflective surfaces like sand. People have gotten lost, crawled in snow or sand for hours seeking help, and could easily have fallen off cliffs or run into other very dangerous situations while snow blind.

The best preventive method to avoid so-called snow blindness is to wear the proper sunglasses and goggles for the weather conditions. Glasses which block out ultraviolet rays are best, although any dark glasses are helpful. Sporting goods shops usually carry a variety of glasses and goggles to deal with various intensities of brightness, overcast weather, and so on.

Any young person who experiences blurred vision should see a physician for evaluation to make sure serious light-induced damage or another medical problem has not occurred. The onset of snow blindness varies from person to person and can therefore occur quickly in one young person while it takes hours for another. Whenever there is bright sunlight or glare from overcast skies, the possibility of snow blindness should be considered and appropriate preventive measures taken.

Cold Injuries

Frostbite is a form of cold injury known to most people to cause loss of or damage to tissue. Much of the time, frostbite can be prevented by using good sense and preparing for the cold. As one is gradually exposed to cold weather, especially below-freezing temperatures, the body adjusts to this change in temperature and problems become less likely. However, not all injuries or problems can be prevented simply through repeated and careful exposure.

Proper protection is a key to preventing frostbite. Wearing warm clothing on all parts of the body (including the head, which can be the source of enormous heat loss), and special protection of small body parts (such as fingers and toes) are a must. Gloves or mittens, warm socks and proper protective shoes are important, as is protection from wetness. Wind increases the risk for cold injury, but proper clothing can usually alleviate this added risk. Use of alcohol, excessive fatigue and lack of good nutrition and conditioning also make a young person more likely to suffer from frostbite and other cold injuries.

Most people think of fingers and toes when talking about frostbite because they are the areas most often affected—and usually affected first. There have also been increasing reports of cold injury to the penis in male runners and cyclists not appropriately dressed for the cold weather. Although there have been no major serious problems due to this and normal function returns quickly, it can be a frightening experience, particularly for the adolescent who is already going through many physical changes as he physically matures. Proper clothing alleviates the risk of this problem, too.

The first symptoms of cold injury to the body are pain, redness and tingling of the affected area. This reaction by the body is caused by its attempt to increase the blood flow to the endangered cold area to increase its temperature. As this fails, the part(s) become white and numb and the pain disappears—a classic warning sign that a problem exists. The part becomes difficult to move and begins to look whiter and waxy. These changes are due to actual development of ice crystals in the tissues—first in the skin, blood vessels and muscles, then deeper, in the bones.

Treatment for frostbite consists of rapid re-warming of the injured part or area indoors where heat and cold can be regulated. Use warm water between 100 and 110 degrees F. (but not higher) to bathe or immerse the area. Once the part or area is essentially defrosted it is vital that it not be re-frozen. Because of the initial trauma the area will be more vulnerable to further cold damage; re-injury increases tissue damage.

As the area or part is re-warmed, it becomes even redder, and may be very painful. Blisters may develop over the damaged area and thick scabs may form during the next several weeks. Sometimes this healing process fails and skin or deeper tissues are lost. (This process is very similar to that which occurs in serious burns.) During the healing process, the frostbitten tissue is likely to develop infection because the blood supply is poor in the area. There may also be permanent effects of frostbite after healing has occurred —increased pain when exposed to cold, unusual sweating and numbness.

After re-warming, the young person should be seen by a physician as soon as possible to evaluate the extent of damage and to determine if other steps need to be taken. Serious cases of frostbite can result in loss of function or even require amputation. Because frostbite can be prevented by careful consideration to clothing chosen, such serious results are most often unnecessary and avoidable.

Hypothermia

Another life-threatening type of cold injury is hypothermia—a severe drop in body temperature. If not recognized and treated immediately, death may occur. Hypothermia results when the body is no longer able to conserve heat and the body temperature falls rapidly. Wetness increases the risk of this serious problem.

Initial symptoms include weakness and slurred speech, along with confusion, shivering and clumsiness. As the body temperature drops further, weakness is replaced by stiff muscles and the young person is unable to move. He or she may become drowsy and might talk about needing to sleep for a little while. A further drop in temperature may result in irregular heart beats and the heart may then stop. When a young person is in danger of having hypothermia, it is critical to stop the process immediately. With the first signs of hypothermia, remove any wet clothing (which retains the cold and wetness) if possible and re-warm the body with whatever is available, including the body warmth of another person or people. If a warm bath is available, have the youngster take one. In any case, the young person should not become cold again, increasing the risk for further problems. With serious hypothermia, after as much re-warming is completed as possible, the young athlete should be seen by a physician.

The dangers of hypothermia are often underestimated and ignored. Those who swim or participate in sports in very cold water (usually below 50 degrees F.) are at special risk, as are mountain climbers, skiiers and others whose activity couples cold, wetness and wind with exertion and sweating. Those involved in any physical activity in cold weather should always be properly dressed with added protection from wetness. Runners and others usually experience little or no problem due to cold weather as long as they are dressed appropriately and take care not to become wet and chilled.

Blisters

Blisters can be bothersome at best and debilitating at worst. Blisters are caused by constant rubbing of an article against the skin. The article may be a shoe or other piece of clothing, or a bat, racket, club, wheel, handlebars, etc. Sometimes blisters are the result of improperly fitted shoes or an improperly fitted glove. Most blisters occur on the hands and feet and can be a problem and painful if they are a constant irritant.

To prevent blisters and to improve grip, properly fitted gloves are often used in golf, baseball batting, racquetball, field hockey, ice hockey, sometimes tennis and many other sports. When it comes to blisters on the feet, some athletes prefer to wear one or two pairs of socks while, in some situations, some prefer no socks at all. What's best for each young athlete depends on his or her own preference and, simply, what works.

It's important to keep blisters clean to avoid infection. Sometimes an antiseptic solution is helpful, as is the application of a bandage (Band-Aid®) to keep it clean and safe from further irritation. If colored socks seem to irritate the blister (due to some dyes used) change to white socks until the blister heals. If blisters develop on the hands, again, the area should be kept as clean as possible to avoid infection. A bandage or Band-Aid® over the blister will also help keep the area clean and protect it from further irritation. Vaseline® is sometimes suggested for blisters on the hand, as a protective, lubricating ointment. If blisters on feet or hands become a constant problem, a change of shoes, the use of a special arch support or the addition of a properly fitted glove may alleviate the problem.

Chafing

Chafing is due to rubbing—skin on skin, skin against clothing or another object—and, usually, some degree of moisture is present. Redness and discomfort result. Cyclists complain of chafing between the legs where there is a constant rubbing motion against the cycle seat; runners often complain of chafing of the nipples (both male and female) due to the rubbing of clothing (or the seams of bras for women); those trying to lose weight in a conditioning program often experience chafing where the inside upper legs as far down as the knees rub against each other or clothing; and sometimes, in most throwing sports, chafing can occur under the arm or in areas where continual rubbing occurs. If left unattended, the redness and discomfort can worsen and pain may result.

The application of Vaseline® (which acts as a lubricant) protects the area and helps alleviate the rubbing affect. Band-Aids® can also be used on small areas, such as the nipples, for further protection. The new, light and extremely smooth clothing now available also helps to lessen some of the potential for chafing.

Calluses

Calluses are usually not a serious problem but can be painful and bothersome while developing. Those on the heel are usually not a problem, but those on the ball of the foot can be. Calluses are hardened layers of skin which form to protect an area that has been subjected to undue pressure. There are many types of callus-removing devices on the market today, but if calluses become too thick to manage, a podiatrist should be consulted. The podiatrist can carefully remove thick calluses with a scalpel and may suggest the use of a special shoe insert to alleviate the problem.

Athlete's Foot

Athlete's foot is a fungal infection which causes uncomfortable cracking and peeling of the feet, especially in the areas between the toes. The infection, which may be acquired in locker rooms and showers, is aggravated by heat and moisture, and may be contagious.

Keeping the feet dry and as cool as possible will not only make the person with athlete's foot more comfortable, but also may help to control the infection. White absorbent socks, changed frequently, along with the use of any of a number of anti-fungal creams or powders (these are available without prescription) are helpful. Particularly persistent or bothersome cases of athlete's foot may need to be evaluated by a physician.

Jock Itch

Like athlete's foot, so-called jock itch is also a fungal infection made worse by heat and moisture. Rubbing by underwear or an athletic supporter (jock strap) worn by males was believed to irritate the fungal infection thereby giving it the name jock itch. However, this same infection is also seen in women, who experience redness, irritation and discomfort in the groin area. Sweating is thought to make the problem worse. Keeping the area as dry and cool as possible helps lessen the discomfort and promotes healing. Non-absorbent materials, such as nylon and other synthetics, can make the situation worse. Tight-fitting leotards or nylon underwear keep the area hot and moist. Therefore, loose-fitting cotton or other absorbent material will be more comfortable and less likely to promote further problems with this fungal infection.

Many times a simple "hot spot" (red, irritated area) develops because of heat and wetness, with no infection present at first. But this type of environment is almost perfect for a fungal infection to develop. Anti-fungal creams available over-the-counter can be used with the first signs of a problem or others can be prescribed by a physician, when necessary.

15.

The Growth Plate—What It Is
and How It Can Be Altered
by Sports

IT SEEMS RATHER CURIOUS that a hard substance such as bone can grow longer and wider, but it is a form of living tissue—just like the other specialized tissues in our bodies: skin, blood vessels, hair, etc. Bone is made up of cells, all going through the cell cycle—multiplying, dividing, dying and being replaced continuously. While the cells in the bone are going through these phases, the material around the cells—called the matrix—also undergoes orderly change. Finally, concurrently, the bone marrow in the center of most bones produces the blood cells that circulate in the vessels.

The long bones—those that make up our arms and legs—have a very remarkable structure called a "growth plate," one almost identically shared throughout the animal kingdom. In essence, the growth plate is the structure that determines how tall we are, and what the shape and size of our skeletal structure will be. An active growth plate is one of the major differences between the adult and the child.

The growth plate determines the longitudinal growth of the bone (height), the width, and the particular configuration of the bones. A unique control mechanism built into the growth plate responds to the hormones in our bodies to shape us in a certain manner. Basically, it allows the bones to grow during the formative years and stop growing as we reach adulthood. When all skeletal growth has been completed, the growth plate becomes inactive and "closes" completely. This growth takes place while the youngster runs, jumps, bends, jerks, falls and flips.

As the body grows and develops, the growth plate does a great deal of work. It is a structure through which tremendous stresses pass as the young child participates in running, jumping and contact sports. During childhood, the growth plate has great healing and restorative characteristics when fractures involve the ends of the bones. These unique powers are decreased forever once puberty is completed and the growth plate closes.

In order to understand why injury to the growth plate can be significant, especially if not treated appropriately, it is important to understand how the growth plate functions and what it looks like.

A normal growth plate is seen in the illustration below. Notice the arrow which points to what looks like a line near the top. If this were seen on an X ray of an adult, the doctor would say the bone was broken or fractured. In fact, those who are not familiar with X rays of children's bones might also mistake this for a fracture or break. But it isn't.

The growth plate of the bone is seen as a clear area on an X ray. The growth plate is made up of cells and cartilage that have not as yet had calcium salts deposited, which cause hardening, as mature bones have. Simply put, the cells and surrounding matrix of the bone's growth plate respond as the hormones of the body tell them to grow. The cells multiply rapidly. As the new area grows, lengthening the bone, the bottom area of the growth plate fills in with

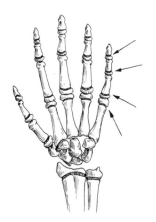
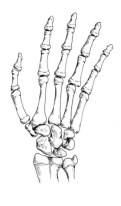

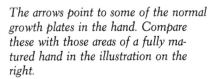

The arrows point to some of the normal growth plates in the hand. Compare these with those areas of a fully matured hand in the illustration on the right.

Fully matured bones in the hand. Notice that all growth plates have closed and the bone hardened.

blood vessels and calcium, that part of the bone hardens, and the process continues. Once the total length of the bone is reached, the rest of the growth plate becomes hardened bone, and closes completely. The bone then has no clear area visible when viewed by X ray (an example of a fully mature bone is seen in the illustration on page 199) and the bone no longer grows in length.

Bone formation (ossification) doesn't mean cells are no longer living. Without living cells, fractures or breaks in the bones of children or adults could not heal. All bone is living matter, continues to be so throughout the life of the individual, and is able to repair itself but in the adult it loses its growth potential.

There are also growth plates related to the attachments of specific muscles and tendons in the child. In the young athlete who is using the muscles and tendons explosively, these attachments are potentially weak areas, as is the growth plate itself, and susceptible to injury. Since the growth plate is found near the ends of the bones and in close proximity to the joint, any childhood injury in the area of the joint or the attachment of the muscle-tendon unit to the bone must be evaluated and treated as a potential growth-plate injury. Generally, active growth plates are more susceptible to injuries than are the adjacent joint ligaments.

If a youngster sustains an injury to the growth plate, or in the area of a joint at the attachment of the muscle-tendon unit to the bone, there are some terms a parent, coach, teacher, school nurse, or the young athlete will hear the doctor use. It is helpful to understand them.

"Physis" is the Greek word for growth. If you look at the illustration on page 201, you will see a drawing of a child's knee. The "epiphysis" is the cap-like portion at the top of the bone. "Epi" means upon. Epiphysis then is the portion of the bone "upon" the "growth" plate. You will also notice the portion of the bone labelled metaphysis. "Meta" in Greek means "after," so the metaphysis is the portion of the bone "after" the "growth" plate. "Apo" means "offshoot" and apophysis is a growth plate that appears as an offshoot from the bone. The apophysis growth area is usually where a muscle-tendon unit attaches.

The young athlete can have many types of fractures (breaks) or combinations of fractures around the growth plate. The direction of the fracture and its location will determine how it is treated as well as the prognosis (possible outcome). Here are the most common fractures:

Type I—fracture is confined to the growth plate and does not extend into adjacent bone.

Type II—fracture extends through the growth plate and epiphysis.

Type III—fracture extends through the metaphysis and growth plate.

Type I, II and III injuries and fractures account for 90 to 95 percent of all the growth-plate fractures in young athletes.

Type IV—fracture extends across the growth plate into both the epiphysis and metaphysis.

Type V—is a crushing injury to the growth plate.

It should be noted that only a small percentage of growth-plate fractures require surgery. Those injuries that do require surgery often extend into a joint and disrupt or damage it. A Type IV growth-plate injury often needs surgery to realign the growth plate and re-unite the portion of the growth plate which has been separated from the larger portion of bone.

Injuries such as a Type V growth-plate fracture are rare and result in altered growth. Such crushing injuries often do not become apparent until the growth of a bone is disturbed following the injury.

Over half of all fractures that occur in young athletes (pre-teens), whether in organized activities or while at free play, involve a growth plate. Therefore, injuries to or around a joint in the child or young athlete should be evaluated and X-rayed whenever pain, limping or

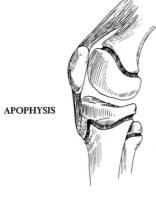

EPIPHYSIS

METAPHYSIS

APOPHYSIS

Notice the areas labeled epiphysis, metaphysis, *and* apophysis.

loss of motion is present. Because there is a high potential for growth-plate fracture, parents and others who work with children should recognize this possibility and make sure an injured youngster is seen and an X ray is taken if the child has had a significant injury.

DO NOT assume the injury is a sprain (injured ligament). Remember, in the child or early teen who is still growing, the growth plates are usually weaker than the ligaments that surround a joint and will tend to be disrupted with injury. On the other hand, an adult whose growth plates are closed will more than likely experience ligament injury rather than injury to the bone itself.

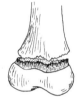

Type I growth plate fracture

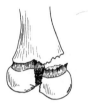

Type II growth plate fracture

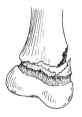

Type III growth plate fracture

Type IV growth plate fracture

Type V growth plate fracture

Specific Problems Related to Growth Plates

Two hip problems, although unique and uncommon, are found in youngsters, and may manifest themselves when the youngster participates in sports. Hip pain in children is always a concern, and such complaints should not be taken lightly.

Legg-Perthes disease is a problem which usually affects youngsters between the ages of five and eight, and is more common in males. In this disease, there is a disturbance in the blood supply to the epiphysis. See the illustration on page 204, for example. The lack of blood flow to this part of the bone causes the end of the bone to change its shape, becoming flattened and fragmented. The ball portion of the hip joint may change its shape permanently, causing an abnormal joint and long-term disability. This problem requires immediate recognition and treatment by an experienced orthopedic surgeon if permanent problems are to be prevented. Rest of the hip is the mainstay of treatment. It may require splinting, and on occasion, surgery.

Another hip problem, *slipped femoral capital epiphysis,* is suspected in a young athlete with hip pain—particularly those between the ages of 9 and 14. An example of this disorder is shown on page 204. In this problem, there is slippage related to the growth plate of the hip, often for no apparent reason. This condition too needs to be recognized and treated early if long-lasting problems are to be avoided. With serious types of slippage, an operation must be done to re-position the slipped area, and the end of the bone must be held in the correct position with a metal pin. In those cases that result in deformity of the hip joint, subsequent reconstructive surgery may be necessary.

Remember, hip pain in an active youngster must be evaluated. Although growth-plate problems related to the hip are rare, one cannot afford to miss one of these disorders. One important point about hip problems—sometimes they cause pain not around the hip, but around the knee. This type of pain, called "referred" pain, may also mean hip disease. Therefore, persistent pain in the knee in a young child or adolescent should be evaluated, looking also for a problem in the hip area.

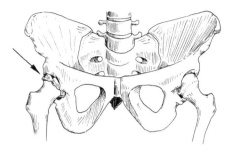

The arrow points to what is called Legg-Perthes Disease found in the hip.

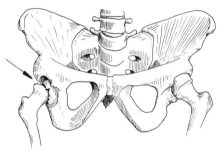

Slipped Femoral Capital Epiphysis is found in the hip.

Little League elbow is a term used for a growth-plate injury in the elbow. This problem, although not one of the most severe of the childhood athletic injuries, has gotten much attention in the news media. The injury may result when a youngster begins to throw hard—especially curve balls—at a very early age. Continued throwing results in fragmentation of the growth plate and permanent damage to the growth centers in the developing elbow.

In the past, these young, muscular athletes tended to throw not only on the baseball team, but also in football, where they often were the quarterbacks. They were throwing hard to please the crowd, and too frequently. Wanting recognition and praise, these youngsters continued to throw even when the elbow hurt.

The new restrictions placed on the frequency and the length of time any youngster can throw in organized baseball, and the discouragement of throwing curve balls before the bony skeleton is mature, have nearly eliminated this problem in young baseball players.

An example of what happens to the elbow with repeated injury is shown in the illustration on page 205. This 12-year-old baseball

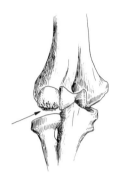

Little League Elbow

player had not been following the recommendations of his baseball program. He had been throwing curve balls since he was very young, and was throwing too frequently in spite of pain. The damage to his elbow will cause him difficulty for many years. This type of elbow problem may be seen in other sports as well (gymnastics, weight lifting, etc.) and often requires evaluation by a physician to rule it out. A youngster with persistent elbow pain should be seen by a doctor.

The growth plates are also susceptible to injury in the growing youngster. *Osgood-Schlatter disease* is one of the most common disorders associated with this type of growth-plate problem. This injury affects the area around the knee, where the patellar tendon—the tendon of the large muscle in the front of the thigh—attaches to the lower leg, as seen in the illustration on page 205. This type of problem is seen most often in muscular young athletes who use their thigh muscles in explosive running and jumping activities. It is a very common disorder which causes pain around the knee in pre-adolescents and adolescents. It also occurs in youngsters who do not participate in athletics. The condition is aggravated by jumping and running.

With vigorous activity, the very strong tendon of the thigh muscle pulls on its bony attachment, called the tibial tuberosity, located just below the knee. This bony prominence becomes irritated when there is active Osgood-Schlatter disease. The athlete complains about pain in the area just below the knee, especially when he or she is very active.

This problem—not actually a "disease"—of the growth plate is most commonly seen between the ages of 9 and 14 and has affected boys more commonly than girls. But as more girls of these ages are

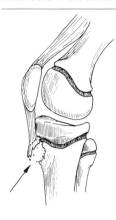

*Osgood-Schlatter Disease af-
fects the area around the knee.*

participating in sports, it is being seen more frequently in them, too.
And the problem will be present in both knees in about 20 percent of
youngsters. The athlete may remember a specific incident which the
pain followed—for example, a jump or fall—or may occasionally
complain of gradually increasing pain. The amount of pain and the
enlargement of the bony prominence may increase if the child continues to play while having problems.

The diagnosis of Osgood-Schlatter disease is easily made by a physician after taking a history and doing an examination. X rays are
often obtained to exclude rarer diseases that may show up in this
area.

Once recognized, the problem is easily treated, simply by restricting activities, especially those requiring vigorous use of the
thigh muscles, until the pain decreases or goes away completely. The
disease is *not* serious, and usually runs a course of several months to
one or two years. The youngster can gradually resume activities after
the symptoms have subsided.

Although rare, the amount of pain might be severe enough in a
few athletes to require more strict rest and restriction of muscle activity. On occasion, with very severe symptoms, some sort of splinting
to restrict knee motion might need to be carried out. Surgery is seldom if ever necessary for correction of Osgood-Schlatter disease.
However, in a very rare situation, the growth plate is pulled away
from the bone by its muscle-tendon unit. But remember, nearly all
cases of Osgood-Schlatter disease will heal with rest, given sufficient
time.

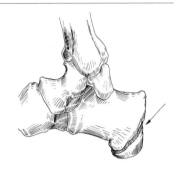

Sever's Disease affects the growth plate in the heel. The arrow points to the area affected.

Sever's disease is one cause of heel pain, and is a growth-plate problem, with the affected growth plate located in the heel. The youngster will usually complain of pain in one or both heels, especially after playing on concrete surfaces for prolonged periods of time, or after strenuous running. This problem, like Osgood-Schlatter disease, is not serious, and improves once the growth of the foot is complete. Placing a ¼-inch soft pad in the heel of the shoe, or providing special footwear may relieve the pain. The discomfort is usually present for one to two hours after participation and does not usually interfere with activity.

Points to Remember

➤ The vast majority of growth-plate injuries will heal without complications, if allowed to do so; the growth plate has tremendous restorative capacity.

➤ While the majority of growth-plate fractures and injuries will respond well, a small percentage will result in permanent alterations in the joint or adjacent structures. Such complications may be minimized by proper medical supervision.

➤ If a serious growth-plate injury is left unattended, growth of the extremity may be affected. In certain injuries, surgery or prolonged restriction may be helpful, but when the blood flow to the area is altered, growth will be affected. The amount of growth reduction of the extremity depends upon the age and development of the youngster.

➤ Ligaments are infrequently torn in a child, so one should be extra careful to pay attention to the possibility of a growth-plate injury being manifested as a sprain or ligamentous injury.

🖝 Growth-plate injuries in association with fractures are fairly common in the young athlete and the child in free play activities at school and at home. Therefore, coaches, teachers and school nurses as well as parents should recognize that when a youngster experiences an injury to a joint and swelling, pain or loss of motion are present, movement should be restricted and the youngster should be evaluated by a physician, so further damage will not occur. In such cases, the physician will often need an X ray to establish a definitive diagnosis and treatment.

🖝 If a parent notices a child limping, or having some discomfort related to a joint or a muscle-tendon unit attachment, he or she should recognize that the possibility exists that this is a growth-plate injury.

🖝 The best thing to do is to restrict use or movement and see a physician accustomed to dealing with these problems so a diagnosis can be made.

🖝 When it comes to joint injuries, an orthopedic surgeon who is familiar with sports injuries and childhood injuries is usually best equipped to treat youngsters and growth-plate problems. Ask your family doctor or pediatrician who would be appropriate to care for this type of problem if it occurs in your child.

The growth plate in the child is a remarkable structure with amazing self-healing properties. It allows a great deal of leeway for injuries, but on occasion needs very specialized treatment. In all cases, especially in the active youngster, it is best to have any injured joint evaluated so necessary steps—immobilization, activity restriction, etc.—can better ensure the recovery of the growth plate.

Be aware, too, that with less serious injury, re-injury can result in long-term damage to the growth plate. Growth-plate injuries can be deceiving, so evaluation of all painful or injured joints, or those with swelling or limited motion, should be evaluated by a physician, preferably one familiar with the specific problems of the young athlete.

16.
Typical Fractures and Dislocations in Young Athletes

ABOUT HALF OF ALL SERIOUS athletic injuries suffered by active youngsters involve a fracture of one of the bones of the arms or legs. A lower percentage of injuries will involve a dislocation at the joint, with or without an associated fracture. The distinction between injuries which are likely or unlikely to result in a fracture is important to parents as well as to others who supervise children's athletic activities.

Fractures of some of the bones in the growing child's skeleton require a great deal of force, usually associated with being struck or falling; others happen because of the wrong force at the wrong angle at the wrong time. The bones of a child's arms and legs, called "long bones," are less brittle than the adult's. Consequently, still-maturing bone is more likely to bend and resist a through-and-through break than a mature bone. This phenomenon accounts for some of the kinds of breaks seen only in children. But the growth plates at the ends of the bones make risk of certain fractures in certain places greater for children, and may affect long-term growth of the bone. However, the child's bone is much more likely to heal faster and better than the same bone in an adult. And the younger the child, the faster the healing progresses. In addition, the bone of the growing child has a much better ability to "remodel"—to readjust its shape depending upon the usual activity of the child and the forces applied to the bone. Therefore, even a considerable amount of bend (angulation) or overlap of the edges of a break in a child's bone may eventually be unnoticeable because, with normal activity, the bone will gradually change shape and straighten.

Even with the amazing restorative power of the youngster's skeleton, it is vital that a fracture be identified early and treated appropriately by someone who is familiar with children's injuries. Appropriate care can prevent some of the long-term results of more severe injury. This allows the youngster to return to his normal level of activity with the best possible result and the least chance for long-term damage.

Defining Types of Fractures

General Types

First of all, a *fracture* is simply a break in a bone—no more and no less. Although there are many types of fractures, and many ways of describing the same fracture, the terms "broken bone" or "break" or "fracture" are interchangeable.

A *simple fracture* is one in which the break is "clean"—it goes straight through the bone, and there is only one break, as seen in the illustration below. In children, several kinds of simple fractures are seen which usually don't occur in adults. One of these is the *"green-stick" fracture*. In this injury to the bone, the relatively bendable growing bone breaks only partially—because it can bend. This type of fracture is shown below. If you think about what happens

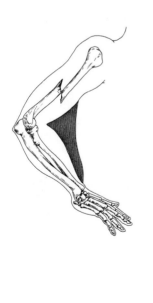

LEFT.
A simple fracture is a "clean" break through the bone.
RIGHT.
Greenstick fractures are those where the bone breaks only partially.

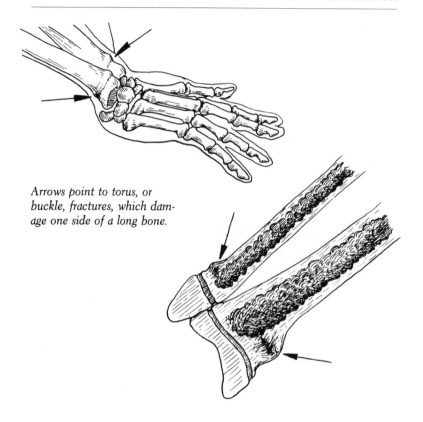

Arrows point to torus, or buckle, fractures, which damage one side of a long bone.

when you try to snap a living branch of a tree, you can visualize what a greenstick fracture looks like. The outer surface may break and splinter, but the tougher, inside layers only bend, without breaking off.

Another type of simple fracture is called a *"torus"* or *buckle fracture*, shown in the illustration above. With this injury, one side of a long bone "buckles" without breaking through, leaving what looks like a wrinkle in the outer surface or cortex of the bone. This break can be very difficult to see on an X ray.

A *"compression" fracture* is a similar hard-to-see injury: the ends of the bone are forced together, shortening the broken bone by compressing it.

There are several types of *complex fractures* seen in youngsters,

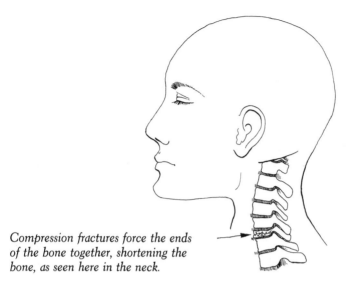

Compression fractures force the ends of the bone together, shortening the bone, as seen here in the neck.

too. A *comminuted fracture* has several broken areas in the same bone; the bone has shattered with the force of the injury and there are visible splinters of bone around it.

Another kind of complex fracture is always serious—the *compound fracture,* seen on page 212. In an injury like this, the bone breaks and the ends separate, and the broken ends of the bone poke out of the skin—or at least did at the time of the injury. This kind of fracture is potentially serious because the bone has been exposed to contamination (dirt, clothing, and bacteria) and is at risk of developing a serious infection (called osteomyelitis) as a result. Treatment of this type of fracture is crucial to producing the best possible outcome.

And remember *growth-plate injuries.* Evaluation of these injuries is necessary whenever there is pain, swelling and limited range of motion of any joint of the body after an injury. Details are found in Chapter 15.

The doctor may use several other terms in describing broken bones. A *non-displaced fracture* is one in which the bone, although broken, is not out of alignment; the crack is present, but the broken ends of the bone are still in contact and lined up. A *displaced frac-*

 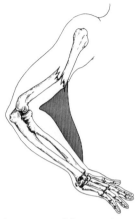

A *comminuted fracture* is a complex fracture which has several broken areas in the same bone.

A *compound fracture* is another complex fracture where the bones separate and the ends poke through the skin.

ture can be either angulated, separated or rotated or all of them. An *angulated fracture* leaves a bend in the bone—visible to the naked eye or on X ray. A *rotational injury*, on the other hand, might be more subtle: the bone was twisted during the break, so the parts of the break are not lined up.

Common Fractures of the Upper Extremities

The most common fracture in the active youngster is a fracture of the lower part of the forearm, near the wrist. This kind of fracture typically involves a *break in one or both bones of the forearm*—the radius and ulna—and can be any of the kinds of fractures already mentioned. Forearm fractures usually occur when a child falls on the outstretched arm and reaches out in an attempt to protect the head and face. In doing so, he or she breaks the bone.

Some of these fractures will be obvious by simply looking at the arm—it looks crooked. Others will be suspected only when the child complains of pain, or when swelling and limited motion are evident. These fractures of the forearm generally heal very well, with a mini-

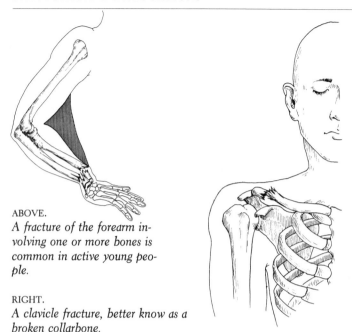

ABOVE.
A fracture of the forearm involving one or more bones is common in active young people.

RIGHT.
A clavicle fracture, better know as a broken collarbone.

mum amount of disability.

Another common fracture is the *clavicle fracture,* better known as a broken collarbone. With the clavicle attached to the front of the breastbone and to the shoulder, this break can be quite painful, but the fracture is usually not serious. A lump or a tender, bruised area over the bone indicates the possibility of such a break. Occasionally the ends of the bone "override" or overlap.

Most of the time, however, just keeping the bone immobile while it heals is all that is needed. It should be noted that the bone heals by producing a "callus" over the broken ends, leaving an even larger lump as healing progresses than was noticeable when the injury first was noticed. Don't worry—this bump will gradually become smaller within several months of the injury.

More serious fractures of the upper extremity occur around the elbow. (Fractures in the middle or top of the larger bone of the upper arm, the humerus, are less common in children than are those which occur around the elbow joint.) *Breaks around the elbow* (see the

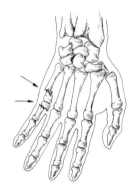

ABOVE.
Fractures of the bones of the hands

LEFT.
Breaks around the elbow have a potential for injuring one of the many growth plates in the area.

illustration above) have a potential for injuring one of the many growth plates in this area, and may result in temporary or permanent damage to the nerves and blood vessels that cross the joint, either because of actual damage or from pressure due to swelling. *Any* elbow injury in which there is loss or limitation of motion, or a large amount of swelling, should be looked at as a potentially serious fracture. Some of these injuries need to be treated by surgery to best preserve the growth plate and joint.

Injuries to the hand commonly result in *finger fractures*, but it's important to distinguish between an actual fracture and other injuries. A common nonfracture injury is the *"jammed finger."* It is usually the result of being hit on the end of the outstretched finger by a ball. This injury causes pain, tenderness and some swelling over the *joint* (knuckle) between two bones in a finger. Pain with motion is also common.

On the other hand, a true finger fracture will cause pain and tenderness *between* the joints of a finger rather than over the joint. The importance of this distinction is in the treatment of the injury. Both require immobilization. However, with a fracture, immobilization may be necessary for several weeks, while a "jammed finger" usually requires a shorter period of immobilization. X rays are usually necessary to rule out fractures or chip fractures.

Other injuries to the hand include *fractures of the bones of the hand* (which cause local pain and swelling) and *tendon injuries.* All hand injuries that cause a significant amount of pain, or any loss of ability to move a part of the hand, or loss of feeling, *must* be evaluated by a physician experienced in the care of this type of injury. Loss of function of the hand is a very serious, lifelong problem resulting when some of these injuries are not recognized early enough, or treated appropriately.

Common Fractures of the Lower Extremities

Among the most serious fractures of the lower extremities are those of the *femur*—the large bone of the upper leg, shown in the illustration on page 216. Obviously, great force is required to break this bone. If the femur is broken, usually as a result of a forceful and direct blow to the leg, the injured athlete knows immediately that a serious injury has occurred. In general, the youngster hears or feels a snap, and the pain is usually rather intense. Often there is a significant amount of bleeding and swelling in the thigh, and deformity due to the break. And the injured youngster is unable to put weight on the leg. This type of injury needs rapid transportation to an emergency care center of a hospital. Calling the paramedics or an ambulance is best and most comfortable for the injured child.

A *fracture of the hip* is another serious injury seen in athletics. Fortunately it is infrequent. Again, a significant amount of force is usually necessary to fracture the hip, which is the top part of the femur (see the illustration on page 216). A hip fracture prevents the athlete from bearing weight on the leg, and usually causes severe pain. This fracture often requires surgical reduction for treatment (see treatment section of this chapter). The injured child must be moved to a hospital emergency facility with the lower extremity splinted or immobilized.

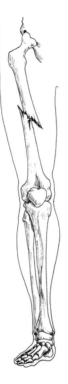

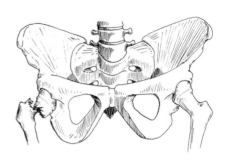

ABOVE.
A fracture of the hip is a serious injury.

LEFT.
Fracture of the femur—the large bone of the upper leg

The majority of *injuries to the knee* are, fortunately, not fractures, but involve varying degrees of damage to the cartilage, ligaments, and tendons surrounding the knee in both young and adult athletes. In general, athletes with persistent knee pain should be evaluated by an experienced physician before play is continued. Knee injuries and disability are among the most common injuries in sports for all age groups.

Fractures of the lower leg are fairly common in contact sports, and, like femur fractures, cause a significant amount of pain and disability at the time of the injury. Often the *tibia* (the larger of the two bones—the shin bone) is broken. Some injuries of the tibia occur when a combination of a blow or fall and a twist, such as in skiing, occurs. Some of these breaks have been prevented by modifications of equipment, such as better binding releases on skis.

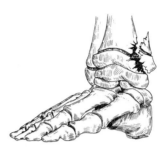

ABOVE.
Ankle fractures are commonly
growth plate injuries and
should be evaluated carefully.

LEFT.
Fractures to the tibia and the
fibula in the lower leg are
fairly common in contact/col-
lision sports.

Breaks of the *fibula*, the smaller bone of the outer side of the lower leg, unlike other fractures of the leg, can be relatively silent and without symptoms. This bone can be broken with contact injuries, or in twist injuries, or as a result of a direct blow. It usually heals with a minimum of problems.

Because of the very common occurrence of growth-plate injuries in children and adolescents, *ankle fractures* must be carefully evaluated. While ankle injuries in adults are often sprains, similar injuries in growing youngsters often involve fractures through the growth plate. (See Chapter 15.)

Fractures of the *foot bones* (see page 218) are not uncommon in youngsters and can cause a fair amount of discomfort. They are manifested by local pain and swelling over the particular bone fractured, often with a bruise or diffuse swelling noted over the top of the foot. Foot fractures may result from a jump to a hard surface, or a fall on the outside of the foot.

 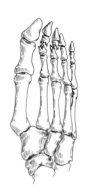

RIGHT.
Fractures of the bones of the foot are not uncommon in youngsters.

FAR RIGHT.
Toe fractures are quite common but usually not serious.

Toe fractures, while common, are usually not serious, and heal readily (shown in the illustration above). They most often happen when the youngster kicks an object. The major problem with these breaks is pain. Treated by taping the injured toe to the toe on either side for two to three weeks, they can be painful enough to prevent an athlete from continuing play or training. Although these are not usually serious injuries, a toe fracture which is obviously displaced, or in which the toe has lost sensation, should nevertheless be evaluated by a physician.

Fractures of the *skull, neck and lower spine,* although uncommon, do occur in young athletes. These serious injuries deserve special and separate discussion, and will be treated in Chapter 17.

Stress Fractures, a Special Type

Normally, with exercise and activity, a bone gradually adapts to the stresses placed on it. For example, if a youngster begins a new activity which places more stress (repetitive loading and increased muscle action) on a bone than it is accustomed to, the bone will gradually "toughen" and might even change shape (thickening of the cortex) slightly to adjust to the new stresses. In certain cases, a *stress fracture* (fatigue fracture) of a bone might result.

Stress fractures are common in certain bones of the body, and develop in a typical manner. Stress fractures of the bones of the feet, for example, are more common in the youngster who starts running programs too rapidly. The so-called "march fracture" of military re-

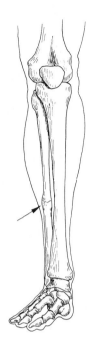

ABOVE.
A normal elbow joint

LEFT.
*Arrow points to a stress frac-
ture of the fibula, in the lower
leg.*

cruits is also a stress fracture of a foot bone. The *fibula* (shown above) can also be broken because of stresses to which it is not accustomed. More stress fractures have been seen in young female athletes recently, as they have become involved in sports year-round. With appropriate conditioning, the female athlete has no higher incidence of stress fracture than the male.

Initially, the symptoms of a stress fracture may be easy to overlook. Dull bone pain is often the first thing a youngster is likely to experience. This at first goes away or diminishes when the activity (usually walking, running or jumping) is stopped. However, after a week or so, the pain begins to be more persistent, and the presence of a more serious injury is obvious to the youngster.

Because stress or fatigue fractures result from repetitive "microtrauma," they can be difficult for even professionals to recognize early, unless evaluated by a physician experienced in such injuries. Fatigue fractures may not be visible on an initial X ray, and may only be seen on a repeat X ray 10 to 14 days after the start of pain.

Therefore, the fracture must be suspected even without any identifiable break in a youngster who has recently started a new and intense activity or has been pushing too fast. The doctor may suggest a bone scan, a test which may be able to detect this kind of break before it would be visible on a conventional X ray. (See Chapter 19 for a more comprehensive description of a bone scan.)

Treatment for stress fractures requires rest from the aggravating activity until healing of the involved bone has taken place. This may include immobilization of the injured area. After healing is complete, the athlete may gradually resume conditioning and activity based on the physician's instructions.

Recognizing and Treating Fractures

Most fractures in active youngsters can be suspected simply by paying attention to a youngster's complaint of pain or limited motion—even if these seem less than severe at the time of an injury. Swelling and tenderness over the injured part will be present in some cases, and a deformity may be obvious. All these indicate that injury requiring further evaluation may be present. Remember, pain is nature's warning signal. Unexplained, persistent pain should be evaluated to find the cause.

The mainstay of emergency treatment of possible broken bone is immobilization of the injured part. This is accomplished by use of a splint (anything sturdy which keeps the injured part still and in the same position in which it is found). Sophisticated splints are available at many locations and through paramedics and ambulance companies, but use of something as simple as a pillow, boards or cardboard will suffice. Splinting protects the injured bone ends, prevents further distortion of the fractured bone and lessens pain. Application of ice immediately (if available) is desirable to minimize swelling. If ice is not available, then proceed with immediate transportation to the appropriate facility for further evaluation and treatment. The athlete should not be allowed to use the area of the body that may be fractured until the injury is properly evaluated and full treatment initiated.

Evaluation of a fracture by a professional includes assessment of the position and angle of the broken bone fragments. Whether or not there has been injury to surrounding blood vessels and nerves must be determined. X rays are usually in order, and may include views of the non-injured side for comparison if the damage is near a joint and its growth plates. These comparison films allow the physician to better tell if a growth-plate fracture is present, and the extent of the injury.

How Fractures Heal

Immediately after a fracture takes place, healing begins. Some bones are very small and fractures may be difficult to see on an X ray. During the first few days following the break, the living bone re-absorbs the bone along the edge of the fracture. (This makes the break actually look worse on an X ray about 10 to 14 days after the injury, so it's more easily identified than at the time of the first film.)

After this re-absorption takes place, the bone begins to form fibrous tissue around the fracture end. It is this process that joins the bone together again. And this will take place even if the bone is not in perfect alignment. As this continues, a callus (fibrous tissue plus bone formation) is formed around the break and the fracture is held firmly together. This callus gradually blends in with the normal bone and disappears by "remodeling" over the course of several months or years. Once the callus is firm, the bone ends will no longer move, and the bone progresses to healing. This healing time varies, depending on which bone has been broken (larger bones take longer to heal or "knit" than smaller ones) and the severity of the break.

In order for healing to end in normal function, the ends of the broken bones must be in appropriate alignment, and held so they do not displace (slip) as healing progresses. Two steps in fracture treatment accomplish this: *reduction* and *immobilization.*

First of all, a fracture which is not in line must be reduced or "set." This can be done in several ways, depending upon the fracture. The easiest way to align the bone in simple fractures is for the doctor to "set" the fracture by manipulating the broken bones. This method is most commonly used when breaks involve the smaller bones of the arm, lower leg or hands. The bone must be lined up as straight as possible, without being rotated or twisted.

Larger bones may require traction to help line up the two ends of the broken bones. Hospitalization is necessary and the young athlete is bedridden. Traction involves pulling steadily on the ends of the bone. This is done to overcome intense muscle contraction which will result in overriding of the bone ends and overall shortening. When a large bone is involved, traction is commonly needed for several weeks. Traction is usually required for femur fractures, and sometimes is used for elbow fractures. It is continued until the ends of the bones are in good alignment and some healing has taken place, so they will not slip and shorten or angulate. At this point casting of the injured area is done to provide protection for the healing bone and to allow complete repair.

Difficult fractures may require surgery to reduce them. This is most often needed for hip, elbow or ankle fractures. This form of reduction is done only when necessary, when the risk of permanent damage or deformity is greater without the surgery than with it.

After a fracture has been reduced (put into the best possible position), the broken bone must be immobilized until it has healed completely. This can be done in several ways, but is most often accomplished with a cast made of plaster or one of the newer, lighter materials. Some of these materials hold up better when exposed to water. Casts are usually applied so that the joints on *both* ends of the fractured bone cannot move; they are designed to prevent motion of the broken ends. Further protection and comfort can be achieved by use of crutches with leg injuries and slings with upper extremity fractures.

Rehabilitation after a Fracture

In general, children and adolescent athletes or others who have experienced a relatively simple fracture have no serious disability after the injury is healed. They will usually resume their pre-injury status by means of gradual conditioning.

And, in general, youngsters who have sustained most types of fractures will recover easily and without extensive rehabilitation needs. This is in sharp contrast to the adult with a fracture, who takes much longer to recover and often has need for specific physical therapy.

The goal of rehabilitation in all cases is to re-establish a full and painless range of motion of the joints of the injured extremity, as well as the recovery of full strength. Gradual conditioning is important before returning to full activity. Inclusion of specific exercises in the conditioning process under the supervision of a physician and/or a physical therapist is beneficial after certain injuries.

Complications of Fractures

Prevention of complications is one of the goals of fracture treatment. But, even with appropriate treatment, some fractures do not heal as well as would be considered ideal. Some of the complications of childhood fractures include: residual pain due to disruption of joint surfaces; limited motion of a part (if the break was near or included a joint); disruption of normal bone growth (the injured bone may end up shorter than the noninjured one); bony deformities; failure of the bone to heal (requiring a bone graft); and infection of the bone.

Angulation and rotation deformities may also occur if breaks are not correctly aligned. It is therefore important that all childhood fractures be recognized promptly and treated by a physician experienced in these injuries. Then the result will be the best possible, considering the specific injury and the specific child.

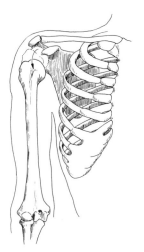

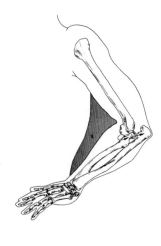

A dislocated shoulder   *A dislocated elbow*

Dislocations

The normal joint is formed when two ends of bones *articulate* with each other, resulting in the best possible efficiency of movement. Joints consist of matched surfaces that are held in proper alignment and supported by the ligaments and capsules (protective covering). They are crossed by tendons which allow them to move, but at the same time aid in their stability. Certain forces, however, can overcome the supporting structures, resulting in a joint dislocation. Such a dislocation is painful and must be recognized and treated quickly for the best possible result. These injuries are associated with varying degrees of tearing of the ligaments and damage to the joint capsule.

In youngsters, dislocations of the *shoulder, elbow, hip* and *knee* can be serious injuries. Those in the *fingers* can likewise be troublesome, but are more easily recognized and treated. For the joint to be realigned correctly, prompt professional evaluation and treatment are necessary.

One serious problem with dislocations in youngsters is the *possibility of growth-plate injuries and fractures* which occur at the same time. These must be carefully treated in order to prevent complications in growth and function. A growth-plate fracture close to a joint may be confused with a dislocation (especially in the fingers). X rays will establish the diagnosis.

Dislocations of the shoulder can become recurrent in most young and active athletes. In this case, the shoulder joint becomes lax, and the bones slide in and out of the socket even when less and less force is applied. Some exercises will help to strengthen the muscle/tendon supports, but in difficult cases, surgical correction is needed to prevent future dislocations.

Dislocations of the patella or kneecap are common. Some girls, in particular, have difficulty with recurrent dislocations, and this can cause significant discomfort and annoyance. This problem is also seen in some male athletes. A recurrent injury can sometimes be prevented with the initiation of specific exercises that strengthen the thigh muscle (quadriceps). Surgery may be necessary in the more resistent recurrent kneecap dislocations.

Hip dislocations are severely painful. They must be treated professionally as soon as possible, in order to prevent serious damage

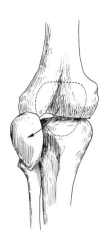

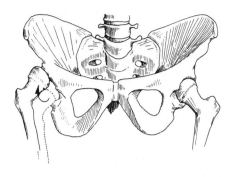

ABOVE.
Notice the normal placement of the hip joint at the right, as compared to the dislocation at the left. Arrow shows movement of the dislocation.

ABOVE LEFT.
Dislocation of the patella (kneecap). The dotted line shows where the patella normal is located. You can see it has been moved (dislocated) to the left.

caused by the disruption of the blood supply to the ball part of the hip bone.

Treating Dislocations

The mainstay of treatment for dislocations is first their recognition, then the replacement of the bones into their normal relationship. Resting the injured joint aids recovery. This is usually accomplished with splinting, casting, or the use of a sling for several days or even weeks.

Care in preventing the recurrence of dislocation is important, as is prevention of recurrent injury to the ligaments and tendons around the joint. This may require specific exercise and rehabilitation in addition to rest and immobilization. Recurrent dislocation might require surgical repair of the joint area to re-establish its stability and usefulness.

Recurrent dislocations may develop even if the best available medical care is given initially. Fortunately most of those that become a problem are amenable to surgery.

Subluxations are less severe displacements of joints (ends of the bones), which start to separate but do not get all the way. Subluxations may become recurrent and be associated with disability. The treatment for subluxations is the same as that for dislocations, including occasional surgery.

Points to Remember

✔ Fractures and dislocations are common in young athletes and can occur in bones and joints throughout the body.

✔ The majority of youngsters have little or no problem recuperating from these injuries and resuming their usual level of activity after rehabilitation and gradual conditioning. Surgery is generally not necessary for the majority of injuries.

✔ Swelling or pain over a bone or around a joint needs to be evaluated for possible fracture or dislocation.

✔ Growth-plate injuries do occur in association with some fractures and require special attention. They should not be mistaken for a dislocation or sprain.

✔ When these injuries occur the area affected should be immobilized (splinted) and the youngster transported to an emergency care facility for appropriate evaluation and treatment.

17.

Head, Neck, and Other Serious Injuries

ALTHOUGH MOST INJURIES young people sustain as a result of sports participation are minor and not serious, at times more severe and potentially disabling problems occur. These deserve special attention.

Some potentially serious injuries can be prevented by using proper protective equipment and common sense. Others happen even though all appropriate protective measures have been taken. They require immediate recognition and treatment in order to minimize their effects, or in some cases, to minimize the risk of lifelong disability and/or chronic discomfort.

Head Injuries

Among the common, potentially serious injuries children and young people suffer are those to the head. The well-known *"bump on the head"* is the most frequent, and usually does not have any serious short- or long-term consequences. On the other hand, more serious injuries to the head should be of concern, as they carry a risk for severe damage to the brain.

Injuries to the Scalp and Forehead

These are very common during childhood, and result from minor and severe trauma to the head. The bruise or contusion to the head results in nothing more than a tender area with or without swelling, which goes away within several days. *Lacerations* (cuts) of the scalp and forehead are also very common. Some may be of concern because of the relatively large amount of blood loss often associated with them; the scalp has an abundant blood supply, so that little damage to the tissue may result in what seems to be an inordinate amount of bleeding. This kind of bleeding—whether it flows out from the laceration—or as seen in the "lump" on the head where the bleeding stops under the skin and subcutaneous tissue—is best managed by applying firm pressure (with as clean a cloth or dressing as possible) with the fingers or hand directly over the area of injury . Direct pressure might be necessary for 10 to 15 minutes in order to control more profuse bleeding.

Application of ice is also helpful. Extensive lacerations require medical attention and suturing (stitches) to close a gaping wound or to control bleeding.

A young person who has sustained a serious laceration or has symptoms of injury to the brain should always be seen by a physician. (Symptoms of brain injury will be described later in this chapter.) Also, if a "bump" (swelling under the skin) seems to be increasing in size after pressure has been applied, the youngster should be evaluated by a physician. This sometimes indicates a more serious skull injury (fracture).

Skull Fracture

This is a break in one or more of the bones of the head, and is usually one of the more feared injuries in most peoples' eyes. While such a break certainly indicates that a significant amount of force was applied to the skull, the break, of itself, may be relatively unimportant. This distinction tends to confuse many people. What *is* important is how severely underlying brain structures were damaged as a result of the injury.

There are several types of skull fractures, from a simple linear (single-line break) fracture (see illustration, page 230) to a depressed break with a laceration over the top (see illustration, page 230). A fracture should be suspected when there is more swelling over a bump on the head than expected, or when there are signs of brain injury. Certain unusual but serious breaks are associated with bleeding and/or leakage of clear fluid (spinal fluid) from the ear or nose.

One of the most common of the infrequent serious head injuries in young people (both sports-related and non-sports-related) is the *cerebral* (meaning *brain*) *concussion.* There are various degrees of concussion, but they share one common feature—an alteration of consciousness at the time of or after the injury. This is probably the

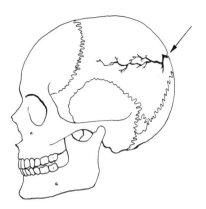

A skull fracture is a break
in one of the bones of the
head.

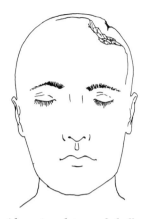

Above is a depressed skull
fracture with a laceration
over the top.

most singularly important symptom to be aware of when evaluating
possible injury to the brain.

Concussion

This is a temporary alteration in the brain which results from the
soft brain tissue being jolted inside of its natural helmet—the skull.
When the head is hit, the brain surface strikes the skull that received
the blow, but also hits the opposite side (from the Latin *concussio,*
to shake violently). After the impact, the brain may react with swelling (just as a bump to the arm may result in swelling) which may be
either mild or severe. If it remains localized (just to the areas which
struck the bone), the symptoms that result will probably be minor
and transient. On the other hand, if the swelling is severe and involves much of the brain, the symptoms will be very disturbing and
may last for longer periods of time.

An *alteration in consciousness* due to concussion may range from
a minor episode of confusion (being dazed or "spacey") to momen-
tary loss of consciousness, to longer periods of unconsciousness.

Any youngster who suffers a blow to the head and shows *any*
change in consciousness should be assumed to have had a concussion—at least until proven otherwise. Another symptom associated

with change in consciousness is a varying amount of loss of memory. The young athlete may not remember what happened or may not remember incidents before or after the injury took place. In general, the longer the time span of memory loss, the more severe the blow to the brain. A person with a concussion may complain of headache, dizziness, a "fuzzy" feeling, nausea, and may vomit. This condition requires medical attention, and if competing or practicing in athletic events, the young athlete should not be allowed to continue to play until a medical evaluation has been accomplished.

Contusion

This is a more serious type of brain injury in which there has been actual damage or "bruising" of the brain. Such injuries usually result in a longer period of unconsciousness than concussions do, and may have other associated signs like weakness, alterations in vision, and prolonged vomiting after the injury. Ordinarily, the amount of force needed to produce this kind of injury is greater than that which causes a concussion.

Most individuals who suffer a contusion of the brain (either of the surface or of the area called the brainstem), recover function after varying periods of treatment and rehabilitation.

Intracranial Bleeding

This bleeding inside the skull, or inside or around the brain is a serious consequence that may develop from head injury. This should always be suspected and the young person evaluated so rapid treatment can proceed, if lifelong disability or death are to be prevented. It is critical to remember that such bleeding can occur with or without skull fracture.

One type of bleeding is arterial (from an artery, and therefore rapid because the heart pumps the blood through the arteries with force). When this occurs, it is called an *epidural hematoma*. With this problem, a person may suffer a short lapse of consciousness, and then wake up for minutes or several hours, and act relatively normal. Thereafter, the young person begins to rapidly deteriorate and loses consciousness again. There is risk to the injured young person of dying quickly—therefore immediate medical treatment is imperative. It's crucial to keep this kind of injury in mind, and to react accordingly if a young athlete who has been injured but seems fine suddenly lapses into unconsciousness.

Another form of intracranial bleeding occurs when the veins of the brain bleed, causing a *subdural hematoma* (a blood clot). This bleeding is usually more gradual, more like seeping, than the epidural bleeding, and usually causes a young person to progressively deteriorate (or not recover as quickly as expected) over several hours or days. This kind of blood clot also requires prompt attention if long-term problems are to be avoided.

One of the most serious complications of any injury to the head—from simple concussion to intracranial hemorrhage—is *brain swelling*. Such swelling causes the pressure to rise inside the skull, with potentially devastating effects. In addition to unconsciousness, such pressure increase can cause weakness in or paralysis of the nerves to the head and neck as well as those of the rest of the body. Most important, deterioration occurs and breathing may stop, resulting in imminent death without emergency medical care intervention. Brain swelling which is not treated has the potential for permanent brain damage and death.

Some sports are potentially more hazardous than others to young athletes in terms of head injury: collision/contact sports such as football and hockey; sports in which speed is involved (skiing, skateboarding, skating, motorcycle racing, bicycling, cycling, tobogganing); those involving heights (diving, sky diving, hang gliding, gymnastics, ski-jumping); and those in which there is risk of being hit by flying objects (baseball, hockey, polo, handball, golf). However, there is risk of head injury in virtually any activity should an accident occur.

When a youngster has sustained an injury to the head, a careful assessment is important. If he or she is not unconscious, it is important to ask questions to determine whether or not a concussion might have occurred (such as: what do you remember, where are you, what happened, how do you feel, do you hurt anywhere?). Determine if the youngster can move all parts of the body, and assure youself that a neck or back injury (discussed later in this chapter) have not occurred. If there has been no loss of consciousness and the young person is feeling fine (and has no other symptoms) he or she may usually safely resume play. However, if there is any question as to the young person's physical status, continued participation in any form should be forbidden until a medical assessment has been performed to assure that serious injury did not result. Youngsters who have sustained an obviously serious head injury should be kept still and calm until paramedics or an ambulance arrive. In other cases of concern about potential head injury, the youngster should be taken to an emergency care center or to his or her personal physician as soon as possible so an examination can be performed and treatment given as indicated. A skull X ray may be warranted, depending on the evaluation and recommendations of the physician.

Any young person who is *unconscious* should be moved as if he or she had an associated neck or back injury. If an unconscious youngster has a helmet in place, it should not be removed—unless there is no other way to assure an airway and he or she is not breathing (there is a discussion on airway management in Chapter 22). Wait for the paramedics to arrive for transport to an emergency care facility. Inappropriate moving or handling of a young person with head and neck injuries can contribute to possible paralysis or other lifelong handicaps, so it's always better to be safe and wait for medical assistance when in doubt.

In all cases of potential head or neck injuries, fluids and food should be restricted until an assessment of the injury is perfomed by medical personnel. Sometimes surgery or diagnostic tests are indicated and liquid or food in the stomach could cause problems. These might also make a young persom vomit in situations of lesser injury.

It is important for coaches, parents and others involved in the supervision of athletic events to be particularly aware of the types of injuries common to that particular sport and to be prepared in the event that they occur. Knowing how and where to alert local medical assistance is vital, as is staying calm when assessing head and other serious injuries.

Neck and Spine Injuries

The bones that make up the spinal column are categorized into five groups according to their locations. The cervical spine (first seven vertebrae or bones) are located in the neck. Just below the neck, the spine consists of twelve thoracic vertebrae (in the chest), five lumbar

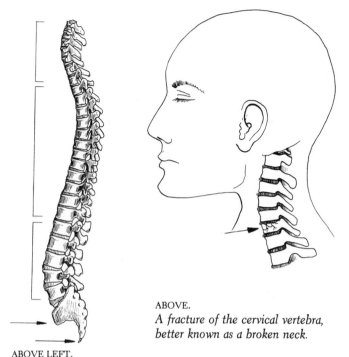

ABOVE.
A fracture of the cervical vertebra, better known as a broken neck.

ABOVE LEFT.
The spinal cord is a tube-like structure found within the spinal column protected by the block-line bodies and protuberant spines.

vertebrae (in the lower back), a sacrum (sacral vertebrae joined together as a platelike "shield"), and the coccyx (tailbone).

Extending through the vertebral canal, (a tube-like area running through the vertebrae), is the spinal cord with its vital nerve structures. Through this pathway, sensory signals are transmitted to the brain via the brainstem from all parts of the body, and motor "direction" signals are sent out to the muscles. These electrical impulses coordinate sensation, motor function and motor reflexes. The brainstem (an extension of the spinal cord at the base of the skull) is a collection of complex circuits which control breathing, heart function, and some eye movements and reflexes, in addition to being a conduit from the spinal cord to the brain.

The vertebrae are bony to protect the delicate spinal cord, and yet have joints with each other in several places to allow maximum motion in all directions, without compromising the spinal cord. The block-like bodies of the vertebrae support the weight of the head and torso, and are separated by intervertebral discs which absorb much of the shock of motion and jarring. Like other bones, the vertebral structures are held together firmly by ligaments, and their motion is controlled by a complex series of muscles. With the assistance of these muscles, tendons and ligaments, the spinal column allows humans to stand erect.

Severity of damage to the bony spine and the spinal cord it protects is dependent upon many variables: the location of the injury (which will determine which areas of function may be affected); the severity of the injury (whether damage to the nerves, bones, discs, soft tissues, or spinal cord is temporary or permanent, involves pressure or actual tearing of structures); and prompt recognition and appropriate treatment (appropriate safety measures after injury and during transport, accessibility to experts for treatment and rehabilitation).

Depending upon many factors, damage may range from less severe, transient problems to various degrees of permanent paralysis. If the spinal cord is transected (severed), paralysis will result, and its extent will depend upon the level at which the cord was severed. Paralysis may include the lower limbs (paraplegia) or all four limbs (quadriplegia), and may affect the control of breathing. (Paralysis of one side of the body (i.e. right arm and right leg)—hemiplegia— usually results from problems in the brain rather than in the spinal cord.) Basically, the higher in the cord the injury is, the more physical functions will be affected; injuries lower in the cord will limit fewer functions.

When the spinal cord is damaged, it may be difficult to determine the extent of the damage, or its long-term effects. This is because a phenomenon called spinal shock, a temporary reaction by the spinal cord to injury, may confuse the picture. Spinal shock may be associated with a drop in blood pressure, collapse, and various derangements of functions of the body, including breathing and bladder function.

Neck Injuries

Injuries to the *muscles and ligaments* of the neck are painful or uncomfortable, but generally are not serious. Muscle strains due to vigorous exercise are relatively common, and sprains of the ligaments of the neck are also possible, but usually will heal with adequate rest. Sometimes a cervical collar is worn to better rest the muscles and/or ligaments, and to support the head and neck. These injuries usually cause pain, especially with motion, but are not associated with abnormal sensations or weakness. Muscle spasm (a "tight" muscle) may occur in the area of injury, and serves as a warning that an injury has happened.

An injury which is relatively common in contact/collision sports is called a *"burner"* or *"stinger."* When a youngster blocks or hits an opponent with the head (for example, in football), the neck may be stretched, and this stretching may injure some of the nerves exiting from the neck to the upper extremities. A "burner" or "stinger" is a temporary injury to the group of nerves in the brachial plexus (a large bundle of nerves which serves the arm, the soft tissues of the neck and the area of the armpit). The young person will usually describe a series of electric "jolts" in the neck and arms. There may also be weakness in the shoulder or arm, lasting for seconds to hours. This injury has a potential for permanent weakness in some of the individual nerves, and should be evaluated. Youngsters with symptoms of a "burner" are usually restricted from play until all symptoms disappear and strength has returned to normal.

Herniation or rupture of an intervertebral disc in the neck is possible. Such an injury, although uncommon, may result in damage to the individual nerves which leave the spinal canal in the neck.

A youngster may have chronic pain or disability due to *repeated minor injury* to the structures of the neck. In these young athletes, there may be associated bony degenerative changes, and sometimes narrowing of the areas through which the nerves leave the spinal canal. Any chronic or recurrent pain or symptoms of neck injury in any youngster deserves careful evaluation to detect subtle injury.

Fractures of the cervical vertebrae (generally called a "broken neck," regardless of the type and severity) can be of many types. A break in a cervical vertebra is always potentially serious, but some injuries are more threatening than others. Injuries in which the fracture is *unstable* (capable of changing position) are particularly dangerous because movement might damage the spinal cord.

A *dislocation or subluxation of the cervical spine* (a slippage of the bones out of the normal alignment) may happen with or without a fracture. This injury can permanently damage the spinal cord, and prompt recognition and careful treatment is essential in order to prevent further extension of the injury and offer the best possible chance for recovery of function.

It is important to remember in this kind of injury that once it has happened, the damage is done, and the point is not to cause further damage or disability by panicking and quickly moving the youngster. *In organized sports, coaches, trainers, or team physicians will handle the situation*, and parents, players and others must do all they can to let them do the work that needs to be done. If, however, this type of injury is suspected and a professional knowledgeable in dealing with it is not present the following steps should be taken:

If the young person is conscious, he or she should not be moved until a determination is made as to the potential for a serious neck injury. Keep the youngster in the same position he or she landed in, telling him/her not to move. If the youngster must be moved because medical help cannot be summoned (to an inaccessible locale, or because phones are not available) all care should be taken to keep him or her in the same position in which he/she was found. It is helpful to have three or more adults help stabilize the position of the injured young person. Then, move the youngster as a "block," taking care not to let the neck and back move. But, whenever possible or practical, it is best to wait for an ambulance and skilled paramedics or a doctor.

If the youngster is unconscious, and has sustained a head injury (and you know exactly what happened), always assume a neck injury has also occurred, and move him or her accordingly. Again, if medical assistance can be summoned, it is best to wait, but in some circumstances, those at the scene will have to initiate first aid measures and transport the youngster so evaluation and treatment can begin immediately. Be sure not to remove protective equipment such as a helmet; this procedure is difficult and requires special expertise if a neck injury or spinal cord damage has occurred.

If, on the other hand, the unconscious youngster is not breathing, the first responsibility of the rescuer is to establish an airway, give mouth-to-mouth resuscitation if indicated and external cardiac compressions if cardiac function has also stopped. These procedures (CPR, or cardiopulmonary resuscitation) should be carried out with as much care as is possible. The youngster should be transported

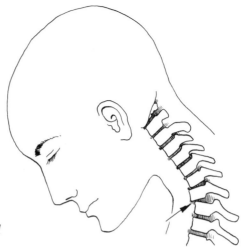

Subluxation of the cervical spine

either by ambulance, paramedics or by private car *only* if there is no other choice as soon as he/she is stabilized. (In serious situations, CPR can be performed while in transport.)

The reactions and actions of those who must aid a seriously injured young person can make the difference between a less serious injury and a lifelong handicap, so it's best to be prepared and know what to do should such an injury occur and professionals not be available.

Players, too, should be advised of the steps to take in case of serious injury of a fellow athlete. This is important for two reasons: the other athletes will know not to move an injured youngster who may have sustained a head and/or neck injury; and, if there is no supervision by professionals at the time of the incident, *they* must be able to follow appropriate steps to ensure the other youngster's safety and well-being. Too often we forget about the important role of the athlete in first aid. Teaching young athletes basic first-aid principles and the ways to deal with potentially serious injuries is too often forgotten. For their own sakes, it is best to make sure that all athletes are confident and knowledgeable about first aid.

Is Risk of Serious Head, Neck and Spinal Cord Injuries Greater in Some Sports than Others?

Serious injuries to the cervical spine, as well as to the head, are more common in collision/contact sports than in other types, simply because of the nature of the activities. Improper techniques and poor supervision can add to the risk for youngsters in almost any sport. It has been estimated that of each 100,000 youngsters who will participate in high school football, one will probably be partially or completely paralyzed as a result of a neck injury, and one per 100,-000 will die as a result of head injury. The risks in sports such as football are well known, but these statistics should also be put into some perspective. Riding a bicycle, for example, can be quite hazardous. It is estimated that there are more than one million injuries annually due to bicycle riding. Of those, 120,000 are fractures and another 60,000 are concussions. Considering these statistics, a young person often runs a greater risk of mild, moderate or serious injury by riding a bike than being involved in a contact sport, which is not to say that there are not inherent risks in contact/collision sports. Simply, there are inherent risks in all physical activities because accidents do happen. More injuries also occur in free-play activities than organized sports. Therefore, proper equipment and supervision, appropriate coaching, and following the rules of the sport or game *do* have an impact on the rate of injury—as well as the severity of injuries that take place.

In recent years, the risk of injury has been reduced in all sports. Such things as better helmets in football, the addition of required helmets in hockey, a baseball catcher's mask with a throat protector, better constructed shin guards, the extension of the helmet to cover the side of the head and the ear in baseball and softball, more protective clothing, shoes and other sports clothing, all aid in preventing serious injury.

Certainly more will be done in the future to ensure safety in sports, and much is available today that wasn't available only a few years ago. Prevention is always the best answer when it comes to serious injuries, and parents, players, coaches and others need to know and do all they can to safeguard young athletes from unnecessary risks or poor conditions which provoke injury.

Other Serious Injuries

Lower Back Injuries and Complaints

Injuries to the lower back are relatively uncommon in young athletes, and most are *muscle strains* and *sprains*. These injuries result in varying degrees of low back pain and limitation of activity for the youngster. They are, in general, not associated with injuries to the nervous system (spinal cord or nerves).

As in the neck, trauma to the lower back, in the form of direct blows or forces applied to the back while it is in an abnormal position, may result in serious and permanent injury. Recognition of the more serious injuries is important for a youngster's long-term well-being.

Fractures of the vertebrae of the lower spine (usually in the lumbar area) may involve the spinous processes (the prominent bony area which protrudes), the small pedicles (spiny areas at the side of the bone), or the body (block-like solid section of the bone). Breaks in these bones may or may not be associated with slippage or instability of the spine. If damage to the contents of the spinal canal occurs in the lumbar spine, it usually involves a single nerve group as it leaves the spinal area, rather than the entire section of spinal cord as it may at other levels, because the cord has already separated into smaller bundles of nerves. *Fractures of the tailbone,* although painful, are not usually associated with serious problems.

Most fractures of the lower back, once recognized, require rest and immobilization until the fracture site has healed. In addition to direct blows during contact sports, such injuries might also occur during gymnastics, on a trampoline, or during other activities which are associated with repeated stresses and strains on the lower back.

Acute rupture of an intervertebral disc of the lower back is a more common injury in the older athlete (and person) than in the younger athlete (see the illustration on page 241), but can occur as a result of athletic trauma. Youngsters with this problem usually have severe back pain which is worsened by certain movements, and muscle spasms in the lower back, near and below the waist. There may be pain in a leg as well, or numbness or weakness of a leg. Whenever such weakness is associated with back pain, a careful evaluation for a disc problem is indicated, and the youngster should not participate in any physical activity until the problem is diagnosed and the physician's recommendation given.

Repeated non-catastrophic injury to the lower back, the stresses of repeated vigorous activity, can be damaging to a young athlete in some cases. Stress fractures and injuries from repeated trauma to the

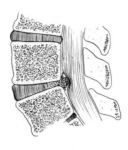
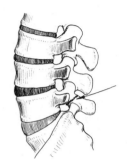

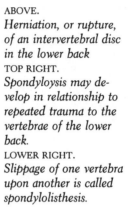
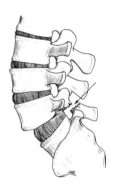

ABOVE.
*Herniation, or rupture,
of an intervertebral disc
in the lower back*
TOP RIGHT.
*Spondyloysis may de-
velop in relationship to
repeated trauma to the
vertebrae of the lower
back.*
LOWER RIGHT.
*Slippage of one vertebra
upon another is called
spondylolisthesis.*

vertebrae are relatively common in certain athletes. For this reason, chronic or repeated back pain in youngsters should not be ignored. In particular, the area of the bone encircling the back of the spinal canal is vulnerable to stress fracture and damage. Such a problem can be difficult to recognize, and even X rays can be confusing. This condition, called *spondylolysis*, shown in the illustration above, is seen in youngsters who are active in football, weightlifting, gymnastics, trampoline, pole-vaulting and other sports in which repetitive, forceful backbends are performed. It is also a risk for certain football players, such as interior linemen.

Certain athletes will develop a slippage of the vertebrae, called *spondylolisthesis*. The vertebra above slips forward off the vertebra below, and may cause continued pain and deformity. With severe

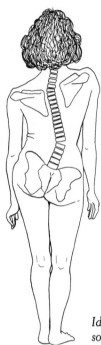

Idiopathic scoliosis, seen most often in girls, may be associated with significant deformity, if left untreated.

degrees of this problem, there may be associated nervous system effects, such as weakness and pain.

Although not arising from injury, certain abnormalities of the spine may be detected as a result of an injury. Essentially, injury calls attention to a hidden problem. Such deformities as *scoliosis* (abnormal side curvature of the spine shown in the illustration above), and *kyphosis* ("humpback" type of deformity) may be first detected after a youngster is injured. Conditions such as *bone tumors, infections* and *arthritis* may also be detected during the young person's activity in sports, but are not caused by that activity.

The bottom line when it comes to back pain and back injury is to make sure the young athlete is evaluated by a physician familiar with these kinds of injuries. Chronic back pain, as well as acute, should be taken seriously in the young athlete.

Abdominal Injuries

Direct blows to the abdomen in young people may be associated with serious injury, which should be recognized and treated promptly. An especially common abdominal injury is to the spleen (a fist-sized organ located in the upper left part of the abdomen), which has a very rich blood supply. A direct blow to the abdomen—from a kick, a punch, a fall onto bicycle bars, etc.—may result in bleeding under the capsule (protective covering) of this organ. Bleeding around the spleen or rupture of the spleen should be suspected if a young person complains of abdominal pain, especially in the left side, and has any symptoms of faintness, weakness or pallor, and has any tenderness when the abdomen is gently pressed. Such an injury requires careful assessment, observation (usually in a hospital) and sometimes emergency surgery to repair or remove the damaged spleen. Rupture of the spleen is more common if the spleen is already enlarged due to such things as infectious mononucleosis and other viral or blood diseases. Youngsters with enlarged spleens, therefore, should be excluded from rough, contact sports while the spleen is enlarged, to prevent possible rupture. They can usually return to the sport once the spleen returns to normal size and illness has ended.

Similar damage—rupture or laceration (tearing or cutting)—to the liver (the large organ located in the upper right side of the abdomen), is also possible with blows to the abdomen. Pain, shock and tenderness are signals of this potentially lethal injury. This injury requires prompt medical attention and control of bleeding, usually through emergency surgery.

Located in the center of the abdomen is the pancreas (a vital organ to both digestion and insulin production), which is occasionally damaged because of direct trauma to the abdomen. Inflammation due to trauma usually causes severe abdominal pain and vomiting. Sometimes associated with injury to this organ is damage to the intestine, often in the form of hematomas (blood clots) in the walls of the intestine. Rupture of an intestine happens only rarely with blunt injury to the belly.

Kidney Injuries

Often resulting from a direct blow or hit to the area between the rib cage and backbone, or to the side of the abdomen, kidney injury can be potentially disabling for the young athlete. Bleeding under the capsule (protective covering) of the kidney, as well as actual tears in the kidney tissue, are possible, and cause pain in the kidney area (either described as deep abdominal, side or back pain). With this injury there is usually blood in the urine which may be visible with the naked eye or may be seen only through microscopic examination of the urine sample. Permanent damage to the kidney, although unusual, is possible. Diagnosis of such problems may require an emergency kidney X ray study called an intravenous pyelogram (IVP) and other sophisticated tests. (IVP and other tests are described in Chapter 19.)

Traumatic Amputations

Although rare, some youngsters while at free play or in organized activities may experience loss of a finger, toe or even arm or leg. This is alway shocking and frightening for all concerned, and usually leads to panic. The first priority must be to control bleeding, since blood loss can be great in some instances, and serious blood loss can result in death. Direct sustained pressure over the wound with as clean a cloth as possible (or just the hand if you have to) will sometimes suffice, but with a serious amputation, there is often enough bleeding to warrant the application of a snug tourniquet-like wrap. Use a shirt, pant leg or any cloth available which can be wrapped around the remaining part near the site of the amputation. As soon as bleeding is controlled or a paramedic or other medical help arrives, the youngster should be transported to an emergency care center as quickly as possible. Although the idea of doing this is upsetting to many people, it is important to take the amputated part to the emergency care center with the youngster. If ice is available, immediately pack it in the ice which might help preserve it. The success with reattachment of severed digits (fingers and toes) and limbs in the past few years is quite encouraging. Sophisticated microsurgery techniques and refined equipment and instruments have made reattachment of amputated tissue possible in some, but not all, cases. Even though the situation is difficult and frightening, quick thinking by those near the youngster may result in reattachment and various degrees of function in the severed part or tissue. Care should be taken in handling the tissue.

Heat Stroke

Heat stroke is almost always preventable, and yet can and has killed. Statistics show that the second leading cause of death in high school athletics is heat stroke. Why such a problem if it can be prevented? Much of the time players don't want to admit they are having a problem, or wish to continue conditioning or training whether it's terribly hot or not. Many others simply do not know about the problem—including not only the athletes, but also parents and other adults who are responsible for supervising youngsters, whether in organized sports or in other recreational activities.

Strenuous physical exertion in high temperatures, especially if humidity is also high, is wise only with proper conditioning to the weather and with appropriate precautions. Most experts agree that when temperatures rise above 90 degrees Fahrenheit with an equally high percentage of humidity, strenuous activity (and for some, simple exercise) increases the risk of heat stroke. Indoor workouts or limited, less strenuous ones with proper precautionary measures are reasonable alternatives dictated by extremely hot weather.

When temperatures rise, loose-fitting, cool clothing is vital, as are adequate water intake and reasonable cool-off periods. Sweat suits, plastic sweat suits (much worse), long-sleeved shirts or long pants will only make matters worse, as will tight-fitting clothing.

Cases of heat stroke are seen in non-athletes as well, and are due to exposure to high temperatures—even without activity. Although each person's tolerance is different and response to heat varies, many of those who experience heat stroke are outside in the sun for long periods without adequate water, and little time has been spent in shaded or cooler areas to allow the body to cool off. Heat stroke can also take place inside a building or home which is not air conditioned when the weather becomes intolerably hot. In all cases, the body's fluids are depleted (dehydration occurs), blood pressure drops rapidly, shock occurs and the brain and tissues essentially "cook." Use of various medications, such as tranquilizers, amphetamines, some high blood-pressure medications, diuretics (water pills), antiseizure medications and others, can be factors causing some occurrences of heat stroke.

Symptoms include nausea, dizziness, headache, confusion, and sometimes listlessness. The person stops sweating (the body's protective cooling-down mechanism) and the skin becomes hot and dry. Body temperature rises quickly, sometimes as high as 106° or 107°. Obviously, there are degrees of these symptoms, but steps to cool the youngster down should take place at the first signs of a problem. The young athlete should be immediately taken out of the heat (either to a shady, cool area or inside an air-conditioned room), and water poured over him or her. The youngster should be encouraged to drink a substantial amount of water to replenish the body's fluids. If symptoms persist after this initial step, pack the youngster in ice or place loose ice over all areas of the body, then immediately transport him or her to an emergency facility either by paramedic, ambulance or private car, if necessary.

As always, the best treatment for anything is prevention—and heat stroke is no different. Ensure proper clothing, adequate water intake, periodic cool-down periods, and advise less strenuous activities on extraordinarily hot, humid days. Advise all young athletes that if they experience any dizziness, nausea, headache, or if they stop sweating, they are to immediately say something—long before the symptoms get worse. All young athletes and parents should know about the potential for heat stroke, the steps to take to prevent it, and what to do if it happens anyway.

18.

Injuries Involving Specific Sports and Parts of the Body

THERE ARE INJURIES associated with all sports; in every one, a youngster can be injured to a minor or serious degree. In younger children, injuries tend to be minor—bruises, lacerations, abrasions and the like—with an occasional fracture, dislocation or growth-plate injury. In older athletes, however, the risk of more serious injury increases.

Before age 12, children play with less intensity and simply don't generate the force because of size and strength—or the motivation—to push themselves into possible injury-producing situations. More accidents with associated injury occur at free play or while on a bicycle, skateboard or roller skates, than during organized athletic events. With these younger children, parents should do all they can to teach them "safety" and "respect" for their "toys"—and what can happen if they take chances.

When youngsters reach the junior high and high school levels—and again when young men and women enter collegiate athletics—the injury and risk rates go up. The body becomes larger and muscle forces are greater with increasing age. Older athletes push themselves harder, too. Whenever size and speed increase, risk of more severe injuries exists. Also, the desire to excel can result in a young athlete trying more difficult challenges. Coaches, trainers, teachers, parents—and the young athlete—must be reasonable about training and participation. As with all things, a gradual increase in activity and expectations is the healthiest and least hazardous way to go. But injuries do occur even with the best coaches, trainers, conditioning program and attitudes.

The fact that there is risk of injury in every sport should not preclude a youngster's participation. Walking—and other normal daily activities—also have their risks. However, if the child has a known abnormality, such as unstable shoulder or a bad knee, he or she can be directed to the kind of athletic participation where injuries to that area are infrequent or usually not severe. Bracing and corrective surgery may occasionally be indicated if rehabilitation does not solve the problem.

Listed below are the areas of the body and the sports in which injuries associated with them occur most frequently. However, it should be noted that injury to other areas can occur in all sports— these are just the most frequently injured areas in each.

Head and Neck Injuries

Head and neck injuries are most frequently encountered in sports in which there is significant speed by the participant, opponent, or other object; in those in which players collide with others or with things; or where the potential body forces can be transmitted to the head or neck, as in falling from a height. Sports with a higher incidence of head and neck injuries include diving, parachuting, motorcycle riding, bicycling, skateboarding, roller skating, football, skiing, car racing, hang-gliding, rock-climbing, and hot-dog skiing.

The greatest potential for head injury in organized school-sponsored sports occurs in football, due to the large number of participants. Statistics show that there will be one death in every 100,000 participants, and one athlete sustaining paralysis for every 100,000 players. Interestingly, in organized football, those conferences with participants under 12 years of age demonstrate less risk of serious head injury. Youngsters at this age have a greater risk for a serious head or neck injury from falls from a swing or bicycle. Therefore, an organized sport does not necessarily carry a greater risk for serious injury. And, every athletic pursuit, organized or not, has potential for a catastrophic head or neck injury due to an unexpected fall, collision or accident.

(For further information, see Chapter 17.)

Shoulder and Elbow

Man is the only species which purposefully and repeatedly throws things. All throwing games were designed by man, and all ask the shoulder and elbow to perform repetitive motions for which they were not specifically designed. A young athlete can develop injuries to these areas from either one episode or from repetitive trauma. Most shoulder and elbow injuries are seen in throwing and racket sports. These include volleyball, handball, baseball, basketball, tennis, racquetball, and other sports, such as gymnastics and swimming, in which repetitive motion of the upper extremities is involved.

Injuries may include tendonitis, bursitis, instability of a joint, growth-plate damage and others. Tennis elbow (a muscle and tendon disorder) and Little League elbow (a growth-center injury) are common, but forms of these injuries occur in sports other than those for which they are named. These also occur in individuals who do not participate in sports or arise from situations not related to sports participation.

(See Chapters 14, 15 and 16 for more specific information about injuries to joints, ligaments, muscles and bones.)

Lumbar Spine

With thousands and thousands of youngsters now participating in organized sports, low back pain, previously quite rare, is being seen more and more. Injury again may be due to a single insult or to repetitive trauma. Types of injuries include stress fractures to the lumbar spine, ruptured discs, ligament and muscle injuries (sprains and strains) involving the back.

The majority of back injuries in children will get better with rest. However, they can be associated with other more serious problems. Constant or nagging pain or severe pain should be evaluated by a physician.

Almost any sport which involves twisting, turning or abrupt motion can have lumbar spine injuries associated with it. Certain sports carry a relatively high risk for injury. But as long as they are done with care and conditioning, and a professional evaluation is sought when necessary, most are reasonably safe.

Low back pain is seen most frequently in weightlifting, gymnastics, wrestling, football, high jumping, pole vaulting and sports like tennis, in which there is repetitive use of the lower back.

Hips

The hips can be injured in explosive running sports in which muscles may be pulled from their attachments. Growth-plate injuries of the hip can also occur when a sport requires jumping from a height, which could entail a fall or in which a collision might be involved. Hip injuries are seen in those involved in motorcycle riding/racing, car racing, skateboarding and roller skating (although the risk can be lessened by use of hip pads and other protective equipment), as well as in running sports.

Knees

The human knee is the largest single joint of the body, quite vulnerable to injury and virtually unprotected by adjacent structures. A complex structure, the knee flexes and extends, and has some rotational and sliding properties associated with its motion. The knee must remain flexible yet stable for best function. Because of the constant demands placed on it and because of its vulnerable position, it is one of the most commonly injured areas in sports.

Injuries to the knee are found in two kinds of sports: those that require abrupt stopping and quick starting, changes of direction, turning, twisting or jumping and in contact sports in which there is a likelihood of forceful collision with the knee.

Knee problems and injuries are therefore seen most frequently in football, basketball, skiing, gymnastics, wrestling, and running (because of the repetitive motion demanded of the knee).

Running and jumping take most of their toll on not only the knee but the remainder of the lower extremity of the body.

Lower Extremity Bones

The bones of the lower extremities—femur, tibia, fibula and bones of the feet—may sustain stress fractures. These are usually related to running sports such as track and field, cross-country and basketball and are also associated with the rigors of training for other sports.

Ankle

Injuries to the ankle are the most frequent and common joint injuries, but full function is usually recovered. Such injuries occur in any sport in which a person moves around—essentially *all* sports. There are significant numbers of ankle injuries in running and jumping sports.

Foot

Stress fractures and other numerous problems affect the many bones and joints of the foot and their supporting ligaments, tendons and muscles. Foot injuries and afflictions affect all athletes, and occur in all sports. From a loose toenail to a broken toe or foot, from calluses to plantar warts, from arch pain or strain to heel pain—all can be debilitating to an athlete because the foot is so vital to good performance in almost any sport or play. Basically, it is the area of contact and the interface through which the body weight is transmitted to the surface or ground.

Hand

The same kinds of tendon systems and structures are found in the hand as in the foot, and similar kinds of injuries can occur. Hand injuries can be disabling to the athlete if the athletic endeavor requires fine motor movement, and can also affect other aspects of a youngster's life as well.

The effect of a hand injury on athletic performance may not be as great as with a foot injury, because it is not a weight-bearing structure. However, for the football quarterback, baseball pitcher, racket user, gymnast and others, a hand injury even as minor as an infected fingernail can limit participation.

Thumb injuries—fractures and tendon injuries—can be particularly devastating. The thumb is essential in normal hand function. "Jamming" injuries, fractures and dislocations of the fingers, including the thumb, are common. Tendon injuries and damage to the nerves from lacerations may have long-term disability associated with them.

Abdomen and Chest

Although uncommon, injuries to the chest and abdominal structures are potentially life-threatening. These may result from either blunt trauma, as occurs in contact sports, or when a youngster falls or strikes an object and receives a penetrating blow. Whether broken ribs or a penetrating wound, these serious injuries need immediate emergency medical evaluation and treatment.

Genital Injuries

The line drive in baseball, the speeding hockey puck, the unsuspected overhead smack coming off the tennis racket—all are potentially threatening for direct blows to the genitalia. Although serious problems rarely result, the associated bleeding (internally and externally) can result in intense pain and temporary disability. If pain or swelling is marked, the youngster should be seen for evaluation by a urologist.

Many injuries to the male genitalia can be prevented or lessened by the use of athletic supporters (jock straps), and further protection is afforded by the addition of a protective plastic cup into the supporter. Athletes engaged in high-risk contact sports—or playing certain positions (catcher, pitcher in baseball; any hockey player, for example)—should be encouraged to use protective cups.

The most common injury to the female genitalia is the "straddle" injury, which occurs when the girl falls onto the relatively unprotected vulva. This can happen in gymnastics (doing "splits," or performing on a beam) or in cycling, as well as during falls in other sports. The local bleeding from the injury causes bruising and pain in the genital area, and occasionally some vaginal or vulvar bleeding and laceration. A strain (muscle pull) of some of the inside leg muscles might also be associated, and cause considerable temporary disability.

Skin

Abrasions and lacerations are a common result of almost any active sport. Floor burns and grass burns result from falls, and sliding injuries are common in both individual and team sports. Rashes and fungal infections may require dermatologic treatment. They may be aggravated by sweating and the equipment more than the given sport.

Breast

Irritation of the nipples is common in both male and female athletes, especially in runners. Rubbing of clothing on the nipples is the usual cause. Adolescents, boys as well as girls, complain of this because of the normal prominence of the nipples. Female athletes may likewise be troubled by breast discomfort during many athletic events. A supportive bra is helpful.

The breast may be bruised by direct contact, but responds as any other tissue to this type of injury. The "old wives' tale," that if a young girl injures a breast, she will develop cancer later, has not been substantiated and should not be a concern in athletic participation. Serious breast injury is rare.

Dental Injuries

In boxing, hockey, football and other sports it is required or recommended that the young athlete use a mouthguard to protect teeth from being knocked out or broken. Youngsters with dental problems, or those with a great deal of expensive dental work, should consider using a mouthpiece for any sport, in order to protect their teeth and mouth. These can be purchased ready-made, or can be custom-made by the youngster's dentist. Broken or damaged teeth should be evaluated by a dentist or oral surgeon.

Eye Injuries

Eye injuries most commonly occur in sports from a finger or from a small ball which can strike the eye directly—tennis, handball, racquetball, baseball and others. Serious damage to the eye structures can be caused by such an injury. However, most injuries are not serious, and involve bruising of the eye or its surrounding structure, or scratching of the cornea. Application of ice, a patch and a physician's careful evaluation for serious damage are in order.

Points to Remember

↗ Injuries occur in all sports, but most are minor to moderate in severity, and full recovery is the rule rather than the exception.

↗ Persistent pain is nature's warning signal to the athlete and parent that something may be wrong, or that the athlete needs to be seen by a physician.

↗ If a youngster has a tendency for recurrent injury in one place (such as the elbow, shoulder or knee), he or she might be directed to an area of athletics where that body part receives less demand or stress.

19.

Special Diagnostic Procedures for Sports Injuries

THE GOALS OF INJURY recognition and treatment are accurate diagnosis, appropriate, timely treatment of injuries, prevention of further disability, and the return to full function and participation by the youngster. Over the past several decades, modern technology has enhanced the physician's ability to recognize and treat injuries in a much more accurate way than in the days when diagnosis relied solely upon the athlete's description of what had happened, what the injury felt like at the time of the evaluation and the results of a physical examination. Now in addition to these time-honored methods, new technology enables more precision.

Components of Injury Diagnosis

History and Examination

Even with the current advances in diagnostic tools and techniques, the history of an injury (what happened) remains the cornerstone of accurate diagnosis. The physician's (or coach's, trainer's or parent's) knowledge of the kinds of stresses and activities encountered in a given sport, coupled with the athlete's description of what actually happened, will allow for the best determination of what might be wrong, and therefore what might be done to confirm that suspicion.

It is always important that the description of an injury be as detailed and accurate as possible: what exactly happened; what the athlete was doing at the time; in what direction a hit or a fall occurred; how the injured area came to rest; and how it felt both at the time of the injury and at the time of evaluation. Answers to such questions are critical as the first step in injury assessment of the youngster. Without an accurate history of the injury, the physician is left to deduce what *might* have happened, rather than determining all that *did* happen. This is especially important in orthopedic injuries, because it allows the physician to determine what forces might have been involved. Expecting the doctor to "figure it out" may often leave some part of the injury not fully explained or treated.

After a careful assessment of the forces involved in an athletic injury, the sports medicine expert will proceed with a thorough physical examination, paying particular attention to the injured area or part of the body. The physician will also rule out other possible injuries of which the athlete might have been unaware. When injuries involve the musculoskeletal system (bones, joints, muscles and supporting structures), the physician will want to carefully examine the injured part for swelling and tenderness, carefully assess the resting position, and test the range of motion (both active by the youngster, and passive by the examiner). Special maneuvers may be required to fully identify the extent of injury, or to determine whether other specialized tests are required.

When injuries involve parts of the body other than the musculoskeletal system, the physician must concentrate on these areas in detail. Each area requires special care. (For information regarding these injuries, see Chapters 17 and 18.)

Only after careful physical assessment is it possible to determine how significant an injury is, what further studies might be indicated in order to assess the degree of disability, and how to best guide the course of treatment. The physician may want to perform various diagnostic tests to gain additional information.

X rays

The use of conventional X rays has long been a mainstay in the diagnosis of injuries to the bones and joints. The X ray is an excellent aid in assessing and verifying injuries, when the injuries potentially involve breaks (fractures) of a bone, dislocations (disruption of the usual relationships of joints) or growth-plate injuries (damage to the growing ends of the bones in young children).

An X ray is produced when a special film is exposed to a small amount of radiation. When an area of the body is exposed to this radiation, the areas which are most dense (thickest) will be more resistant to the X rays which are passing through. Bones are the most dense, so they show up on X rays as very white areas. Muscles, tendons, ligaments and other less dense materials are seen in lighter shades of gray. Because bones are so dense, they can easily be visualized in great detail. With the less dense muscles, tendons and ligaments, detail is lost, so X rays are not especially helpful in complete diagnosis of injuries to these structures.

The primary purpose of taking X rays in childhood sports injuries is to determine if a fracture has occurred and if there has been a growth-plate injury. Because a youngster is growing, and therefore the potential for growth-plate injury is high, a physician is likely to request X rays of any injury near a joint. He or she has an ethical and medicolegal responsibility to assure (as far as possible) that such a problem does not exist. Often X rays will include not only the traumatized part of the body, but also the same part on the other side, for sake of comparison. Sometimes comparison views are invaluable in determining subtle variations from the norm which might otherwise go unrecognized.

Often, the evaluation of an athletic injury will include an X ray not only because of its inherent value in assessing the injury, but also because of the expectations of parents and others, who want to be certain about whether or not a fracture has occurred. Because a physician is expected to always be "right," he or she will usually want to verify the presence or absence of a fracture.

Conventional X rays of body parts other than the musculoskeletal system might be performed, depending upon the nature and extent of an injury. X rays are particularly helpful in determining the presence or absence of skull fractures, and may be used to evaluate chest and abdominal injuries as well.

Stress X rays

In certain injuries such as those which disrupt ligaments and tendons, modification of conventional X-ray techniques can assist in determining whether or not a joint is stable. If a ligament has been torn extensively, a joint may "open up" (the surfaces will separate abnormally) when stress is applied to it. If this force is applied while an X ray is being taken, the injury's extent can be verified and documented.

Stress films are most often used to examine ankle and knee joints, which frequently sustain ligamentous injuries, especially in the older child. Occasionally such films will also elucidate a previously unsuspected growth-plate injury. Depending upon the amount of discomfort the youngster is experiencing, such X ray films may be taken with local or general anesthesia or other types of pain relief, to allow sufficient stress to be placed on the joint to ensure careful, complete evaluation.

Tomograms

Tomograms are X rays which show "slices" of the bone. With this technique, the physician has a picture of each section of the bone—at five or more millimeter intervals—to carefully evaluate. This close scrutiny of each small area of the bone is helpful in determining the extent of a problem, or in better identifying a problem in an area which appears suspicious on a regular X ray. These studies are especially helpful in differentiating between tumors and other problems of the bone, and injuries. They may be useful in diagnosis of stress fractures and other subtle injuries as well.

Arthrograms

A useful procedure in evaluating a joint problem is the arthrogram, a study in which a contrast "dye" is injected directly into a joint. After the injection, special X rays are taken to determine exactly where the dye went, whether the joint structures are normal, and whether or not there are tears in ligaments or cartilage.

Arthrograms are most commonly performed in the diagnosis of injuries to the knee, ankle, shoulder and elbow. They are very useful in identifying a torn cartilage, because the contrast (dye) leaks into the tear, where it collects and can be visualized on X ray. Although the procedure can be somewhat uncomfortable, it can be very useful in making a differential diagnosis of certain injuries, and can be especially useful prior to surgery on a joint.

Arthroscopy

Arthroscopy is one of the newest techniques in orthopedic diagnosis, and shows the greatest promise for both diagnosis and treatment of injuries to and around joints. Available only for the past ten years or so on a large scale, the technique has been used most extensively with knee injuries.

With this procedure, an orthopedic surgeon inserts a special arthroscope, a fiberoptic tube system (which allows the surgeon to see inside the joint) into a small incision in the joint. The joint surfaces and structures are visualized under great magnification, and can be seen on a special television screen by the surgeon. The images can also be recorded on videotape or regular film. This procedure allows the physician to see even the most minute tears in ligaments and cartilage, for example, and repair them.

Perhaps one of the most impressive features of the arthroscopy technique is the ability to repair or remove damaged tissues with tiny instruments inserted through or at angles to the viewing instrument. The surgeon guides the instruments by watching the screen and its magnified image. With this technique, there are no large incisions, and very little residual pain and disability from the surgery.

This new technique is being used more and more widely, and has particular advantage for the athlete, where a limited amount of time away from the sport, as well as quick and accurate diagnosis and treatment, are important. The technology involved in arthroscopy reduces the length of hospitalization and the cost as well as the length of time required for recovery. Its usefulness is also being evaluated for shoulder, elbow and ankle injuries. Presently, arthroscopy is not used to treat all joint injuries, but its use is increasing.

Bone Scan

A bone scan is a procedure in which a minimal amount of radioactive material is injected into the bloodstream so that the bones of a certain area can be evaluated in terms of their uptake of the radioactivity. From this test, a physician can get a better picture of what is happening in a bone. It shows how much "activity" is occurring in the bone, especially with regard to blood flow and the production of new bone.

The radioactive material which is injected actually "fools" the bone, which picks it up and processes it as if it were the usual chemical materials used in bone formation. Several hours after it is incorporated into the bone, a scanning camera is run over the body and identifies any areas of abnormal radioactivity. Bone scan is invaluable in many instances, in that it can identify problems in the bone much earlier than standard X ray. Areas which are undergoing rapid change show as "hot spots" on the scan, and may represent sites of fracture, infection or tumor. The scan is particularly useful in the diagnosis of stress fractures. Many times these subtle breaks are identified within days with a scan, while they would not be visible on conventional X rays for several weeks. The bone scan can provide useful definition of other subtle fractures, too, and may serve to differentiate an area of injury from another bony problem which might mimic it in the young athlete. Again, early, accurate diagnosis is extremely important to the active athlete, who is concerned about continued disability, and time missed from conditioning and performance.

CAT Scans

Computerized axial tomography (CAT) scans are sophisticated studies which depend upon computer technology to produce images of various parts of the body. As in conventional X ray tomography, this technique has the capability of taking "pictures" of thin slices of tissue—bones as well as soft tissues. Then it reconstructs a three-dimensional impression of the area.

CAT scans are most useful in studying the head (diagnosing intracranial bleeding due to injury, for example), as well as identifying other abnormalities inside the skull. It is also used for examination of the chest, the abdomen and, in certain situations, for evaluation of the spine and other bony areas.

CAT scan technology is a milestone in non-invasive diagnosis and evaluation. It provides information to the physician quickly and accurately—and presents information heretofore obtained only through invasive diagnostic studies requiring hospitalization and/or exploratory surgery. Its use in the future will, no doubt, increase.

Myelograms

A myelogram is a study which may be used to outline a potential problem involving an intervertebral disc in the back or a tumor. Contrast dye is injected into the spinal column in the lower back, and X rays are performed to reveal disruptions or alterations in the column of dye. A myelogram is often performed prior to determining the need for disc surgery or operative exploration and repair of other injuries or removal of tumors. The procedure bears risks as well as benefits, however. Risks include reactions to the dye, discomfort, spinal headaches, and possible nerve damage.

Normally, a standard X ray visualizes the discs (the cushions between the vertebrae of the back) as gaps, rather than as defined structures. With injury, the disc can rupture and protrude into the spinal canal, impinging on nerve roots and causing pain and other neurological problems. (These injuries are uncommon in children, but occur more commonly in older athletes.) A myelogram essentially outlines the area where the nerve roots leave the spinal canal, and may show the area where the ruptured disc or tumor is pressing on a nerve.

This diagnostic procedure usually requires hospitalization. Although it is commonly performed before disc surgery, it may not be indicated in some individuals.

Electromyogram (EMG)

Certain tests are available to help in the determination of the function of the nerve-muscle unit. Such information can be gained from an electromyogram (EMG), a study which tests the status of the peripheral nerves (the small branches which serve the individual muscles) and the muscles they control. In this test, small needles (electrodes) or surface patch-like electrodes are placed in or over the muscle to be tested, and the electrical activity of the area is recorded. (Normally, there is a "background" of electrical activity in a nerve-muscle unit, and with stimulation of the nerve, the amount of electrical activity increases.) Electromyograms can detect certain abnormalities of the muscles themselves, as well as help to determine the degree of damage to the nerve supply to an area. They can also be helpful in identifying certain diseases involving the muscles themselves.

Other Types of Contrast X rays

The myelogram, mentioned previously, carries with it certain risks (as discussed), and may not be desirable in all young people with symptoms of disc disease. For these youngsters, an *epidural venogram* might be recommended instead. In this study, a contrast dye (visible on standard X ray) is injected into a blood vessel of the lower leg, and picked up by the veins surrounding the spinal cord. When there is pressure from a protruding lumbar disc, there is distortion of the vein pattern in the spinal cord area, suggesting disc protrusion or tumor. Such types of techniques might be more commonly used in the future to assist in diagnosis, especially in the younger athlete.

When injuries to the abdomen and flank areas (near the back) occur, it may be necessary for a youngster to have a kidney X ray to determine whether or not there has been damage. Such an X ray, an *intravenous pyelogram* (*IVP*) involves injection of a contrast dye into a vein. The dye travels through the body, and X rays are taken to follow its progress through the kidneys. Such a study will show leaks of the dye outside the kidney, and abnormalities of function which might have resulted from injury. Another study, a *cystourethrogram* may be used to examine the lower urinary tract as well. Here the physician is looking for tears in the urethra and bladder, particularly when injuries to the genitalia or lower abdomen have occurred. This study involves the introduction of contrast material (dye) into the bladder through a catheter (a special small plastic tube inserted into the urethra).

The upper and lower intestines can similarly be evaluated by either swallowing contrast material (upper gastrointestinal series) or by a barium enema of the colon.

Blood Studies and Other Tests

Often when an injury has occurred, especially a serious one, a physician will order a blood test on the young athlete. The (*complete blood count*) CBC gives several types of information. Parts of the CBC, the *hematocrit* and *hemoglobin*, identify the number of red blood cells in the body, and allow a physician to determine if there has been significant blood loss due to injury or subtle bleeding within the body. These may also detect previously existing anemia in the young athlete. The *white blood count* is also a part of the CBC, and helps to determine whether or not there is unusual or marked inflammation in the body. This is important in determining whether a youngster's symptoms are due to injury, or might rather be due to another condition which is mimicking trauma. Other *tests for inflammation* may also be useful in establishing whether or not arthritis or infection is present.

Urinalysis is a study of the urine, used most often in athletes to detect blood cells in the urine (unseen by the naked eye) after injury has occurred. It might also detect an unusual condition, myoglobinuria, in which a blood-like pigment from the muscle is excreted in the urine after very vigorous exercise or muscle injury. (This condition, if very extensive, has a potential for causing kidney damage and failure.) There are many other uses for the urine study, of course, not necessarily related to athletics. One common use is to test for abnormal sugar in the urine in the diabetic.

Occasionally a serious problem of the musculoskeletal system (or other body area) will mimic a sports injury, and be identified during diagnosis for the potential injury. The presence of such problems as tumors (masses or lumps) might be noted because of examination for an injury. When this occurs, a special surgical evaluation may be necessary. *Biopsy* is one technique used to remove a tissue sample to determine whether or not it is abnormal. A tissue sample can be obtained by inserting a needle into the suspicious area, or a section of that tissue can be surgically removed for microscopic examination.

20.
Rehabilitation and the Long-Term Effects of Injury

THE ONLY DIFFERENCE between rehabilitating an injured youngster who is involved in athletics, and rehabilitating one who is not is the urgency by the young person, parents and/or coaches to get him or her back into competition as soon as it is safe. This usually means that the intensity of rehabilitation is greater than for a non-athlete and the young person is more highly motivated to participate actively in a prescribed rehabilitation program set up for him or her.

Today everyone hears of the wide variety of specialized equipment available on the market that's designed to hasten recovery from athletic injuries. The young athlete and parent can, however, achieve the same rehabilitation goal without much of this equipment.

Most athletic injuries today receive no specific program of rehabilitative care. Although the ideal is to be rehabilitated through a program prescribed by a doctor, a sports medicine specialist, an athletic trainer, or physical therapist, many times the young person is supervised by school personnel or a coach (if it is not a school-sponsored sport), and the rehabilitation program is performed with minimal equipment. In some cases, a hospital's physical therapy department or the doctor's physical therapist will supervise the rehabilitation program. Therapy can also take place at home with very simple equipment, as long as the recommended program is followed carefully and judiciously.

The principles (the Four Ps) of rehabilitation from athletic injuries are easy to remember and depend on common sense. They are: (1) Protecting the injured area, and resting until healing is complete; (2) Performing again at prior level; (3) Preventing of re-injury; and (4) Preventing or postponing the onset of degenerative processes. Let's look at these separately, in more detail.

Protecting and Resting the Injured Area

Obviously, the extent of rehabilitation time and effort needed is directly related to the extent of the injury. The shorter the time period a young athlete must remain at rest, the shorter the rehabilitation period will be. The longer the youngster must remain at rest, the longer his or her rehabilitation time will be. If surgery is necessary, rehabilitation time may be even longer, but the principles of restorative therapy for both non-surgical and surgical injuries are the same. They are also similar regardless of what limb was injured.

In the initial injury phase, exercise is limited. Rest is the primary prescription until a reasonable amount of healing takes place. Depending upon the location and extent of injury, it may be protected by a cast or splint, tape, use of crutches, sling or other means of restricting motion or weight-bearing. In all cases, a rehabilitation program begins as soon after the injury as possible, when it is safe and the danger of aggravating the injury or re-injury is diminished.

During the time before rehabilitation exercises begin, while rest is prescribed, the young athlete is usually anxious. Coaches, trainers, parents and the athlete's peers need to do all they can to be supportive. Many youngsters have a tendency to "overdo it" or become frustrated because the injury has limited their activity. These young people are used to being very active and involved, and find it difficult to have to rest. The "rest" entails only the injured structures. The remainder (uninjured portion) of the body is kept active and exercising as long as this does not prolong the recovery period.

Performing Again at Prior Level

Three Types of Exercise

After the initial healing (rest) phase of rehabilitation is complete, a carefully planned exercise phase begins. Three types of exercises help reinstate muscle tone and strength. They are isometric, isotonic and isokinetic exercises, and are utilized in most rehabilitation programs to varying degrees, depending upon the extent of injury.

Isometric Exercises

These force the muscle to contract without shortening the length of the muscle; there is no movement in the joint. Muscles are strengthened and built by tension and resistance against an immobile object. These can be done simply by flexing and tightening a muscle for ten seconds, then relaxing it, then repeating the routine. All voluntary muscles of the body can be strengthened and toned through isometric exercises. Because these exercises do not involve the movement of joints, they are a very important part of most early rehabilitation programs.

Isotonic Exercises

These strengthen muscles by shortening and lengthening them by moving a resisting object. This usually involves repetitive lifting of weights. As a weight is lifted (by whatever body part is being strengthened), the muscles flex and shorten. As the weight is allowed to return to the resting position, the muscle lengthens. This aspect of rehabilitation is gradual, starting out with light weights and few repetitions, then increasing both slowly as the injured area heals and strengthens.

Isokinetic Exercises

These exercises are performed on a sophisticated machine (Orihotron and Cybex units). This type of exercise trains explosive muscle power, and can also be achieved by participating in the athlete's usual sport.

Or, muscle strengthening can be accomplished through the careful use of simple weights, either made at home or purchased. However, the parent and young athlete should discuss a plan of action with the doctor, physical therapist, athletic trainer or physical educator (whoever is involved) to design a safe program which adequately meets the needs of the young athlete. Usually the "home" rehabilitation program takes longer than the more sophisticated ones, but all goals can still be achieved.

Isometrics, isotonics and isokinetics all start at an entry level in rehabilitation, and exercises are intensified as endurance, stamina and strength increase. (For more information on isometric, isotonic and isokinetic exercise, see Chapter 4 on Conditioning.)

Anyone in a rehabilitation program should not perform physical therapy tasks when significant pain or swelling exists. An increase in pain and/or swelling usually means the program is either too strenuous or that exercise was initiated too soon after the injury. Because rehabilitation is not only a science but also an art, it is virtually impossible to prescribe a general program. Programs are specifically designed for each youngster, depending on the extent and type of injury, healing time necessary before exercise can take place, and the motivational level of the young person. The regimes must be frequently re-evaluated and modified according to repeated assessments of the youngsters' progress.

Rehabilitation must be very specific and individualized, so that balance is met between muscle movements, endurance, strength, cardiovascular fitness, speed, flexibility and agility—and paying special attention to avoiding re-injury. With certain injuries, all parts of the body may be forced to rest for a period of time—so all parts of the body may require rehabilitation as much as the injured area. For example, during rest the young athlete can't expect to maintain the same cardiovascular fitness as before the injury, and must slowly regain this. This principle applies to other aspects of fitness and training as well. Therefore, the extent of rehabilitation will theoretically be based on the length of time the youngster was not active.

On the other hand, many injuries allow athletes to exercise all but the injured member. So, sometimes, the youngster may need to be directed to other athletic areas to retain fitness while in the process of rehabilitation. For example, if the injury were to the leg, the young person might be directed to swimming or rowing to maintain physical fitness until running could safely resume. Likewise, if an injury involves an arm, the youngster might be directed to running or the stationary bicycle as an alternative in order to stay fit during the rehabilitation process. All such programs depend, however, on the recommendation of the youngster's physician.

As the young athlete rehabilitates the injured area, and reconditions and trains, he or she will begin to close the gap between present status and the performance level before injury. Once the injury is totally healed and reconditioning of the entire body has taken place, the goal is to return the athlete to participation at the same level he or she left when injured.

Preventing Re-Injury

One of the biggest problems in rehabilitation is re-injury. The young person, highly motivated and wanting to participate as soon as possible, may begin strenuous activity too soon, when the injury is not totally healed and conditioning is not complete. Although rehabilitation can be exasperating for many young athletes, it is important that they understand that going back too soon, when they are really not ready, can result in re-injury. Re-injury will keep them out even longer—and, in fact, the residual effects (more extensive damage) may make return to the previous level of performance difficult or impossible.

Preventing or Postponing Degenerative Processes

One goal of rehabilitation is to prevent or postpone the onset of arthritis and other potentially debilitating processes, such as chronic pain or limited function of joints, tendons, muscles or ligaments. If the young athlete returns to participation too soon or overstresses the injured area, on the other hand, the potential rises for chronic injury and degenerative processes to begin Muscles, tendons, ligaments, cartilage and bones have the potential for recovery, but recurrent injuries increase the resultant effects of injury and disability may become permanent.

Ice, Heat and Other Treatments

In addition to exercises, a rehabilitation program may include ice massage, application of dry heat (heating pad) or wet heat (whirlpool or hot packs). Such treatments as ultrasound, diathermy and transcutaneous electrical nerve stimulation have very limited value in the young athlete, and are more often used to aid the mature adult. Because a youngster has such tremendous natural healing powers, it's hard to justify the expense of using these more elaborate modalities, when the benefits of physical therapy are so much greater, and so much less costly.

Medications and Drugs

The use of medications and drugs in rehabilitation programs for young athletes is different from use for adults. Cortisone, anti-inflammatory medications, Dimethyl Sulfoxide (DMSO) and other drugs are not recommended for use in young people, because of their limited benefit, and their side effects.

Pain medications should be taken only to relieve the discomfort caused by an injury, and only when the youngster is at rest. They should never be used in order to allow a youngster to participate or rehabilitate despite pain. If pain is masked, further participation can lead to re-injury and potential long-term problems for the young person.

(Information about useful pain medications, as well as about the uses and abuse of other drugs, will be found in the next chapter.)

Successful Rehabilitation

Successful rehabilitation from injury involves the return of muscular strength and endurance, balance and coordination, full motion and function of the injured area, overall physical fitness, and re-training in the specific skills required for the sport, in order to return to the previous performance level.

After this is achieved, care should be taken to avoid re-injury. If re-injury does not occur and the performance level is the same as or better than before the injury, then rehabilitation has been successful. If performance level cannot be re-achieved, the young athlete may need to be directed to another sport in which he or she can achieve a high level of performance or enjoyment, in spite of the lasting effects of the injury, and without causing further injury or damage.

In some cases in which re-injury is predictable because of the nature of the sport, the young athlete might best be directed early in the recovery process to another sport in which the risk for re-injury or life-long damage is decreased. This would allow the youngster to stay active in a sport in which he or she can perform well, without fear of chronic injury or a resulting degenerative process.

21.
Medications—Uses and Abuses

IN GENERAL, THERE ARE a number of medications that are proposed to hasten the recovery from an injury and to allow individuals to perform in the face of injury or pain. They offer little or nothing to enhance performance, or promote healing in children. They may, on the other hand, cause problems. Simply stated, in children the risk of taking certain medications for athletic injuries is usually greater than any potential benefit that can be derived from their use.

Parents and others interested in the well-being of children and youth in sports and athletics should be particularly cautious about medications and drugs recommended for their children. The risk/benefit ratio of each recommended drug should be determined carefully and critically. Obviously, if the benefits of using a medication negate the risks involved, then it may merit use. But, when the risks outweigh the potential good, there is no indication for the use of the medication, in athletes or others.

Of all the categories of drugs used in treating athletic injuries the following deserve particular attention and scrutiny: anti-inflammatory pills, cortisone injections, pain pills and injections, testosterone and anabolic steroids, medications (enzymes) to decrease swelling, stimulants (pep pills), and diuretics (water pills and injections).

Anti-Inflammatory Drugs

Aspirin adds the benefit of reducing pain to that of reducing inflammation in joints, tendons, bursas, and tissues surrounding them. It also has value in lessening the severity of aches and pains due to vigorous participation. Yet, even as safe as aspirin is when correctly used, it can be overused and abused. In cases of childhood rheumatoid arthritis or other specific medical situations for which the child is under the care of the physician, the use of large amounts of aspirin or other related anti-inflammatory drugs is acceptable—as long as the parent is careful to ensure that the child is not given more than is prescribed and that doses are given at the correct time intervals. Bleeding from the stomach or aggravation of an underlying ulcer are potential problems with increased use of aspirin.

Butazolidin® is also an anti-inflammatory medication generally used for tendonitis, bursitis and some forms of arthritis. Stronger than aspirin, this drug has a very limited value for the very young athlete and should be used only for limited lengths of time and under medical supervision. It can have side effects such as gastrointestinal (GI) upset or bleeding, and it can suppress the production of blood cells, potentially causing numerous other problems.

When Butazolidin® is prescribed, it is usually used for five to ten days under close medical supervision, and is taken by mouth with food or milk. In general, this and other related drugs now available or soon to be generally available, will be used rarely in treating youngsters. Their use should always be discussed frankly with the doctor.

DMSO is yet another drug advocated by many as offering great resolution of the inflammation and pain associated with sprains and tendon injuries. Not available in the United States by prescription because it has not yet been released for general use by the Food and Drug Administration (FDA), the drug has been shown (in some studies) to be acceptable for human use. However, there is no reason for DMSO to be used in childhood injuries, even if someday approved for general use. The child has such great healing capabilities that, given time and a chance, most injuries will heal rapidly.

Cortisone does not hasten tissue healing as some people think. It can, in some instances, hasten the resolution of inflammation in the tissues, and it's possible the inflammation may not return. But cortisone can have some very deleterious effects on joints and tendons when injected repeatedly into them. It can hasten the wear and tear changes and contribute to premature arthritis. And, when used by mouth, the drug affects almost every system in the body. It's almost never taken by mouth for a childhood athletic injury.

Cortisone is a corticosteroid which is naturally produced by the body's endocrine system and its continued use can result in changes in the adrenal glands. It has the potential (orally) to reduce the body's natural response to infection and resistance to infection and may cause changes in certain aspects of the body's metabolism, among other effects.

The most popular use of cortisone and related synthetic compounds is for dealing with inflammatory problems, by injecting it directly into the affected area. Cortisone injected locally has little effect on the rest of the body, but it is rarely used in childhood. Its ability, in some instances, to hasten the resolution of inflammation in the tissues is transitory. If someone suggests its use for a childhood athletic injury, there should be serious questioning of the reasons, risks and benefits—and a second opinion should be considered if multiple injections are proposed. The use of such medications adds little to what rest and time and youth's fantastic healing capabilities can accomplish.

Pain Medications

Pain is nature's way of telling us that we should not be doing what we are doing, or that something may be wrong. The use of any artificial substance that overrides the body's warning system is potentially damaging and foolish, especially when dealing with athletic injuries in children. Yet we see cases in which young athletes use a medication to relieve pain so they can continue participating in a sport, or to push the body past its limits. In these cases, there's enormous risk of further injury, and of serious permanent damage or disability.

Insofar as pain medications go, aspirin and acetominophen (for example, Tylenol®, Datril®, and others) are most commonly used for children; aspirin offers an added benefit of giving some relief of inflammation. These are relatively safe if used prudently and infrequently. And they should be used for relief of pain that is present at rest, not during participation. When a child is in pain, we need to heed the warning signs and insist that the youngster rest. If pain persists it should be evaluated and explained by a physician, and appropriate measures taken to insure recovery.

Stronger pain medications such as codeine, Darvon®, Demerol®, Talwin®, and morphine should be used *only* for short periods of time, when a serious injury causes severe pain, and *only* under the direction of a physician. Although adults often use these drugs, they should *not* give their own prescription medication to children unless advised to do so by a physician.

These medications, like the others, should not be given in order to allow further participation, or to produce enough increase in pain tolerance for a youngster to play or work out. *Overriding the body's warning signals has no place in childhood athletics.* It can result in more serious permanent damage when continued participation is added to the stress of injury.

Injecting a joint, muscle or tendon directly with pain relieving medication (numbing shots) so a youngster can play is not consistent with the advisable medical care of a young person.

Pills to Decrease Swelling

There are a few specially developed medications—enzymes—which work very much as meat tenderizers do, breaking down blood products and reducing the swelling results from injury. These supposedly hasten the body's resolution of tissue damage from injury. Taken orally, these drugs are not particularly effective, and their injection into injured tissue is also of questionable value.

Hyaluronidase (tissue-spreading enzyme) is supposed to help spread out the swelling so the body can absorb it faster. It is sometimes mixed (in a "cocktail") with cortisone, another anti-inflammatory drug, or an anesthetic agent such as xylocaine or novocaine. Injected into an injured area to block pain, while it reputedly also reduces the amount of swelling and decreases subsequent inflammation, it has no place in childhood athletics. Its use (at least in a novocaine or xylocaine mixture) simply stops pain from being felt. The tissue may sustain more severe damage as participation continues.

Testosterone and Anabolic Steroids

Testosterone is the male hormone associated with the development of greater muscle bulk. Because of its known effects, some people have recommended its use to build bulk and strength in athletes. However, there is controversy in the medical literature as to the validity of claims about testosterone and increased muscle function and mass. Although there are athletes who take the drug and insist that there is benefit, this has not been proved scientifically in the United States.

The question arises—will a female using testosterone show greater effects than the male and become stronger? Some countries use this drug selectively for their female athletes to strengthen them. Some of the changes the women sustain are irreversible—that is, they do not disappear completely when the hormone is stopped. The female who uses this hormone often experiences an increase in facial and body hair, develops a deeper voice, and may have a cessation of menstrual periods. Likewise the drug may be problematical for the young preadolescent boy who uses it. Although this is a normal hormone for boys and men (and even in girls, the adrenal gland produces a small amount of this hormone normally), its use prior to puberty may start puberty early. In addition, the boy may grow to less than his predicted height. The effect of the testosterone on parts of the body other than muscles simply does not warrant its use. Anyone who suggests its use to enhance athletic performance in a young person (male or female) should be questioned seriously and another opinion should be sought.

Anabolic steroids are synthetic male hormones which are used (as testosterone) to build muscle mass. Like testosterone, they also develop the male secondary sex characteristics, although this aspect is said to be decreased. Essentially, they have the same effects on males and females that testosterone has, as well as the same potential side effects and risks. The effects of testosterone and anabolic steroids on part of the body (other than muscle) do not warrant their use in males or females.

Increasing muscle mass or strength can be achieved naturally through proper conditioning and weight training methods, without unnecessary side effects and undue risks. This is obviously a much healthier and safer way to improve strength and athletic performance. And young athletes should understand that there is still controversy among experts as to whether or not testosterone or anabolic steroids even do what they are claimed to do.

Stimulants (pep pills)

There has been recent publicity concerning the use of stimulants—both prescription and of street origin—by professional athletes. Those who use them believe that their ability to perform is enhanced, and that they have more strength and endurance for longer periods of time. Studies have shown this belief to be an illusion—in general, performance may be worse rather than better with drug use, and judgment probably suffers as well.

The use of stimulants by the young athlete has no place in sports or in good health. Parents and others should be aware of the potential for abuse of newer compounds (speed, uppers, "bennies," etc.) which are available over-the-counter in stores and on the street. (For more information see Chapter 6.)

Diuretics for Weight Control

Although not officially sanctioned, the use of diuretics or water pills has been a common practice for quick weight loss in athletes. This is particularly so in wrestling, boxing and other sports in which weight class is important in competition. But the use of these drugs, which can cause serious disturbances of salt and water balance in the body, should be condemned. This chemical disturbance in the body can be further accentuated by the profuse sweating associated with exercise.

Points to Remember

➤ In general, the injured young athlete heals well and usually responds to rest and protection alone. Once the rehabilitation period, whether long or short, is complete, the young athlete is usually able to re-establish full performance.

➤ The use of medications to enhance performance, to control severe pain, or to hasten recovery from injury is seldom, if ever, indicated in the young child or adolescent.

➤ If a drug for pain or healing is indicated, a frank discussion with the doctor should reveal why the drug is recommended, its benefits, its risks, and its possible complications.

22.

What Everyone Should Know about Safety and First Aid

WHEN A YOUNGSTER IS injured in an athletic event, whether organized or not, the most important thing to remember is that the damage has already been done. Panic and overreaction will help no one. The point of first aid *in every situation* is to evaluate the problem, then take appropriate steps to ensure that more damage does not occur because of hasty movement. Simply, the goal is to control the existing problem without compounding it.

In organized sports, there should always be someone in control of the situation—either the coach, the trainer or a physician. Parents and others should try to remain calm and let these professionals do what needs to be done. In unorganized events or activities, someone needs to take control of the situation and direct others who might be of some help. It may be a parent or other adult, or even a responsible young athlete.

The Importance of First Aid Knowledge

Most athletic injuries in youngsters will require the administration of basic first aid. It is highly recommended that parents take the time to complete a course in basic first aid, including training in CPR (cardiopulmonary resuscitation), even if their child is not particularly athletic or active. *All* children are hurt from time to time, and need informed, capable on-the-spot attention.

It's important to know what to do—and what *not* to do. Less panic and more control over the situation is the goal. And, when serious injuries occur, or those rare life-threatening situations happen, parents will be equipped to take vital action, instead of standing around helplessly. This is particularly important when one is faced with accidents which occur in remote areas where paramedics or other emergency assistance is very distant, or totally unavailable.

Classes are available through the American Heart Association (for CPR), the American Red Cross and many community hospitals as well as other community and civic organizations. Youngsters, at about the age of 12, can also benefit from training in both first aid and CPR, and should be encouraged to learn. Knowing how to perform basic cardiac life support and basic first aid is important not only for those involved in sports, but also may be useful in saving a life under other circumstances. Having the knowledge and skill to determine what can and cannot be accomplished is reassuring to anyone.

Life-threatening Emergencies and Their Management

The ultimate emergency is one in which a person is not breathing, and in which the heart is not circulating the blood. If breathing and circulation are not resumed, attention to other injuries or problems will be useless. The first goal of first aid is *to determine whether or not the person is breathing and has a heart beat. The next goal is to start these two functions if they are not present.*

The youngster who is not breathing and has no heartbeat (has *arrested*)—is unconscious and usually pale or blue. When you find a person like this, first *check for breathing.* Feel for air movement in front of the nose or mouth or watch for chest movement. If there is none, first *clear the airway.* Check the mouth for any material that is blocking the throat and remove it. Begin resuscitation, as taught in the basic CPR courses.

Sometimes, there is obstruction to air flow in the respiratory system, and just clearing the mouth is not successful in re-establishing breathing. If the person is choking, *and unable to talk,* attempts to clear the airway should be made. This may be done by giving the person sharp blows on the back between the shoulder blades, or by squeezing the person's abdomen sharply—as in a "bear-hug"—so air rushes out of the mouth. (See basic cardiopulmonary resuscitation (CPR) course material for further details.)

After assuring that the airway is clear, *check for a heartbeat* by checking the pulse in the neck, just under the large muscle that runs from the chin to the shoulder (the carotid pulse). If there is no pulse, *chest compressions* must be started as well, and CPR continued

*Direct pressure over a wound will
usually control bleeding.*

until assistance arrives, or until the person resumes breathing and has
a heartbeat.

NOTE: The successful resuscitation of a person who has no
heartbeat is based on prompt recognition of the problem, and quick,
competent institution of basic life support. In order to do these maneuvers correctly, one *must* learn them in a certified CPR course,
and practice the techniques until they are "second nature." This
brief summary is *not* intended to replace a course, or to be complete
in teaching one the necessary techniques to save a life. Don't wait—
complete a course in CPR.

First-Aid Basics

Controlling of Bleeding

Bleeding of most wounds can be controlled on the spot with direct
pressure over the wound. Place a clean (sterile, if possible) cloth,
gauze or piece of clothing directly over the wound and apply even,
firm pressure for *10 to 20 minutes* without releasing the pressure to
check the bleeding. If it is apparent that bleeding has not slowed or
stopped appreciably, a bandage (cloth, tape, etc.) can be wrapped
snugly around the bleeding area, and medical help sought.

If it appears that a major artery or vein has been severed, direct
pressure over the laceration or injury should continue until medical
help arrives, or the youngster can be taken to an emergency care center for specific repair. There is almost no place for the use of a tourniquet to control bleeding—direct pressure is more effective, and

To help control shock when there is no head or neck injury, keep the young person calm and elevate the legs.

tourniquets can be dangerous if applied for long periods of time (gangrene may result).

Serious wounds of the chest can interfere with adequate breathing, especially if there is air entering through a wound. Both to control bleeding and to help with the ability to breathe, firm pressure should be applied to any chest wound.

With wounds of the eye, abdomen, the throat and front of the neck, and the male genitalia, only gentle or moderate pressure is indicated. It is important in these cases to seek medical attention immediately, or call paramedics if there are any in the area. Paramedics in most cities respond within a matter of minutes.

Treating Shock at the Scene

Shock is a condition in which the heart is unable to circulate enough blood to the rest of the body. It can be caused by many things, but with an injured person, loss of blood is usually the most pressing of its causes. Control of obvious bleeding is the cardinal principle of treatment of this kind of shock.

Another kind of shock may occur with injury—shock caused by the fright, pain and suddenness of the injury. This may be called a "visceral reaction," in which much of the blood is directed to the internal organs instead of to the brain and heart. This kind of "shock" often results in a simple "faint." It may also be noted as pallor, or a "green" look after injury, and the child may become nauseated, sweaty and even vomit.

The basic goal of shock treatment, regardless of its cause, is the return of better blood flow to vital organs. Control bleeding, if there is any, first. Have the injured person lie down. This allows better blood flow to the head. If there is no head injury, elevate the legs so even more blood is allowed to go to the head, but if there is a head injury, the person should lie flat. Keeping him or her calm is also essential, especially if the cause of the shock is thought to be the "visceral reaction." Beyond this, treatment requires specific medical attention of the injury. This means doing all possible for safe and rapid transport to a medical facility.

Caring for Head, Neck and Spinal Injuries

These more serious injuries deserve special consideration, and are dealt with specifically in Chapter 17. But the cardinal rule is, "First, do no harm."

Among the most serious of injuries are those in which an athlete has lost consciousness. The youngster must be approached carefully, so as not to further injure the brain or nervous system.

When approaching an unconscious youngster, if the airway is clear, and breathing and blood flow are adequate, then *proceed slowly.*

If the injured youngster is unconscious, *always assume that there may be a serious head or neck injury.* Do not move the youngster until professional help arrives, unless *absolutely* necessary. Inappropriate movement can, at times, mean the difference between a less severe and treatable injury, and a lifelong handicap. Even if the young person "comes to," he or she should not be moved or allowed to move until there is some assurance that there is no weakness or paralysis. Be especially wary of neck or spine injury if there is numbness or tingling of a body part, or if there is weakness or paralysis of one side of the body or the whole body. Be careful also if there is no movement of one body part, such as arm or leg, in the absence of known injury to that part. It is usually best to keep the injured person lying down, calm, still and warm until help arrives.

If it is necessary to move an unconscious person, try to immobilize the neck and back in the position in which the unconscious person was found, and move the victim as a block or log, supporting all parts. If the airway is partially blocked, move the neck *very* carefully to straighten the airway. Try not to pick up a child, even a very small one, to carry him or her alone.

Using Ice, Compression, Elevation (ICE)

An easy way to remember how to treat the common athletic injuries, in which there is swelling and/or bleeding is *ICE*—I for ice, C for compression and E for elevation.

ABOVE RIGHT.
*Ice aids in minimizing bleeding
and swelling.*

RIGHT.
*Compression applied by an elastic
wrap, as seen here on the ankle and
foot, will help control bleeding
and/or limit swelling.*

Ice applied to the injured area helps to minimize bleeding and swelling.

Compression over lacerations, muscle contusions, sprains and strains by an elastic wrap, will help control bleeding and also limit swelling. If an elastic wrap is not available, use any kind of cloth (as clean as possible), and wrap it around the area. Do not wrap the compression dressing so tightly that it blocks the returning blood flow from the rest of the extremity. With a laceration a clean cloth can be placed over the bleeding area and firm pressure applied to limit blood loss.

Elevation is extremely helpful as well in limiting swelling and controlling some pain. However, with injuries to an arm or leg, it is very important that the injured part not be allowed to hang down below the level of the heart. If the injury is to the trunk, the victim should be placed flat. (Head injuries are treated separately—see Chapter 17.)

In free play activities and other unorganized sports, as well as in organized activities, it is ideal to have equipment available to do these simple things in case of injury. Simple availability of elastic

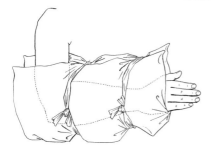

Splinting can be performed with special splinting materials or by use of cardboard slabs, wood, magazines, or a pillow (as shown here). The point is to immobilize the injured area.

bandages and proximity to a source of ice will make treatment of many athletic injuries much easier and more successful.

Splinting

If a fracture or dislocation appears to be the problem, no one except a physician should try to reduce (realign) it. Sometimes fractures or dislocations can damage a nearby growth plate, and motion or force may only increase the damage.

Splinting an injured part—arm, leg, hand or foot—limits motion and gives the area some protection so the athlete can be moved and transported with less pain, as shown in the illustration above. Although special splinting materials are available for purchase, cardboard slabs, wood, a pillow wrapped around an injury, or a stretcher can be used when professional equipment is not available. Use common sense and ingenuity in keeping an injury immobile.

As always, the first-aider should aim to prevent further injury, although splinting will minimize pain and discomfort. And, if the person assisting the victim is not sure whether an injury is a fracture, dislocation, strain, sprain or muscle bruise, it's best to splint the injury as a safety precaution. Ice, compression and elevation are helpful after splinting is completed to minimize swelling and bleeding. Remember, even if the damage is deep in the muscle or in the bone, swelling and bleeding are a normal response to injury.

Caring for Face, Eye and Nose Injuries

The face and scalp have a rich blood supply, so laceration to these areas may result in a frightening amount of bleeding. In most cases, these lacerations are not serious, and bleeding can be controlled with firm, steady pressure. Ice can also help in limiting bleeding. Stitches

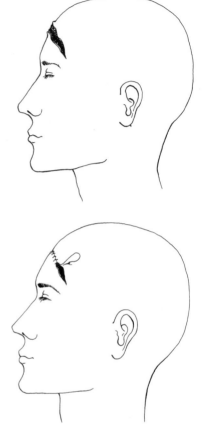

This open cut on the forehead is gaping and will need to be sutured (stitched up).

Suturing this same gaping wound will hasten healing and lessen scarring.

or other forms of closing a wound by a physician may be necessary to finally control bleeding.

Injuries to the eye can obviously be serious. Direct blows to the eye can cause bleeding inside the eye and damage to delicate internal structures. If an eye injury occurs, and pain or blurry vision result, patch the eye and take the injured youngster to an emergency care facility for further evaluation. If there is a penetrating injury to the eye, or a laceration to the eyeball itself, *do not* attempt to manipulate the eye. Cover it (or preferably both eyes) and go to an emergency facility immediately. Keep the injured youngster as calm and quiet as possible.

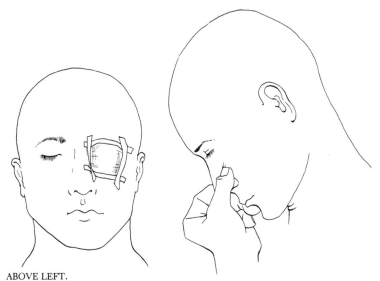

ABOVE LEFT.
Patching an injured eye protects it.

ABOVE RIGHT.
Pinching the nose minimizes bleeding and swelling when a nose bleed or broken nose occurs.

First aid for a broken nose is quite simple, although the effects of the injury may look awful. If a direct blow results in nose bleeding, pinch the nose to control bleeding and apply ice to minimize swelling and bleeding. Packing the nose may also be necessary, but should only be done by trained personnel. Alert the youngster to breathe through the mouth. See a physician for evaluation. It is difficult to know if a nasal fracture is present unless there is an obvious deformity. It often requires an X ray to know for sure if a nasal fracture is present. As a nose injury heals, there may be bruising and discoloration under the eyes as well as over and around the nose.

Caring for the Injured in Remote Areas

With the increase in backpacking and other sports and activities in remote areas, the possibility of injury occurring while a person is far from emergency assistance is present. When an injury is serious and help is limited, it is very difficult to decide what to do, especially with an unconscious victim. Given that each situation is different, here are some factors that merit consideration in making the decision about whether to go for help or wait for someone to arrive, or whether to attempt to transport the victim:

✓ The distance from the nearest emergency assistance, and response time.

✓ The condition of the injured person (including breathing and heartbeat, severity of shock, consciousness, bleeding and extent of obvious injuries).

✓ The size of the victim and the number of persons available to help, if any.

✓ The equipment available (stretcher, splints, cervical collar, etc.).

If more than one other person is present, and a telephone is fairly near, it might be best for one person to stay with the injured person, and the other to go for help. If, on the other hand, the child is very small, and assistance cannot be obtained in a reasonable amount of time, it may be necessary to carefully and judiciously move the child. For suspected fractures, neck or back or head injuries, care should be taken to keep the youngster in the same position in which he or she was found, with as many people as possible helping to control and maintain the body's position.

Giving Medications

In general, medications should not be given to any injured athlete on the scene by anyone other than a physician or trained paraprofessional. Pain medications might mask a serious injury, or interfere with the doctor's assessment of the injury as to its severity or the presence of other damage, especially when the head or internal organs are injured.

Likewise, the administration of liquids or fluids to an injured person is not wise. One of the effects of a serious injury is nausea and vomiting, and food or liquid in the stomach could be aspirated (inhaled into the lungs) during vomiting. These factors are even more important if an injury is severe enough to require surgery. The presence of food or liquid in the stomach increases the risk from anesthesia and surgery.

First Aid Tips

- Stay calm.
- Evaluate the situation quickly but carefully, looking for hidden as well as obvious injury.
- Check to see if the youngster is breathing and the heart is functioning. If not, begin CPR without delay.
- Control any external bleeding.
- Do not give medication, food or liquids.
- Immobilize injured areas.
- Transport an injured person as expeditiously and carefully as possible, waiting for paramedics or ambulance when necessary and advisable.

Important:

- Learn CPR (cardiopulmonary resuscitation).
- Take a first aid course.
- Keep a simple first aid kit available. This should include bandages and dressings, elastic wraps, splint material and possibly antiseptic wipes. Availability of ice is ideal in caring for athletic injuries.

Safety First

Not all injuries can be prevented, even under the best conditions. But all care should be taken to make sports as safe as possible for our young people. A few simple safety rules help control injuries and lessen the potential severity of others.

The fact is, a significant number of athletic injuries to youngsters occur in unorganized sports where trained personnel are not available. But even in some organized sports there is a lack of attention to prevention.

Parents should ensure that organized sports in which their children participate have a safety plan in case of injury, and a person who will be responsible to see that it's carried out. Availability of necessary first aid equipment and safety equipment is likewise essential. This may be just knowing the response time of the paramedics and how to obtain their assistance. Indeed, these should also be considered ahead of time for unorganized sports.

Plan Ahead—Develop a Communications Network

The key to a successful safety and first aid program is a good communications system, based on the following:

➤ Know where an event will take place (field, track, etc.) ahead of time. Write down the cross streets.
➤ Find out where the paramedics or an ambulance can enter the field, so instructions can be given. If a locked gate is involved, who has the key and how can they be reached?
➤ Know how you'll contact emergency medical care—where's the nearest phone, is it a pay phone (you'll need change), who will go for help, and where is their car if transportation is necessary?
➤ If an injured player will be transported to an emergency facility by private vehicle rather than paramedics or ambulance, do you have the number of the nearest emergency facility so you can notify them that a seriously injured athlete is on the way?
➤ A responsible adult should have on hand a "consent to treat" form for each athlete, signed by a parent, and the names and telephone numbers of contact persons in case of injury. These should be available at the event, not in a file or a desk drawer.
➤ Coaches and trainers and other supervising adults should be aware of any medical problems of youngsters, and any medications being taken by them.

Points to Remember

➤ Someone should be responsible for ensuring that playing conditions are safe (equipment, fields, floors, etc.)
➤ Proper protective equipment must be available and worn by each participant. Shin guards, face guards, helmets, hip and knee pads, mouth guards and the like must fit properly, and participants must be dressed appropriately and safely for the event and weather.

Coaching should be appropriate for the age and competition level. Children should not be pushed to perform beyond their ability, and workouts, training and conditioning should be reasonable and directed toward good health, physical fitness and fun, particularly in younger age groups.

⌒ Injured children should not be allowed to participate until enough time for recovery and reconditioning have passed, and return to function is complete.

⌒ Parents should ensure that medications to lessen pain or enhance performance are not permitted during sports participation.

⌒ Rules in sports are designed for safety as well as fairness. Good officiating can result in fewer and less serious injuries—and more fun.

⌒ Time for stretching and warm-up before an activity or competition is important in lessening injury occurrence.

⌒ Plenty of water and fluids should be made available to the young athlete during workouts and competition.

Glossary

Aerobic metabolism—The body's "burning" of fuel by a mechanism which depends upon oxygen to convert glucose (sugar) to energy

Abrasion—Superficial scraping damage to the skin, usually caused by falling or sliding

Aggression—The intent to inflict harm on another person; to show hostility

Amputation—Loss or severing of a limb or part of a limb

Anaerobic metabolism—The body's mechanism of energy production from a special carbohydrate, glycogen, without oxygen

Anemia (Anemic)—A condition in which a person is low in red blood cells and hemoglobin, the oxygen-carrying material in the blood cell

Angulated fracture—A break in a bone in which the two ends of the break are bent at an angle

Amphetamines—"Uppers," stimulants which increase the body's rate of metabolism. May have harmful effects on the cardiovascular system

Antihistamines—Medications used for allergy problems. Sleepiness is a side effect for many people

Anti-inflammatory Drugs—Medications used for injuries to reduce inflammation. They may be especially useful in some joint problems

Apophysis—A growth plate that appears as an "offshoot" from the bone; often an area where a muscle-tendon unit attaches in the young athlete

Arterial bleeding—Bleeding from an artery, a blood vessel that carries blood from the heart to various parts of the body. Bleeding is rapid and may spurt from the lacerated vessel, because blood is pumped through arteries with force

Arthrogram—Special X ray used in evaluating joint problems. A contrast dye is injected directly into the joint; an X ray is taken to determine the distribution of the dye, whether the joint structure is normal and whether or not there are tears in capsule, ligaments or cartilage

Arthroscopy—A procedure in which a fiberoptic lens system is inserted through small incisions and allows a surgeon to see inside a joint. The joint surfaces and structures are visualized directly or may be visualized on a television screen

Aspirin—A commonly used and readily available drug to ease pain. It has an anti-inflammatory effect on joints, tendons and some of the tissues surrounding them

Asthma—A chronic respiratory disorder which may be associated with labored breathing and wheezing

Baseline nutritional requirements—Minimum daily food intake for good health

Biopsy—Surgical removal of a tissue sample for microscopic examination to determine whether or not it is abnormal

Bone scan—A special diagnostic test in which a small amount of radioactive material is injected into the body so that the bones undergoing rapid change in a certain area can be more fully detailed. Radioactive material accumulates around the affected or injured area of bone

Brain swelling (Cerebral Edema)—A very serious condition usually caused by a contusion or intracranial bleeding; the brain swells, causing a rise of pressure inside the skull.

Brainstem—An extension of the spinal cord located at the base of the skull; controls breathing, heart function, some eye movements and reflexes

Bruise—Contusion; an injury to a body tissue caused by external force

Bulking up—Term used in athletics for weight gain, usually interpreted to be an increase in muscle mass

Burner—Temporary injury to the bundle of nerves which control the shoulder and arm. May be associated with soft-tissue injuries of the neck and area of the armpit. Electrical shock sensations and muscle weakness in the shoulder and arms may occur

Bursa—Fluid-filled sac between moving tissues such as bones and tendons. Serves to lubricate and reduce friction where a tendon passes adjacent to a bony structure

Bursitis—Inflammation of the bursa

Caffeine—A stimulant which increases heartbeat and reaction time; causes insomnia, restlessness and stomach disorders

Caloric intake—Amount of potential energy eaten as food by a person

Calorie—A unit of available heat or energy. Food value is often spoken of in terms of calories

Callus—1. A fibrous tissue formed over irritated portions of the skin. 2. A fibrous tissue formed during healing of a bone fracture. This callus holds the bone firmly in place, and is later itself converted into bone

Carbohydrate—One type of food substance usually easily digested and converted into energy. Sugars and starches are carbohydrates

Carbohydrate loading—Increasing intake of carbohydrates before an athletic event to increase glycogen in muscles, thereby increasing energy available for those muscles. Only minimally effective unless the athlete is performing for long periods of time

Cardiopulmonary Resuscitation (CPR)—Revival of a person who has no breathing and/or heartbeat by instituting Basic Life Support techniques

Cardiovascular—Referring to the heart and blood circulation system

Cartilage—A substance softer than bone which forms a cushion where bones form joints. Important in joint function and wear. There are different types of cartilage with specialized functions

Cast—A fully encircling, rigid device used to protect an injured part. Traditionally made of plaster and used to immobilize broken bones. Some newer forms of cast material are lighter and more resistant to water

CAT Scan (Computerized Axial Tomography)—A new diagnostic technique which makes "pictures" from thin slices of tissue—bones as well as soft tissues. May be used to examine the head, abdomen, spine and bones in greater detail than allowed by other forms of X ray

Cerebral—Referring to the head or brain

Cervical—Referring to the neck

Cervical collar—A soft neck brace used to support and limit motion of joints, muscles and/or ligaments of the neck

Cervical vertebrae—First seven vertebrae or bones located in the neck

Chondromalacia—Condition in which the articular (joint) cartilage becomes worn and irregular, usually because of repeated injury or altered mechanics of the joint

Clavicle—Collarbone

Closed reduction—Repositioning or "setting" a fracture without making a surgical incision

Cocaine—An illegal drug which gives the feeling of extra energy and euphoria

Coccyx—Tailbone

Competitive—Vying with another; enjoying a challenge; expressing excellence; striving to be the winner

Complex Fracture—Two types—1. *Comminuted fracture*—several broken areas in the same bone; shattered; 2. *Compound fracture*—the bones break and the ends separate, with broken end(s) puncturing the skin

Complete Blood Count (CBC)—Blood analysis to determine the number, shapes and kinds of red and white blood cells, as well as other components of the blood

Compression fracture—Ends of the bones are forced together during the injury, shortening the bone or altering its shape

Concussion—Head injury which results in loss of consciousness and temporary changes in brain function

Congenital disorders—Disorders which exist at or from birth

Consciousness—Level of alertness and orientation

Contusion—Bruise; injury to skin, muscle or bone usually caused by an external force (e.g. blow or striking a fixed object)

Cortisone—One of a group of naturally occurring hormones of the body; sometimes injected into joints or soft tissues to reduce inflammation.

Often effective, but may have undesirable side effects and is used sparingly in children

Cystic Fibrosis—A hereditary disease which affects many body functions, most often seriously affecting the lungs as well as other organs

Development—Increase in complexity of function; maturation rather than increase in size

Diabetes Mellitus—A disease of the body's metabolism in which sugar is excreted intermittently or continuously in the urine and is elevated in the blood. It may require use of insulin to control the abnormality

Diathermy—A type of deep-heat treatment for rehabilitation of musculoskeletal disorders

Diskitis—Inflammation of the intervertebral discs (soft structures between vertebrae which act as cushions)

Dislocation of a joint—Slippage of the bones of a joint out of normal alignment. Commonly referred to as "out of joint"

Displaced fracture—A broken bone in which the major pieces are out of normal alignment. May be angulated, separated, shortened or rotated

Diuretics—"Water pills" which dehydrate (dry out) the cells of the body and cause the kidneys to excrete extra water. Used for quick weight loss; can cause disturbances of salt and water balance

DMSO—An anti-inflammatory medication not licensed for use in the United States at the present time

Dysmenorrhea—Cramping associated with the menstrual cycle

Ecchymosis—Bluish discoloration of soft tissue and skin associated with bleeding in the tissue. Often the bleeding is caused by a blow to or tearing of the deep tissue

Electromyogram (EMG)—A test of muscles and peripheral nerves where small needles or surface patch-like electrodes are placed in or over a muscle, and the electrical activity of the muscle is recorded

Endurance—Quality of sustaining performance over a period of time

Epidural hematoma—Arterial bleeding inside the skull over the surface of the brain. Such bleeding causes increased intracranial pressure and may be life-threatening

Epidural venogram—A test for disc disease or epidural tumor in which contrast dye is injected into a blood vessel of the lower leg and travels into the area of the spine. If there is a protruding disc, there is a distortion of the vein pattern in the spinal canal area, suggesting disc disease

Epiphysis—A cap-like portion at the end of a bone in a child

Estrogen—Female hormone

Femur—Large bone of the thigh

Fibula—The smaller of the two bones in the lower leg

Fine motor skills—Abilities which requires use of smaller muscles, especially hands

Floorburns—Skin burns or abrasions resulting from falls or sliding injuries

Fracture—Break in a bone

Glucose—A simple sugar used by the body for energy production

Glycogen—A storage form of sugar, stored in muscle and liver

Greenstick fracture—An incomplete break in a bone. The outer surface breaks or splinters, but the bone is not cracked through and through

Gross motor skills—Ability to control large movements of the body and wide movements of the trunk, arms and legs

Growth—Increase in physical size

Growth plate—The area of the bone where growth takes place. In long bones, it is located at the ends of bones, near joints

Heart murmur—An extra noise heard during heart action. May be loud or soft, significant or insignificant.

Heat stroke—A serious, life-threatening condition caused by exposure to extreme heat. The body's temperature regulating system fails and the body temperature rises to dangerous levels. Symptoms are dizziness, nausea, lack of sweating and headache, followed by loss of consciousness

Hemiplegia—Paralysis of one side of the body

Herniation of intervertebral disc—Damage to the cushioning disc between vertebrae causing it to rupture out of place. It may cause pressure on an adjacent nerve (i.e. pinched nerve)

Hormone—Complex chemical substance produced by many parts of the body; circulates in the blood and stimulates functional activity

Hyaluronidase—An enzyme (chemical) which works as a tissue-spreading factor and permits wider infiltration of injected medication

Immobilization—Prevention of motion of a portion of the body; often used after an injury

Infection—A disease process caused by the invasion of germs (bacteria, viruses, fungi). With bacterial infection, there is often formation of pus and sometimes tissue destruction results

Internal fixation—Insertion of pins, screws or plates to hold the ends of a broken bone together while healing occurs

Interval Training—Combination of aerobic and anaerobic conditioning which is used to increase speed

Intracranial bleeding—Bleeding inside the skull, inside or around the brain

Intramural—Within a given school, as opposed to against other schools

Intravenous Pyelogram (IVP)—an X ray test to determine kidney function. Contrast dye is injected into a vein, and as the dye travels through the kidneys, X rays are taken to follow its progress

Isokinetic exercise—Specialized form of muscle building and conditioning in which the resistance remains constant through the range of motion

Isometric exercise—Exercise which builds muscles through tension and resistance against an immobile object. No joint motion takes place

Isotonic exercise—Exercise which builds strength and muscle mass by shortening and lengthening of the muscle with resistance and joint motion

Kidneys—Two fist-sized organs which remove waste products from the blood and produce urine. Located deep in the abdomen on each side of the spine, just under the rib cage

Kyphosis—Humpback deformity

Laceration—Cut in skin and/or underlying tissue

Lactic acid—By-product of the use of glycogen. Builds up in muscles and causes feeling of muscle fatigue and discomfort

Legg-Perthe Disease—Condition in which there is a disturbance in blood supply to the epiphysis (cap on the end of the bone) of the femur. May result in a change in shape of the hip joint

Ligament—Tough, elastic structure which connects bone to bone

Little League elbow—Fragmentation or injury of the growth plate in a developing elbow. Caused by overstraining the elbow, especially by throwing too often and too hard at a young age. Throwing "curve balls" should be discouraged in the childhood pitcher

Liver—A large organ located in the upper right side of the abdomen. A "factory" which purifies blood and makes proteins and many other crucial body substances

Loose joints—Term used to describe the laxity and flexibility associated with certain body types

Lumbar vertebrae—Five vertebrae in the lower back

Marijuana—An illegal drug which is smoked or eaten for pleasure. Causes feelings of euphoria, altered perception, a sense of unreality and slowing of reactions

Menopause—A woman's change of life, during which estrogen production by the ovaries ceases

Menstrual cycle—Monthly shedding of blood and tissue of the uterus, caused by hormone fluctuations in women

Metabolism—Process of converting body fuel to energy

Metaphysis—The portion of a bone shaft adjacent to the growth plate

Musculoskeletal system—Bones, joints, muscles and their supporting structures

Myelogram—An X ray study of the spine in which a contrast dye is injected into the sac around the spinal cord, then X rays are taken to look for disruptions in the column of dye

Myositis ossificans—Complication of a muscle bruise in which abnormal bone deposits occur in a muscle often associated with swelling, pain and restricted adjacent joint motion while the new bone is forming

Neuromuscular—Referring to the interaction between the nervous system and the muscles

Nicotine—A drug found in cigarettes. A mild stimulant which increases heart rate, and may cause headache and nausea

Nondisplaced fracture—A broken bone that is not out of alignment

Open surgical reduction—Repositioning or "setting" a fracture by surgery

Osgood-Schlatter Disease—A disorder of the growth plate just below the knee, where the tendon of the quadriceps muscle attaches to the tibia. Causes pain and tenderness, but is not serious

Pancreas—Small organ important in both digestion and insulin production. Located in the middle of the abdomen

Paralysis—Loss of ability to move a portion of the body as a result of nerve dysfunction

Paraplegia—Paralysis of the lower limbs

Patella—Kneecap

PCP (Angel dust)—An illegal and dangerous drug which creates a feeling of total control. Hallucinations of feats of extreme strength are common

Pedicles—Special areas at the sides of the vertebrae forming a portion of the spinal canal

Pigeon-toed—The toes and feet turn inward toward each other. Usually is not a problem but in its more severe forms may cause difficulty in running

Placebo—"Fake" drug containing no active ingredients

Placebo effect—Helping effect seen when a person takes a placebo. Thinking a drug will be helpful often makes it so

Psych up—Mental preparation for a competition

Puberty—Time of development of sexual maturity. Boys usually reach puberty between 12 and 15, and girls between 10 and 14, on the average

Quadriplegia—Paralysis of all four limbs

Reduction—Realignment or repositioning of an altered body structure. "Setting" of a broken bone or repositioning of a dislocated joint

Rehabilitation—Reestablishment of full function and strength after an injury or illness

Resistance exercise—Exercise in which muscles work against a weight or force

Rotational injury—Twisting injury. May be associated with varying degrees of soft-tissue injury, torn ligaments and fracture of bones

Sacrum—Platelike shield of bone at the lower end of the spine

Scoliosis—Curvature of the spine. A condition most commonly affecting adolescent girls

Sedative—A drug which decreases reaction time, calms and/or induces sleep

Seizure—Convulsion. Jerking of limbs and torso in response to an electrical or chemical imbalance in the nervous system

Sever's Disease—Irritation of the growth plate of the heel. Aggravated by the shock of running or playing on hard surfaces, and resulting in heel pain. Not a serious condition

Shin splints—Pain experienced in the shin following running, and often associated with training errors

Shock—A condition in which the heart is not able to circulate enough blood to the rest of the body, usually caused by injury or loss of blood. May be life-threatening unless treated immediately

Sickle Cell Anemia, Sickle Cell Trait—Chronic, hereditary anemia or blood disorder most often found in black people

Simple fracture—Break which goes straight through a bone

Skull fracture—Break in one of the bones of the head

Slipped capital femoral epiphysis—Slippage of the growth plate area in the hip, which may result in a malformation of the hip joint

Spina bifida—Congenital malformation of the spine, associated with varying degrees of nervous system damage, including paralysis and sensory loss

Spinal cord—A highly organized nervous structure located in the spinal canal. Formed of bundles of nerves which transmit signals to and from the brain and all parts of the body

Spinal shock—A temporary reaction by the spinal cord to injury. Results in varying degrees of dysfunction of the spinal cord

Spleen—A fist-sized organ of the immune system, located in the upper left part of the abdomen; contains blood and bleeds easily when injured

Splint—One-sided, rigid material applied with a wrap to an injured part in order to immobilize it

Spondylolisthesis—A condition in which there is slippage of one vertebra upon another

Sprain—Injury to a ligament

Stamina—The ability to function steadily over time

Straddle injury—Injury resulting from falling with the legs apart over an object. Common in gymnasts and cyclists, and may result in a genital injury

Strain—Injury to a muscle-tendon unit

Stress fracture—Break in a bone due to repeated stress rather than from one episode of trauma

Stress X ray—X ray taken while a joint is stressed to try to "open up" an area of disruption. Shows damage to ligaments and tendons because they would normally give the joint stability with the stress

Subcutaneous tissue—Structures under the skin and above the deep structures

Subdural hematoma—A blood collection inside the skull over the surface of the brain. Results in increased pressure on the brain

Subluxation—Partial displacement or slippage of a joint out of correct alignment

Tailbone fracture—Breaking of the lowest portion of the spine (tailbone)

Tendon—Tough but elastic structure which connects muscle to bone

Tendonitis—Inflammation of a tendon

Testosterone—Male hormone

Thoracic vertebrae—Twelve vertebrae of the back in the chest area. Vertebrae to which the ribs are attached

Tibia—the larger of the two bones of the lower leg. Shin bone

Tight joints—Term used to describe relative lack of ligamentous laxity characteristic of certain body types

Tomograms—X rays taken to focus on specific areas of a body part. Produce small "slices" (1 to 2 millimeter intervals) of the tissue

Torus fracture—"Buckle" fracture. One side of a long bone "buckles" without breaking all the way through the bone, leaving a "wrinkle" on the outer surface of the bone

Traction—A procedure which uses weights to pull the broken ends of a bone back into position

Traumatologist—A specialist in the care of injuries

Ultrasound—A diagnostic test which uses high-frequency sound waves to "visualize" structures of the body

Undescended testicle—A testicle which did not drop down into the scrotum early in development

Urinalysis—A study of the urine. Used to detect its components, both normal and abnormal

Vertebra (plural, Vertebrae)—One of the bones of the spine

Vertebral canal—Tube-like area running through the bones of the spine to encase the spinal cord

Walking tandem—Walking with one foot directly in front of the other

X ray—An outline produced when a special film is exposed to a small amount of radiation. Areas which are most dense are more resistant to the X rays, and block them out, leaving a white shadow on the film. Bones are very dense, so they show up white on X ray

Recommended Reading

Sports in America, James A. Michener, Fawcett, 1977.
Women & Sports, Janice Kaplan, Discus/Avon Books, 1979.
The Complete Book of Running, James J. Fixx, Random House, 1977.
The New Aerobics, Kenneth Cooper, Bantam Books, 1970.
Treatment of Injuries to Athletes, Don Horatio Donaghue, Saunders, 1970.

Bibliography

Adams, J.E. "Bone Injuries in Very Young Athletes." *Clinical Orthopedics* (1976): 58: 129.

Alderman, R.B. *Psychological Behavior in Sport.* Philadelphia: W.B. Saunders Company, 1974.

Balazs, Eva K. "Psycho-Social Study of Outstanding Female Athletes." *Research Quarterly* 46 (1975): 267–273.

Berkowitz, Leonard. "Sports Competition and Aggression," in *Sports Psychology: An Analysis of Athlete Behavior,* Straub, William F., ed. Ithaca, N.Y.: Mouvement Publications, 1978.

Borostrom, L. "Anatomic Lessons in Recent Sprains." *Acta Chin Scand* (1964) 128: 483–495.

Burke, Edmund J., and Kleiber, Douglas. "Psychological and Physical Implications of Highly Competitive Sports for Children." *The Physical Educator* (May 1976).

Calvert, Robert, Jr. "A Report on Athletic Injuries and Deaths in Secondary Schools and Colleges, 1975–1976." Department of Health, Education, and Welfare, 1976. 1–40.

Carron, Albert V. *Social Psychology of Sport.* Ithaca, New York: Mouvement Publications, 1980.

Chick, R.P., and Jackson, Douglas W. "Tears of the Anterior Cruciate Ligament in Young Athletes." *Journal of Bone and Joint Surgery,* Vol. 60A (October 1978): No. 7: 970–973.

Cohen, Ivan, et al. *The South African Textbook of Sports Medicine.* Johannesburg, South Africa: Sports Medicine Clinic, 1979.

Cohen, Sidney, "Angel Dust." *Journal of the American Medical Association.* August 1977. 238: 515–516.

Committee on Pediatric Aspects of Physical Fitness, Recreation, and Sports. "Injuries to Young Athletes." *Pediatrics* 1980. A53–A54.

Committee on Youth, American Academy of Pediatrics, and Committee on Adolescent Medicine, Canadian Pediatric Society. "Alcohol Consumption: An Adolescent Problem." *Pediatrics,* April 1975. 55: 557–559.

Committee on Youth. "A New Approach to Teenage Smoking." *Pediatrics,* April 1976. 57: 465–466.

Cooper, Lowell. "Athletics, Activity, and Personality: A Review of the Literature." *Research Quarterly* 1969. 40: 17–22.

Corran, Robert. "Violence and the Coach." *Coaching Review.* July 1978. 40: 45.

Crase, Cliff. "The 24th National Wheelchair Games." *Sports 'N' Spokes.* July/August 1980. 17–25.

Dominguez, Richard H. *The Complete Book of Sports Medicine.* New York: Charles Scribner's Sons, 1979.

Godshall, R.W. "The Predictability of Athletic Injuries: An Eight-Year Study." *Journal of Sports Medicine,* 1975. 3: 50–54.

Guyton, Arthur C. *Basic Human Physiology, Normal Function, and Mechanisms of Disease.* Philadelphia: W.B. Saunders Company, 1977.

Hunter, Letha Yurko. "The Female Athlete." *Resident and Staff Physician,* June 1980. 68–79.

Hurwitz, Samuel. "Medical Aspects of Adolescents Participating in Sports." *Western Journal of Medicine,* November 1974. 121: 443–447.

Jackson, Douglas W., and Feagin, John A. "Contriceps Contusions in Young Athletes: Relation of Severity of Injury to Treatment and Prognosis." *Journal of Bone and Joint Surgery,* January 1973. 55A: 95–105.

————, Ashley, Robert L., and Powell, John W. "Ankle Sprains in Young Athletes: Relation of Severity and Disability." *Clinical Orthopaedics,* July 1974. 101: 203–215.

————, and Wiltse, Leon L. "Low Back (Lumbar) Pain in the Young Athlete." *Clinical Orthopaedics,* July 1974. 101: 203–215.

————, and Bailey, Daniel. "Shin Splints in the Young Athlete: A Non-Specific Diagnosis." *The Physician and Sports Medicine,* March 1975. 3: 45–51.

————. "Myositis Ossificans in the Young Athlete." *The Physician and Sports Medicine,* October 1975. 3: 56–61.

————. "Athletes and Ankle Sprains." *Consultant,* October 1975. 15: 177–178.

————. "Shin Splints: Common, Painful, and Confusing." *Consultant,* February 1976. 16: 75–79.

————. "Ankle Sprains in Young Athletes." *Orthopaedic Audiosynopsis,* May 1976. Vol. 8, #2.

————, Wiltse, Leon L., and Cirincione, Robert J. "Spondylolysis in the Female Gymnast." *Clinical Orthopaedics,* June 1976. 117: 68–73.

————. "Chronic Rotator Cuff Impingement in the Young Athlete." *American Journal of Sports Medicine,* November 1976. 4: 231–240.

————, Jarrett, H.F., Bailey, D., Kausek, J., Swanson, J., and Powell, J.W. "Injury Prevention in the Young Athlete (A Preliminary Report)." *American Journal of Sports Medicine,* January 1978. 6: 6–14.

————. "Injury Prevention for the Athlete." (West Point program), 16mm optical sound production. American Academy of Orthopaedic Surgeons Film Library, 1974.

————. "Shoulder Impingement in the Athlete." *Orthopaedic Audiosynopsis,* June 1978. Vol. 10, #3.

————. "Videoarthroscopy: A Permanent Medical Record." *American Journal of Sports Medicine,* September 1978. 6: 213–216.

————. "Low Back Pain in Young Adults: How Useful Are Diagnostic Tests?" *Consultant,* September 1978. 18: 184–185, 188.

————. "Shin Splints: An Update." *The Physician and Sports Medicine,* October 1978. 6: 51–64.

————. "Shoulder Problems in Overhead, Overuse Sports (A Symposium)." *American Journal of Sports Medicine,* March 1979. 7: 138–144.

Kaplan, Janice. *Women & Sports.* New York: Avon Books, 1979.

Klavora, Peter, and Daniel, Juri V. *Coach, Athlete, and the Sport Psychologist.* Toronto: University of Toronto School of Physical and Health Education, 1979.

Kock, Raymond, Jackson, Douglas W., and Jones, Al. "Rehabilitation of Anterior Cruciate Ligament Injuries." (Houssels Foundation) Memorial Hospital Medical Center, Long Beach, California, 1979.

Krupp, Marcus A., and Chatton, Milton J. *Current Medical Diagnosis and Treatment.* Los Altos, California: Lange Medical Publishers, 1978.

Larsen, R.L. "Epiphyseal Injuries in the Adolescent Athlete." *Orthopedic Clinics of North America,* 1973. 4: 831–851.

————, and McMahan, R.O. "The Epiphysis and the Childhood Athlete." *Journal of the American Medical Association,* 1966. 196: 99–104.

Long-Hansen, N. "Fractures of the Ankle: Clinical Use of Genetic Roentgen Diagnosis and Genetic Reduction." *Arch. Surgery,* 1952. 64: 488.

Lorin, Martin I. *The Parents' Book of Physical Fitness for Children From Infancy Through Adolescence.* New York: Atheneum, 1978.

Louria, Donald B., et al. "Epidemiology of Drug Abuse with Some Comments on Prevention." *Pediatric Annals,* February 1973. 11–17.

Mathis, James L. "Psycho-Social Aspects of Drug Abuse by Modern Youth." *Medical College of Virginia Quarterly,* 1970. 6 (4): 187–190.

Michener, James A. *Sports in America.* New York: Fawcett Books, 1977.

Milman, Doris H., and Su, Wen-Huey, "Patterns of Illicit Drug and Alcohol Use Among Secondary School Students." *Pediatrics,* August 1973. 83: 314–320.

Mirkin, Gabe, and Hoffman, Marshall. *The Sports Medicine Book.* Boston: Little, Brown and Company, 1978.

Morgan, William P. "Personality Traits of Women in Team Sports vs. Women in Individual Sports." *Research Quarterly.* 38: 686–690.

————, et al. *Psychological Correlates of Success in Candidates for the 1972 Olympic Wrestling Team.* Seattle: American College of Sports Medicine, 1973.

————. "Prediction of Performance in Athletes," in *Coach, Athlete, and the Sports Psychologist.* Toronto: University of Toronto School of Physical and Health Education, Publications Division, 1979.

Morse, Robert M., and Hurt, Richard D. "Screening for Alcoholism." *Journal of the American Medical Association,* December 1979. 242: 2688–2690.

Nicholas, James A. "Injuries to Knee Ligaments: Relationships to Looseness and Tightness in Football Players." *Journal of the American Medical Association,* 1970. 212: 2236–2239.

Parish, Peter, M.D. *The Doctors' and Patients' Handbook of Medicines and Drugs.* New York: Alfred A. Knopf, Inc., 1977.

Pascoe, Delmer J., and Grossman, Moses, eds. *Quick Reference to Pediatric Emergencies.* Philadelphia: J.B. Lippincott Company, 1973.

Pescar, Susan C. "Adolescence—A Disease?" in *Memorial Mercury,* Memorial Hospital Medical Center, Long Beach, California, March/April 1978.

———— "The First Step," in *Memorial Mercury,* Memorial Hospital Medical Center, Long Beach, California, May/June 1978.

————, "20/20 Vision With My Fingertips," in *Memorial Mercury,* Memorial Hospital Medical Center, Long Beach, California, Volume 1, #2, 1979.

Rachum, A., and Associates. "Standard Nomenclature of Athletic Injuries." American Medical Association, Chicago, 1966, p. 21.

Reis, Harry T., and Jelsma, Beth. "A Social Psychology of Sex Differences," in *Sports Psychology, An Analysis of Athlete Behavior*, Straub, William F., ed. Ithaca, New York: Mouvement Publications, 1978.

Ryan, Allan J., moderator. "Alcohol and Athletes, A Round Table." *The Physician and Sports Medicine*, July 1979. 7: 39–51.

————. "Women In Sports—Are the 'Problems' Real?" *The Physician and Sports Medicine*, May 1975. 49–56.

Salter, R., and Harris, W.R. "Injuries Involving the Epiphyseal Plate." *Journal of Bone and Joint Surgery*, April 1963. 45A: 587–662.

Schonberg, S. Kenneth, et al. "Somatic Consequences of Drug Abuse Among Adolescents." *Pediatric Annals*, February 1973. 22–41.

Scott, J.P. "Sport and Aggression," in *Sports Psychology, An Analysis of Athlete Behavior*, Straub, William F., ed. Ithaca, New York: Mouvement Publications, 1978.

Shiller, Jack G. *Childhood Injury*. Briarcliff Manor, New York: Stein & Day, 1977.

Shneidman, M. Norman. "Soviet Sport Psychology in the 1970s and the Superior Athlete," in *Coach, Athlete, and the Sports Psychologist*, Klavora, Peter, and Daniels, Juri V., eds. Toronto: University of Toronto School of Physical and Health Education, 1979.

Singer, Robert N. *Coaching, Athletics, and Psychology*. New York: McGraw-Hill Book Company, 1972.

Smith, N.J., ed. *Sports Medicine for Children and Youth*. Columbus, Ohio: Ross Laboratories, 1979.

Smith, Nathan J. "Nutrition and the Young Athlete." *Pediatric Annals*, October 1978. 7: 49–63.

Staheli, Lynn T., ed. "Symposium on Common Orthopedic Problems." Pediatric Clinics of North America, 1977. Volume 24.

Straub, William F., ed. *Sports Psychology, An Analysis of Athlete Behavior*. Ithaca, New York: Mouvement Publications, 1978.

Suinn, Richard M. *Psychology in Sports, Methods and Applications*. Minneapolis: Burgess Publishing Company, 1980.

Tandy, Ruth E., and Loflin, Joyce. "Aggression and Sport, Two Theories." *Journal of Health, Physical Education, and Recreation*, June 1977. 44: 19–20.

Tashkin, Donald P., et al. "Subacute Effects of Heavy Marijuana Smoking on Pulmonary Function in Healthy Men." *New England Journal of Medicine*, January 1976. 294: 125–129.

Thorndike, Augustus, Jr. "Myositis Ossificans Traumatica." *Journal of Bone and Joint Surgery*, April 1940. 22: 315–323.

Torg, J., and Quendenfeld, T. "The Effects of Shoe Type and Cleat Length in Incidence and Severity of Knee Injuries Among High School Football Players." *Research Quarterly*, 1971. 42: 203.

Tullos, H.S., and King, J.W. "Reasons of the Pitching Arm in Adolescents." *Journal of the American Medical Association*, 1972. 220: 264.

Tutko, Thomas A., and Richards, Jack W. *Psychology of Coaching*. Boston: Allyn and Bacon, Inc., 1971.

Ungerleider, J. Thomas, and Bowen, Haskell L. "Drug Abuse and the Schools." *American Journal of Psychiatry*, June 1969. 125: 105–111.

Wetli, Charles V., and Wright, Ronald K. "Death Caused by Recreational Cocaine Use." *Journal of the American Medical Association*, June 1979. 241: 2519–2522.

Williams, Jean M. "Personality Characteristics of the Successful Female Athlete," in *Sports Psychology, An Analysis of Athlete Behavior*, Straub, William F., ed. Ithaca, New York: Mouvement Publications, 1978.

Wilmore, J.H. "Exploding the Myth of Female Inferiority." *Physician and Sports Medicine*, 1974. 2: 54–58.

Wiltse, Leon L., and Jackson, Douglas W. "Treatment of Spondylolisthesis and Spondylolysis in Children." *Clinical Orthopaedics*, June 1976. 117: 92–100.

Wise, Arnold, Jackson, Donald W., and Rocchio, Patrick. "Preoperative Psychologic Testing as a Predictor of Success in Knee Surgery." *American Journal of Sports Medicine*, 1979. 7: 287–292.

Index

Numbers in italics indicate illustrations